Iroquois Warriors
in Iraq

Steven E. Clay

Combat Studies Institute Press
Fort Leavenworth, Kansas

Library of Congress Cataloging-in-Publication Data

Clay, Steven E., 1957-
  Iroquois warriors in Iraq / Steven E. Clay.
    p. cm.
  Includes bibliographical references and index.
  1. Iraq War, 2003- 2. United States. Dept. of the Army. Division (Training),
98th. I. Title.

  DS79.76.C587 2007
  956.7044'3420973--dc22

                                                        2007016154

First Printing May 2007
Reprinted June 2009

For sale by the Superintendent of Documents, U.S. Government Printing Office
Internet: bookstore.gpo.gov   Phone: toll free (866) 512-1800;   DC area (202) 512-1800
Fax: (202) 512-2104 Mail: Stop IDCC, Washington, DC 20402-0001

ISBN 978-0-16-078425-5

Foreword

The role of the Organized Reserves in the history of the US Army has taken many twists and turns since the nation's founding. The organization and missions of the Army's reserves, both the National Guard and the Army Reserve, are once again undergoing fundamental change to meet the needs of the 21st century. In *Iroquois Warriors in Iraq*, Mr. Steve Clay analyzes the role played by the "Iroquois Warriors" of the US Army Reserve's 98th Division (Institutional Training). In an unprecedented move, the soldiers of the 98th were called on in mid-2004 to deploy to Iraq and to fulfill a critical role in the building, training, and advising of the new Iraqi Army.

Prior to 2004, a US Army Reserve institutional training division had never deployed overseas to a theater of operations, nor were they designed to function as unit trainers and combat advisors. The author highlights the challenges faced by the 98th Division as it trained for and deployed to Iraq for this unusual mission. Among those challenges were how to train and prepare for the mission, who to send, how to integrate reservists into the new Multi-National Security Transition Command-Iraq (MNSTC-I), and whether to deploy the 98th as a unit or as a collection of individual soldiers.

Throughout the turbulent period of 2004 and 2005 in Iraq, the soldiers of the 98th Division added to the proud legacy of the US Army Reserve. *Iroquois Warriors in Iraq* tells the story of the history of the 98th Division (IT), it is a compelling narrative of the earliest phases of the Army's efforts to build the Iraqi armed forces, and it offers a number of key insights for the Army as it conducts the Long War. CSI is pleased to recommend this study for your professional reading. *CSI—The Past is Prologue!*

Timothy R. Reese
Colonel, Armor
Director, Combat Studies Institute

Acknowledgments

This book was a pleasure to write because it gave me an opportunity to relate a part of a story that is often overlooked in American military history—the story of the US Army Reserve. Since World War I, the combat history of the Regular Army and the National Guard has been fairly well documented, while that of the Army Reserve has been spotty at best. I hope this monograph helps make up for that shortfall in some small way.

I wish to acknowledge the help and contributions of all the Iroquois Warriors and other soldiers associated with the 98th Division's deployment to Iraq who made this book possible. They cooperated in this effort by participating in numerous interviews, telephone calls, and e-mails. They also sent me many documents that provided much of the framework and context of what happened. Without their assistance, this book would have been impossible to write.

In particular, I would like to thank LTC Jim DiRisio for providing me copies of numerous briefings, orders, rosters, e-mails, and memorandums he had collected throughout his period of active duty at Rochester and for the time he was in Iraq. Jim has a historian's eye and made a pointed effort to preserve those documents for future use. Those documents certainly came in handy for this project. Jim also patiently answered my countless e-mails pestering him for information on a host of topics relating to various aspects of the mission. As a member of the tactical operations center (TOC) and then as the executive officer to the Coalition Military Assistance Transition Team (CMATT), he was particularly well positioned to observe many key events and actions and thus able to provide excellent commentary on most of the subjects.

Other soldiers also provided superb information and documents and patiently fielded my many queries as well. These included MAJ Matthew Jones, COL Gus Stafford, COL Jody Daniels, MAJ John Vernick, MAJ Scott McConnell, and LTC John Curwen. In addition, Matt Jones went to great lengths to set up numerous sessions with most of the people interviewed for this project, and COL Stafford spent a great deal of his time on phone calls and e-mails detailing the negotiations and complex issues surrounding the development of the redeployment training plan and its subsequent execution at Camp Atterbury.

Finally, I would like to thank those here at CSI for their help, advice, and support. In particular, I would like to express my appreciation to COL Timothy Reese and Dr. William G. Robertson for assigning me this project and for their invaluable input to the final product. Their advice and recommendations on the analysis chapter were particularly welcome and appropriate. I also wish to thank Ms. Betty Weigand, my editor, for her patience and superb editing skills. She performed yeoman work on the manuscript and made it eminently superior to the initial draft. Any mistakes or omissions, however, are my own.

Contents

Figures

Introduction

In August 2004, the 98th Division (Institutional Training) was formally assigned the mission of deploying approximately 750 soldiers to Iraq to reinforce the newly formed Multi-National Security Transition Command-Iraq (MNSTC-I), commanded by Lieutenant General (LTG) David H. Petraeus. The MNSTC-I mission was to enable the Iraqi armed forces to take over the mission of fighting and defeating the insurgency that had developed in Iraq since the summer of 2003. Major General (MG) Paul Eaton who commanded the under-resourced Coalition Military Assistance Transition Team (CMATT), an agency owned by the Coalition Provisional Authority (CPA), had undertaken the initial effort in 2003–2004. When MNSTC-I was organized as a separate command under the Multi-National Forces-Iraq (MNF-I) in June 2004, CMATT was subsumed by the new headquarters. Nevertheless, MNSTC-I, like CMATT before it, was not sufficiently manned to conduct the mission adequately. The challenge was to find units and personnel to reinforce the command to enable it to satisfy its mission requirements. Ultimately, the solution was found in assigning the mission to the US Army Reserve's 98th Division.

In the summer of 2004, virtually all of the US Army's active and National Guard combat brigades were in Iraq or Afghanistan, had just returned from an overseas mission, or were currently slated for an overseas assignment. Additionally, the various Special Forces (SF) groups in the same two components were equally committed. There seemed to be no good option for reinforcing the MNSTC-I. However, a concept that had its genesis in the desire to reorganize the US Army Reserve (USAR) training divisions to be capable of supporting current world realities rather than those of the Cold War paradigm was coalescing at the same time the planners in the Pentagon were grappling with how to support Petraeus' new command. That idea, termed the Foreign Army-Training Assistance Command (FA-TRAC), was the brainchild of LTG James R. Helmly, the Chief of the Army Reserve and the commanding general of the United States Army Reserve Command (USARC).

This monograph is the story of how that concept evolved and how it came to form a nexus with MNSTC-I that resulted in the use of a USAR training division for an overseas combat mission for the first time in US Army history. The monograph presents issues connected with the mobilization, deployment, training, and integration of Reserve Component (RC) units and personnel in general; the use of units to perform tasks not part of their mission essential task list (METL); and issues associated with the major task assigned to the 98th Division—training and advising a foreign

1

army. It finishes with an analysis of the overall mission and provides conclusions and recommendations for consideration. The intent of this monograph is to expose leaders and soldiers to the issues described above, so in future conflicts, and perhaps even for the current conflict, they might gain insights that will enable them to develop solutions should similar problems arise.

Chapter 1

The 98th Division and the Foreign Army-Training Assistance Command

Go do it.

LTG Richard Cody

The story of how the 98th Division, or more properly how *soldiers* from the 98th Division, a table of distribution and allowances (TDA) organization designed to train and educate leaders and soldiers on basic and advanced individual skills at Army training centers, was selected and deployed to support the efforts of the MNSTC-I to train and advise the Iraqi Army in collective combat tasks seems unusual at first blush. However, when one views Army history, one will find numerous examples of Army units and soldiers assigned missions for which they were not originally organized, equipped, and trained. It has often occurred in past wars and is certainly true in the current conflict. Moreover, it will likely occur again in the future.

When the 98th Division received its mission in August 2004 to go to Iraq and support the MNSTC-I, the priority of requirements as designated by LTG Petraeus were: first, to fill numerous staff vacancies in the command; second, to provide various training capabilities to establish and develop institutional training for the Iraqi Army (officer and noncommissioned officer academies, Military Occupational Specialty schools, etc.); and third, to advise and support Iraqi Army units on "operations and training management issues."[1] The operative words in the last priority are "advise" and "operations." Within these two words lie the reality of the mission conducted by the soldiers who performed the division's most controversial task—advising the Iraqi Army.

It is useful at this point to explain the difference between training and advising. Training units and individuals in the sense that the 98th Division was designed to do entails the instruction of specific individual and collective (e.g., squad, platoon, company, etc.) tasks using the various tasks, conditions, and standards defined and detailed in the US Army's various training manuals. Most 98th Division advisors believed they were going to Iraq to train the units of the Iraqi Army in a garrison environment. Advising a foreign army, however, is not the same as training it. Although advising can include training, it primarily consists of the effort to establish trusting relationships with the unit leaders and advise them on the best ways to perform missions. As an advisor, one coaches his counterpart and recommends options or courses of action before and during combat operations. Advising usually involves exposure to potentially lethal situations. This scenario is closer to what the advisors of the 98th Division would actually experience.

Before reviewing what the division's soldiers did in Iraq, it is helpful and important to understand the history of the division and how it became involved in the mission.

History of the 98th Division

The 98th Division is nicknamed the "Iroquois Division" for its shoulder insignia, which depicts an Iroquois warrior with five feathers that symbolize the five civilized tribes of that nation. The blue and orange colors of the patch represent the House of Nassau for the Dutch settlers who originally settled the upstate New York area where the division has been historically located.

The 98th has the dubious distinction of being the only division still on the rolls of the Army that has no official combat experience. It began its existence as a National Army division mobilized at Camp McClellan, Alabama, beginning on 1 October 1918. The division was one of a number that were being organized and trained to participate in the great Allied offensives envisioned to take place in the spring of 1919. Colonel (COL) Jennings B. Wilson was assigned as the division's chief of staff and took command of the personnel assembling at Camp McClellan pending the assignment of a commanding general. As things turned out, other than the division headquarters, the 26th Trench Mortar Battery at Del Rio, Texas, was the only unit assigned to the division to be organized during the war.[2]

The division's initial connection to the northeast United States was loosely established that fall when two New York National Guard regiments, the 52d Pioneer Infantry (12th New York) and the 53d Pioneer Infantry (47th New York), both already in France, were slated to be reorganized and redesignated respectively as the 389th and 390th Infantry Regiments and assigned to the division as part of the 195th Infantry Brigade. This action never transpired as the War Department ordered the demobilization of the division on 30 November 1918, and the division's first chance to show what it could accomplish in combat faded to nothing.[3]

The division was reconstituted in June 1921 as an element of the Army's newest component, the Organized Reserves. The division headquarters was established on 18 August 1921 at Syracuse, New York, thus formally establishing its ties to the northeast in general and to the state of New York in particular. The various infantry, artillery, and service units of the division were organized throughout the upstate area. During the inter-war years, division units were composed mostly of Reserve officers and a few enlisted reservists. By law, the Organized Reserves could only enroll up to 33 percent of an organization's authorized enlisted strength. This political constraint was imposed through congressional action secured by powerful National Guard lobbies to ensure the new federal compo-nent would not compete with the nation's second-string team of ground forces.

Regardless of the problems encountered with manning, the leaders of the division busied themselves by attending various drills, classes, and schools during the inactive training period. An interesting point to note here is that unlike their counterparts in the National Guard, reservists were not paid for their attendance at training events during the inactive training period that generally ran from September to June. The only time reservists were paid was when they attended active duty training, which typically consisted of a 2-week training camp held at a Regular Army installation.

The 98th Division's units attended camps at various locations depend-ing on the branch of the unit. For example, the infantry regiments went to Fort Niagara, Fort Porter, or Plattsburg Barracks in New York, or Camp Dix in New Jersey. The artillerymen went to Pine Camp (now Fort Drum). The quartermasters attended camp at Fort Hancock and the signaleers went to Fort Monmouth, both in New Jersey. Since there were few enlisted men in the division, officers of the various units gained practical knowl-edge in leading soldiers by running the annual Citizen's Military Training Camps at various posts and for some years by taking command of a unit of Regulars on minor maneuvers. Junior officers would later receive invalu-able experience by participating in the running of Civilian Conservation Corps (CCC) companies during 6-month stints on active duty at various CCC camps. These training cycles went on year after year with only a few exceptions, most notably the participation of many of the division's personnel in the large First Army maneuvers in 1935, 1939, and 1940 as umpires and fillers for Regular Army and National Guard units.

As World War II approached, training vastly increased for members of the division as did opportunities for tours on active duty with the Regular Army. As more Regular Army units were activated, individual reservists, including many from the 98th, were called to the colors. As a result, per-sonnel assigned to the 98th Division were not mobilized as part of the division when it was finally activated in 1942—there were too few reserv-ists left in the 98th to mobilize as units. The division, in essence, had been "cherry-picked" to the point that it made more sense to start from scratch rather than try to build it around a cadre of a few junior officers not yet called to duty and World War I-era senior officers who would likely be relieved for age.

When the division was activated at Camp Breckinridge, Kentucky, in September 1942, it was composed of personnel from all over the country, but it still did not lose its northeastern flavor as many of the assigned draftees were from New York and New England. After undergoing its post-mobilization training and "D" series tests, the Iroquois Division was sent to Hawaii in April 1944 to further prepare for combat in the Pacific. As in World War I, the 98th was slated to participate in one of the last great offensives of the war—Operation OLYMPIC. For OLYMPIC, the division was to land on the island of Kyushu and help reduce the remaining armed resistance in Japan. Just as in the previous war, the fighting ended before the "Iroquois Warriors" got their chance to prove their mettle. The division did participate in the demilitarization of Japanese forces and occupation activities in the areas around Osaka. In February 1946, the colors were once again cased and returned to the United States.

The following December saw the unfurling of the colors at Syracuse when the division was again organized in the Reserves. Members of the unit spent the next 12 years attending drills and annual training (AT) at Fort Dix and Camp Drum and otherwise preparing for mobilization as an infantry division. In May 1959, however, the 98th Division received a change of mission that would be the focus of its attention for the next 48 years. It was reorganized and redesignated as a training division.

Under this new guise, the 98th Division was responsible for taking over a replacement training center and assuming responsibility for conducting basic combat training (BCT), advanced individual training (AIT), and common specialist training (CST). The Iroquois Division's wartime mission was to assume control and operate Fort Leonard Wood, Missouri, as an infantry training center. That focus remained static until 1968 when the division's AIT mission was changed to engineer-specific training and the regiments were reorganized as brigades. In 1994, under a major transition of Army Reserve training divisions, the 98th was reorganized as an institutional training division or DIVIT. Under this concept, the division, which retained its engineer BCT and AIT missions, picked up a wider array of training and education missions that were once the responsibility of the United States Army Reserve (USAR) schools. These included the Primary Leadership Development Course (PLDC), noncommissioned officer (NCO) basic and advanced courses, officer basic and advanced courses, the Command and General Staff Officer Course

(CGSOC), nursing courses, civil affairs courses, and a number of others. Because of this reorganization, the division assumed command of units all over the northeastern United States as some elements of the inactivated 76th Division and a number of the USAR schools were integrated into its structure. The 98th Division was in this configuration when it was being considered for a new mission—the Foreign Army-Training Assistance Command (FA-TRAC).

Foreign Army-Training Assistance Command

In the autumn of 2003, LTG James R. Helmly, Chief, Army Reserve (CAR) and CG, USARC was convinced (unlike some in the Pentagon who were already talking about demobilizing the National Guard and Army Reserve) the situation in Iraq would be a long-term obligation for large numbers of US troops to perform nation-building and security duties. He believed the active force was too small to fill all the requirements and the only way to meet the need was with the assistance of RC units. Helmly also knew that his own component, the USAR, was too inflexible to meet modern warfare demands because much of it, especially the 11 Reserve training divisions, was still structured for a Cold War type scenario. Thus, he began to look for ways to transform the USAR, or at least parts of it, to "generate greater capability within existing resources." One of his concepts was what he termed the FA-TRAC.[4]

In the FA-TRAC, Helmly envisioned a standing headquarters commanded by a major general (Regular Army or Reserve) that possessed a robust planning staff consisting of both regulars and reservists. This headquarters would deploy to a failed, failing, or defeated nation to coordinate the planning and execution of rebuilding all or parts of that nation's armed forces. With the assistance of the USAR's DIVITs and/or Training Support Divisions (TSDs) coming into country on a rotational basis, the FA-TRAC would establish what was essentially a mini-version of the US Army's Training and Doctrine Command (TRADOC) and its training base. The established training base would be parts of BCT, AIT, CST, the Officer Education System (OES), the Noncommissioned Officer Education System (NCOES), the Command and General Staff College (CGSC), the War College, lane training, and other special training capabilities to meet the needs of that nation's army. Only those parts of the DIVITs or TSDs called for by the FA-TRAC would rotate to conduct the mission. As the assisted nation stood up its own training institutions capable of assuming the mission, the FA-TRAC would eliminate those requirements from the rotation schedule. On completion of the mission, the command would return stateside and prepare for the next deployment.

In essence, the FA-TRAC concept envisioned a purely training role for any USAR elements attached to it.[5]

Sometime that fall, Helmly went to see LTG Richard Cody, Army G3, to discuss the idea of the FA-TRAC. Cody evidently liked what he heard because he asked Helmly to further develop the concept and brief him on the results. After some frustrating work with his staff (the young staff officers struggled to understand what was needed for the concept), Helmly provided the results in a brief to Cody on 28 April. There had been one minor change to the original concept that was included in the new brief. Because no new force structure or manpower spaces were going to be forthcoming anytime soon, the concept was changed to have a DIVIT headquarters function as the FA-TRAC headquarters instead of an entirely new command.[6]

Cody approved the concept brief. In this concept, Helmly concluded, Cody saw a means to relieve the Army combat units of some of the burden in Iraq with which they had been saddled after the end of major combat operations. Cody (and others) apparently perceived that the Army's brigade combat teams and combat arms brigades (including those of the National Guard) would quickly become stretched thin in terms of scheduled rotations to Iraq to perform just the basic security missions, not including the training of the new Iraqi Army.[7]

Since its inception, the FA-TRAC concept was discussed and debated in the halls of the Pentagon, at USARC headquarters, and within the USAR at large, but the pace of implementation of the idea was slow. Helmly's idea filtered its way to the Army's force provider, US Army Forces Command (FORSCOM), which opposed the concept because it wanted to use National Guard units to train the Iraqi Army. Helmly recalled:

> At the time, the Guard had already assumed the mission of helping to train up the Afghan National Army and they've done an exemplary job of that, but they used the asset of task organizing TOE-deployable Guard brigades. . . . when I first proposed [FA-TRAC], FORSCOM seemed to oppose my concept, saying that they would just use Guard brigades. I kept arguing, though, that that was ridiculous because you're going to end up needing those Guard brigades to deploy to Iraq or Afghanistan or elsewhere. . . . Here again we were victimized all the way down to Army FORSCOM; general officers were believing what the DOD was saying—that we would be down to five brigades in Iraq and one in Afghanistan 6 months from now or whenever.[8]

The pace of progress began to change in late May 2004 when Cody asked Petraeus, who had been recently ordered to take command of the newly formed MNSTC-I, to sit in on a briefing at the Pentagon before he went to Iraq. The briefing, conducted on 1 June by Brigadier General (BG) Gary M. Profit, Deputy Chief of the Army Reserve, covered the FA-TRAC concept. Also in attendance were Cody; Helmly; MG Bruce E. Robinson, the commanding general of the 98th Division; and BG Richard Sherlock, the division's assistant division commander (ADC). Petraeus recalled the brief was "essentially a proposal whereby one of the institutional training divisions of the US Army Reserve could take on the same mission that MNSTC-I was about to embark on" and it presented the idea that this division "could take on substantial portions of the mission."[9] The brief also recommended that a USAR training division take on that mission, which included helping the MNSTC-I headquarters become operational and providing training teams to train three Iraqi divisions. Sherlock recalled that Petraeus' response to the FA-TRAC idea was "Let's do it." Petraeus wanted a survey team to come to Iraq to conduct a requirements and "troops to task" assessment.[10] Cody assigned the survey team mission to Robinson's 98th Division.

Once in Iraq, the new MNSTC-I commander wasted no time in issuing the appropriate instructions for the survey team. On 3 June, the day after his arrival in Baghdad, Petraeus' headquarters issued MNSTC-I Fragmentary Order #15 that outlined the visit of the team to Iraq. It called for a three-person advanced party to arrive on, or about, 3 July, followed by the rest of the team of 10 personnel to arrive on, or about, 20 July. The order included the names of the 98th Division personnel who would make up the team and, in general, the team's activities and the locations it would visit.[11] The stage was set on the Iraqi side of the water to begin gathering information for a decision.

After the 1 June brief, Helmly directed Sherlock to conduct a mission analysis for the survey and brief it to Cody. Sherlock and a small team put together the brief and presented it to Helmly on 15 June. Helmly recollected that the plan was "very solid and I was very pleased with it." He approved the conclusions and gave Sherlock his blessing to present the brief to Cody on 18 June.[12]

The 18 June briefing was attended by Cody; Helmly; Robinson; and COL Frank Cipolla, commander of the division's 2d Brigade, a One-Station Unit Training (OSUT) brigade headquartered in Buffalo, New York. Sherlock's brief depicted a three-phased operation: deploy a survey team to Iraq to conduct the assessment, develop the FA-TRAC's tables of organization and equipment (TOE) to meet MNSTC-I's mission requirements, and stand up the FA-TRAC and subordinate elements in Iraq to assume the mission no later than 15 October. The brief also provided two courses of action regarding the organization of the FA-TRAC headquarters. Both courses envisioned a robust headquarters of 240 to 319 personnel commanded by an Army Reserve major general and detailed the capabilities of each option. It concluded with a series of questions, the command's critical information requirements, which needed answered to complete the planning for the mission.[13]

What was known was that MNSTC-I needed a lot of reinforcements to be able to address the myriad responsibilities of the new command. The major unknown was what the FA-TRAC's actual mission requirements were in terms of the mission tasks and the numbers of personnel and kinds of skill sets needed to satisfy the demands of those tasks. The survey team's mission was to go to Iraq and find out those details and report back to the Army Staff and other agencies for a decision on deploying all or parts of a training division to form the FA-TRAC to support MNSTC-I.

On conclusion of the brief, Cody asked a few questions, and then said, "Okay, the mission is approved. Go do it."[14] Cipolla, who had already been identified as one of the potential survey team members, recalled that Helmly turned to him and said, "I envy you," and then asked, "Are you ready to go?"[15] Of course, Cipolla replied that he was. Now all that was required was to get the survey team to Iraq and start the research.

Notes

1. Headquarters, Multi-National Security Transition Command-Iraq, Support Unit, "Requirements Assessment," 3 August 2004, 5–6.

2. Center of Military History, *Order of Battle of the United States Land Forces in the World War*, CMH Pub 23-4 (Washington, DC: Government Printing Office, 1988), Vol 3 Pt 2, 666–67.

3. Ibid.

4. MG James R. Helmly, telephone interview by author, Combat Studies Institute, Fort Leavenworth, KS, 2 December 2006, 1. MG Helmly was appointed as a lieutenant general during his tenure as the Chief, Army Reserve. When he left that office, he returned to his permanent rank of major general and was serving as such at the time of this interview.

5. Ibid., 4.

6. Ibid.

7. Ibid.

8. Ibid., 5.

9. LTG David H. Petraeus, interview by author, Headquarters, Combined Arms Center, Fort Leavenworth, KS, 11 December 2006, 4.

10. BG Richard Sherlock, interview by author, Office, Chief of the Army Reserve, Pentagon, Washington, DC, 16 November 2006, 1, 10; "Requirements Assessment," 2.

11. Multi-National Security Transition Command-Iraq, Fragmentary Order #15, Subject: Training Support Division Training Assessment, Baghdad, Iraq, Date/Time Group: 032100D June 2004. Apparently the names had been provided by the division to Petraeus before his departure to Iraq.

12. Sherlock interview, 16 November 2006, 1.

13. Headquarters, 98th Division, PowerPoint Brief, "The Foreign Army-Training Command, Proposed Timeline and Operational Concepts," 18 June 2004.

14. Ibid., 1, 4.

15. BG Frank Cipolla, telephone interview by author, Combat Studies Institute, Fort Leavenworth, KS, 20 November 2006, 2.

Chapter 2

Alert and Preparation

How can you do that?

98th Division Soldiers to LTG Helmly
USA Today, 16 September 2004

After LTG Cody approved the mission, Robinson and Sherlock began preparations to send a survey team to Iraq and to mobilize the division. This was not as straightforward as it may seem as the division had to continue its routine operations and, at the same time, plan for an impending mobilization without adequate information. The potential for mobilization created a host of questions that needed answers before any realistic planning could be conducted. Yet, Robinson could not afford to have his staff sit on their hands and wait for those answers before starting to get the division ready should it be mobilized. Robinson and Sherlock also had to concurrently sell the concept of deploying a DIVIT to Iraq to the generals at FORSCOM and USARC, all of whom (except Helmly of course) seemed to be against the idea and who would have a say in the final decision. Both of these situations caused a great deal of uncertainty and confusion among the Iroquois Warriors throughout the summer.

The Tactical Operations Center

On his return, Robinson directed Mr. Todd Arnold, the division's command executive officer (CXO), to activate a planning cell at the Reserve Center headquarters in Rochester. On 21 June, Arnold activated the cell under the division's G3, COL Bradford Parsons.[1] The cell, which came to be referred to unofficially as the TOC (tactical operations center), was to coordinate and plan the alert, home station premobilization training, mobilization, and deployment of division elements (including the survey team) to Iraq. Once the survey team deployed to Iraq, the TOC was to operate on a 24-hour basis to provide the team with a ready communications conduit and response center.[2]

To assist him in executing the TOC mission, Parsons appointed Lieutenant Colonel (LTC) Christopher Semler as the officer in charge (OIC). Semler had one full-time military technician and nine drilling reservists who were brought on active duty initially under 30-day Additional Duty Training orders, and later on short-term Contingency Operation Temporary Tour of Active Duty (COTTAD) orders. Among the latter was Major (MAJ) James DiRisio, who recently transferred to the 98th from the 84th Army Reserve Readiness Training Command.[3]

DiRisio felt honored at having been asked to come on active duty to help plan for this major event in lieu of others, but the division's new chief of staff soon dispelled this feeling. The Department of the Army (DA) had recently directed the American flag patch be sewn on the right sleeve of soldiers' battle dress uniforms (BDUs), and DiRisio had not yet gotten around to having it attached to his uniforms. One drill weekend, soon after reporting to work with the planning cell, the chief of staff called together all the officers to discuss with them the importance of being aware of the realities of the Global War on Terrorism (GWOT). In front of those officers, he then pointed out DiRisio as an example of someone slow to grasp that reality because he had not sewn the flag on his uniform. [4]

Though responsible for establishing the TOC, as the CXO Arnold was primarily in charge of the 98th's active duty staff that took care of the day-to-day operations of the division. While the TOC prepared the division for the deployment mission, Arnold continued to coordinate, plan, and execute the division's normal missions dealing with the Total Army School System (TASS), Initial Entry Training (IET), Professional Development (PD) training, and other missions that had not been removed from the division's plate. To some degree, this situation caused friction between the members of the TOC and the division staff. DiRisio recalled, "Initially, the majority of the full-time support staff looked at what the TOC was doing with varying levels of disinterest or contempt. Many simply could not be bothered by the thought that we were engaged in something that was completely beyond the high levels of competency they had developed in executing the division's traditional missions."[5]

Arnold, however, was not one to let that condition fester. DiRisio went on to say:

> LTC Arnold was the person through whom the TOC interacted with the 98th's full-time staff, and in this capacity, he gradually became more involved and interested in the work the TOC was doing. . . . LTC Arnold was extremely adept at making the linkages between our needs and the full-timers' abilities to make things happen. He met often with COL Parsons and [MAJ Matthew] Jones, and most often took the lead in communicating the effects of our planning to the rest of the division.[6]

Parsons and his small team had other challenges to overcome besides the division staff. The immediate problem was one of gathering information. This was extremely problematic, as Sherlock had forbidden the TOC to coordinate with higher headquarters (USARC and FORSCOM) except under specific circumstances. Sherlock was concerned that these two headquarters, which had staff personnel strongly opposed to the idea of using a DIVIT to reinforce MNSTC-I, would attempt to kill the effort. Also, the TOC was not allowed to contact other Reserve divisions that had already sent people to support the Iraqi Army training effort.[7] Additionally, Parsons had been cautioned on the kinds of information he could share with subordinate units. Thus, the members of the TOC were often dependent on the division's full-time staff to surreptitiously acquire answers to questions in which they themselves were largely disinterested.

Nevertheless, the TOC team went to work trying to get answers through other means. COL Robert Catalanotti, commander of the division's 1st Brigade in Providence, Rhode Island, remembered that Parsons was "intensely trying to pull that information in from outside sources. . . . He was doing everything he could to try and understand the mission and how the mission was to be filled with personnel, equipment, and logistics."[8] Without the advantage of having members of the 98th already in Iraq providing the division with answers to the key questions and with the communications constraints imposed, such a task was proving next to impossible. "We started gathering as much open source information as we could," DiRisio remembered, and "started making contacts over there [in Iraq] and got onto the SIPRNET [secure internet protocol router network] and did a little bit of exchanges of classified information."[9] Still, the information flow was a trickle and certainly not adequate for serious planning efforts. Some help was on the way, however.

On 23 June, just 2 days after the TOC stood up, Cipolla and two other soldiers that made up the survey team's advanced party arrived at the division headquarters. The other members were LTC Phillip McGrath, commander of the 1st Battalion, 304th Regiment, an IET unit out of Londonderry, New Hampshire, and Captain (CPT) Ramin Dilfanian. Dilfanian was assigned to the 6th Battalion (Military Intelligence), 98th Regiment at Fort Devens, Massachusetts, and had been born in Lebanon. He was an Arab linguist and would function as the team's interpreter. The three soldiers conducted their Soldier Readiness Program (SRP) at the Reserve Center and departed for the Continental United States Replacement Center (CRC) at Fort Bliss, Texas, on 26 June.[10]

On 6 July, BG Sherlock and the other 10 members of the survey team gathered at division headquarters. The team included COL William Clegg, assistant division commander for support; LTC Jody Daniels, deputy chief of staff; LTC Anthony Morales, assistant G3; and LTC Lawrence J. Kelly, commander of the 13th Battalion, 98th Regiment; among others. Also included in the lineup was LTC Sean Ryan, a staff officer on loan from the Office of the Assistant to the Chairman of the Joint Chiefs of Staff for Guard and Reserve Affairs, who had worked with Sherlock on a previous assignment. Ryan, whose background in the Reserves had been in Special Operations and then later in mobilization, went along as the G5 Plans officer. The team was organized somewhat along the lines of typical staff functional areas (S1 through 4), but also included personnel who would analyze collective training, security, medical, and TASS requirements.[11] After completing the SRP at the division headquarters, the team departed for Fort Bliss on 10 July. With the departure of the survey team, Parsons and his TOC staff would soon start receiving some of the answers they needed.

Rumor, Confusion, and Concern

After getting the survey team on its way to Fort Bliss, Arnold and Parsons continued preparations to, as they initially understood it, "mobilize the entire division."[12] They were not alone in their belief that the whole division was to participate in the mission. It was a common perception in the early stages of the mission among most of the division's leadership. Indeed, on the day before the survey team left for Fort Bliss, the *New York Times* ran a widely printed Associated Press article that led with the statement, "As many as 3,600 soldiers from the 98th Division could be headed to Iraq . . .," which certainly helped to reinforce the idea in the minds of the rank and file.[13] This impression was to hold sway among most members of the division for some time before the survey team would quash it with its findings later in the summer.

As the G3, and thus a member of the division staff as well as the TOC, Parsons had the responsibility to communicate information on the plans for the possible mobilization to subordinate commanders and staffs. Though he had to be very careful what he provided, he tried to keep the brigade commanders informed. This contact was critical in trying to minimize the rumor mill that begins grinding when units get word of a potential mission. When it first started operations, the TOC went to great lengths to conceal what it was doing. No one outside the command group and only a few people on the division staff even knew of the cell's existence and mission. But, few things stay secret for long. According to DiRisio, "As soon as people heard there was a TOC set up, the word began to get out that things were going to happen—that we were probably going to Iraq or Afghanistan. The word also got out about training a foreign army."[14] Parsons attempted to control the inevitable rumors by providing information to brigade commanders as soon as possible when he received answers he was allowed to pass on. As the G3, he held a weekly conference call with brigade commanders to relay the latest facts, particularly those bits of information that began to trickle in from the advanced party. "Step-by-step along the way we had counseled all our brigade commanders and our division staff as well as our commanding general," Parsons remembered, "of the serious nature of the mission and the risk we had in going forward."[15]

On 12 July, the division initiated "Stop Loss" to prevent a rapid loss of personnel from the division through transfers, separations, and retirements. This action reinforced the idea that the division was about to be assigned a mission. The speed of the rumor mill increased after 16 July when a formal alert notice was received by the division headquarters from the Department of the Army. The order listed the division headquarters and 40 subordinate units, including the band.[16] This event combined with the recent news articles about the possible mobilization and deployment of the division to Iraq shook even the most dubious of the division's soldiers.

Rumor now appeared to be reality, and not all members of the division were happy about it. Many were shocked that what was normally a nondeployable TDA (that is, a noncombat administrative) unit was apparently getting ready to be mobilized to go to a combat zone. Reservists who felt they were safe from having to deploy now faced the real possibility that they might have to soldier in the heat, flies, and bullets of the Middle East rather than the relative comforts of Fort Leonard Wood or Fort Dix. The thought prompted protests from a few of the reservists and from some family members.

Even the most senior Army reservist in the country was not immune to receiving complaints. In a *USA Today* article, Helmly described the reaction he received after the 98th Division was alerted. "I've gotten cards, letters, and e-mails [saying], 'How can you do that?'" He also heard from reservists who said, "I didn't think it would happen to us."[17]

Helmly recalled that at the beginning of the GWOT, the Army Reserve, as an institution,

> . . . had been lulled into believing that they probably wouldn't be mobilized and, if they were, it wouldn't be for long. . . . The problem . . . was that everybody wanted their damn security blanket. Well, my intent was to take that security blanket away. I want you to understand that the world is not amenable to a security blanket. It's different. It's changed. So I was doing everything I could to change the organization to accommodate the demands of war.[18]

He had told many of his subordinate leaders that this was a different kind of war and the Army Reserve had to change to accommodate it. Unfortunately, many reservists either did not hear their chief's warnings or chose to ignore them, believing things would go on as usual. Now, at least for reservists in the Iroquois Division, reality was setting in, and some could not or would not adapt.

Those who had no intention of going to Iraq, providing the division actually received the mission which was by no means certain at this point, could either desert (none did), transfer to the Individual Ready Reserve (IRR), or if they were eligible could request retirement. A number of senior officers and NCOs chose one of these options, some as early as mid-June. One of those quick to transfer to the IRR was the division's new chief of staff—the very same man who had recently chided Jim DiRisio for being slow to grasp the gravity of the GWOT by not having the American flag sewn on his BDUs. Another soldier, a brigade sergeant major, who after being provided a sanitized brief of the potential division mission, went straight to the G1's office to prepare his retirement packet.[19] In a flurry of paperwork, several other seasoned leaders submitted retirement packets and, with the approval of the division commander, these soldiers ended their association with the Army Reserve, which left vacancies in the division's various staffs and units.[20]

Although there were those who chose to leave when the going was getting serious, there were more Iroquois Warriors who had a desire to actually do this mission. When asked later about what went right with the division's experience in Iraq, Arnold reflected, "What went right was the 98th Division soldiers' reaction to the deployment. We had individuals who were slated to retire and they postponed their retirements. We had individuals who were going to PCS [permanent change of station] or end their tour of service and they postponed them. There were a lot of people who wanted to participate in this mission."[21]

Attempting to Bring Order to Chaos

While the staff dealt with the reaction to the news that the division might go to Iraq, the TOC team continued to gather information and develop plans from what they acquired. In the second week of July, Parsons had them develop two briefs with the information they had gleaned thus far. The purpose of these briefs was to update division leaders and higher headquarters staffs on what the division might do in Iraq. Though ultimately not reflective of what the division actually did, and keeping in mind that the survey team had not yet arrived in Iraq, these briefs provide a glimpse into what the impressions were among division leaders at that point.

The first was a mission analysis brief dated 7 July and prepared ostensibly to update MG Robinson on what the mission was thought to be. It began by providing the mission statements for MNSTC-I and CMATT sent back by the advanced party. Figure 1 provides the highlights of the briefing.

Facts:

- The Office of Security Transition owns eight bases[22]
- The 98th Division will be the headquarters for command and control of Iraqi Army training
- The Army G3 had directed attachment of additional assets to the 98th Division

Assumption: FA-TRAC will be a 98th Division mission

Essential Tasks:

- Develop a training force and the FA-TRAC command and control structure
- Deploy
- Execute mission

Constraints/limitations:

- Must retain structure to execute the division's Training Year (TY) 04 and 05 TASS, IET, and PD missions
- 3,110 potentially deployable personnel

Timeline:

- 7 August   Main CP deploys
- 28 August   Mobilization groups begin deployment
- 30 September Assume mission

Figure 1. 7 July mission analysis brief.

The briefing ended with the following restated mission and intent for the division:

> Mission: On order, TF 98, 98th DIV (IT) (-), deploys to Iraq and trains the new Iraqi National Army to support the national sovereignty of Iraq.

Intent: We will deploy TF 98 to Iraq to train the new Iraqi National Army (INA) to rebuild their capability to provide their own National Security capability and reduce Coalition presence in Iraq. Success will be defined by the completion of the training of 3 divisions consisting of 3 brigades of 3 battalions per brigade, and the successful redeployment of TF 98 to home station.[23]

Figure 2. MG Bruce E. Robinson, commanding general of the 98th Division.

At this point, it is clear the division still planned to deploy the headquarters to provide command and control of the division's efforts in Iraq. It is interesting to note that the focus was on *training* and not *advising*. It is also apparent the division was still planning to execute all, or at least some, of its normal training support requirements as it had not been relieved of those taskings. The 30 September date for assuming the mission was based on what was believed to be a mobilization order that would arrive at any moment.

The second brief (figure 3), prepared on 9 July, listed the same basic facts and assumptions, and addressed three courses of action (COAs) for each of three issues.

> **Mobilization sites (for predeployment training):**
>
> - COA 1: Fort Bliss
> - COA 2: Fort Dix
> - COA 3: A combination of Forts Bliss and Dix
>
> **Task Organization for "Training Teams" (for conducting OES, NCOES, BCT, etc., in Iraq):**
>
> - COA 1: Two brigade headquarters, each with four battalion headquarters, each with three BCT companies
> - COA 2: Three brigade headquarters, each with three battalion headquarters, each with three Advanced Skills Training companies
> - COA 3: Two brigade headquarters, each with three battalion headquarters, each with three BCT companies; one additional battalion headquarters with six BCT companies for surge capability
>
> **Subject Matter Expert (SME)/Mentor Integration (for "mentoring" Iraqi Army units):**
>
> - COA 1: SME/Mentor Detachment at brigade headquarters only (28 personnel)
> - COA 2: "Robust" SME/Mentor Detachment at battalion headquarters (20 personnel each)
> - COA 3: "Modest" SME/Mentor Detachment at battalion headquarters (12 personnel each)

Figure 3. 9 July course of action brief.

This brief also illustrated that the planners assumed the predeployment training would occur at Fort Bliss, Texas, or Fort Dix, New Jersey, or a combination of the two. If the latter option was selected, personnel going to staff positions would go through a short train up and processing at Bliss. The remainder of the division personnel, that is the trainers and mentors working with the Iraqi Army, would go through a more extensive train up at Fort Dix. The task organization for the training teams envisioned a training component similar to a DIVIT's typical capabilities as a major part of the division's mission. The SME/mentor COAs also show that the planners at this point did understand there was a requirement for what were being referred to in Iraq as Advisor Support Teams (ASTs). Still, it is interesting to note that the word "advisor" had not yet entered the 98th Division's deployment lexicon.

Premobilization Planning

While the TOC struggled with finding and providing answers, the subordinate units of the division were not idle. Brigade and battalion commanders and their staffs began to prepare their troops for this possible deployment by identifying who was and was not deployable and planning time during drill schedules for processing the soldiers through the standard SRP, conducting limited predeployment training, and holding Family Readiness Group (FRG) meetings.

The first step in deciding who of the roughly 3,300 soldiers of the division would go on the mission was determining who was deployable. Soldiers with retirement orders, PCS orders, or certain types of permanent physical defects were all exempt from the deployable list. MAJ John Vernick, the division's assistant G1 mobilization officer in charge of identifying the pool of deployable personnel, soon discovered that security clearances were an issue. Feedback from the theater of operations was that everybody had to have a current clearance, and not everyone in the division met that requirement. Mr. Jose Santiago, the division's security manager, suddenly found himself deep in paperwork for initiating new security investigations. There were also instances where certain individuals could not be granted clearances for financial difficulties or for prior criminal records and thus became ineligible for deployment. Then there were the provisions of the Lautenberg Amendment. This law, which amended the Gun Control Act of 1968, prohibited anyone convicted of domestic violence from shipping, transporting, possessing, or receiving firearms or ammunition, including military personnel on official business. Thus, Vernick was required to verify all convictions of soldiers in that category, and if found to be accurate, those soldiers were eliminated from the list. Fortunately, only about 10 soldiers met that particular condition.[24]

Due to the lack of hard answers on what the division's actual personnel requirements were for the mission, two assumptions were made for the purposes of developing the initial deployment list or battle roster. First, the division would not be relieved of any of its routine training requirements. Thus, some personnel would have to stay behind to satisfy those requirements and to run the division's rear command post (rear CP). The latter organization would keep the division's headquarters in Rochester open, command the stay-behind detachment, address family readiness and support issues, and provide a communications node with the division headquarters in Iraq. The second assumption was that everybody not needed in the rear CP or for TASS, IET, and PD requirements, or who were not otherwise disqualified, would deploy.[25]

As the mobilization officer, Vernick suspected that once the mobilization order arrived there would be pressure to get an initial mobilization group to Iraq as quickly as possible. By law, the Army had to give RC soldiers 30 days after notification of mobilization to take care of personal issues before they were brought on active duty. Typically, these issues included notifying their employers of the mobilization, taking care of outstanding bills, preparing their spouses and children for their absence, and completing any pending legal requirements. The law also allowed soldiers to waive that right, and so the word went out to the division asking for volunteers to waive their rights to the 30-day delay. Significantly, about 200 volunteers responded to the request. For these troops, the biggest concern was not so much the idea of soldiering in Iraq, but the fear that their employers would find out they volunteered to go early.[26]

At the regular monthly home station drills, units began processing soldiers tentatively identified as deployable through the SRP. This included verification, preparation, or revision of personal documents such as wills, emergency data sheets, allotments, applications for Servicemen's Group Life Insurance, and Family Care Plans (FCP). The process required soldiers to undergo physical or dental examinations if the previous exams were out of date and it allowed the unit administration personnel to help soldiers update their personnel records. Typically, this process would take a soldier about 2 hours of drill time to complete, unless one or both of the medical exams were required. The results of the SRP conducted in mid-July for the 2d Battalion, 390th Regiment were probably typical. During that drill, 35 soldiers went through the SRP. On average, about 46 percent of the documents in each of the files needed some form of revision. This was normal given many of the revisions were things such as updating phone numbers or addresses. Only five of those soldiers had unsatisfactory or incomplete FCPs. Additionally, the soldiers' mobilization files were collectively rated as "Good," although several were missing at least one required document.[27]

In addition to the SRP, units also conducted training on many of the "40 plus 9" tasks. These consisted of 40 common task tests (CTTs) and 9 battle drills required by TRADOC and FORSCOM for premobilization training and testing. Among the events were things such as putting on and wearing the protective mask, first aid, and a number of individual weapons tasks. Some thought this training, or at least part of it, was a waste of time on at least two levels. In the case of the protective mask tasks, people believed that Iraqi insurgents would not use chemical or biological weapons in their own country. Second, all of the tasks were those that drill sergeants routinely taught. It seemed odd that those considered the experts at teaching such tasks were now required to prove their own proficiency performing them.

The soldiers' families were also brought into the premobilization activities. At numerous Reserve Centers throughout the northeast, division units set up Family Readiness Group briefings for soldiers and their loved ones. At these meetings, family members were briefed on a host of issues that dealt with mobilization: how to get ready for the absence of their soldier, Army benefits for active duty reservist families, and the various agencies available that provided support to families of service personnel. MAJ Paul Loncle, who would deploy to Iraq as a member of OES Mobile Team 4, described his impressions of the FRG efforts:

> The family readiness group (FRG) brought [the family members] in and had a series of subject matter experts speak, starting with Mr. John Knope, our FRG director. He had all these various organization representatives come and explain benefits, what they could and couldn't do . . . all [of the agencies were] represented. The Red Cross was there to tell how to get Red Cross notification messages to your soldiers. They explained what [conditions] would really permit emergency leave—that whole process—and I thought they did a very thorough job. They had a lot of handouts. It was very well run and organized and I thought they did a really good job providing as much information to the families as possible.[28]

In addition to the group that Knope assembled to inform the family members, MG Robinson also attended many of these meetings to talk personally with the spouses and children of his troops:

> General Robinson was on the road probably 5 days out of every week for several months. He was going to different locations meeting with families—and anybody who wanted to meet with him, he would make himself available. He would start in Maine and work his way south to New Jersey and western New York. There were a couple times when he would show up at a location with only a few people there. But in his eyes, as long as he met with one person who understood what was happening, he

considered that a success. There were a lot of questions. Some of ours were, 'Why is my father/brother/son, who is not an infantryman, mobilized for infantry duties? What is their mission once they get over there? What is their mission once they come back?' There were standard questions, plus additional ones. The biggest thing was, 'This is something new—what can you tell us [about what] they're going to be doing over there? Yes, you're taking them into harm's way, but what exactly are they going to be doing?'[29]

Though many family members were not thrilled with the prospect of having their soldier deployed to Iraq, these meetings, and Robinson's personal efforts, went a long way toward making them feel they were indeed part of the Army family and were not going to be alone in this adventure.

Opposition to the Mission

As all the division's premobilization preparations were proceeding, the staffs at USARC and FORSCOM were clearly aware that Robinson, Sherlock, and the 98th Division were all leaning forward in the saddle with the intent to participate in this mission. Members of the division, most notably Sherlock and Robinson, had been keen from the beginning to get the Iroquois Division involved in the FA-TRAC business. The division's direct involvement in the series of June briefings in Washington and the deployment of a survey team to support MNSTC-I reinforced the impression. Many of the key staff officers in the USARC and FORSCOM were against the 98th Division, or any Reserve division for that matter, being involved in such a venture. Throughout the summer, while the survey team was in Iraq developing the requirements assessment, staff officers at USARC and FORSCOM brought up reason after reason to the 98th Division staff, to the Office of the Chief of the Army Reserve, and to the Pentagon, why the division should not do the mission.

The USARC opposition developed across a wide spectrum of real and perceived issues: DIVIT soldiers were not trained for a combat mission, the FA-TRAC mission would conflict with training missions in the continental United States (CONUS), other units were better qualified or had more available personnel, and this was a pseudo-advisor mission and many DIVIT soldiers were not combat arms and those that were combat arms were out of practice. The USARC staff also stated that other DIVITs were complaining that if the 98th Division was tagged with the mission, they might have to pick up the 98th's TASS requirements. Opposition from the FORSCOM staff appeared to be based on two main points: first, DIVIT soldiers did not possess the right skill sets for what was shaping up to be an advisor-type mission; and second, the division might not meet its TASS, IET, and PD training missions for FY 2005 due to its reduced drill sergeant and instructor pool.[30] The key point of contention for both appeared to be focused on the advisor aspect of the mission.

In some respects, it was rather odd these two headquarters were so opposed to this idea. The very theater that the division was to support was positively disposed toward the idea. Reflecting on the issue, BG Sherlock related:

> I'd have to say there was much more significant resistance . . . in CONUS than there was overseas. From the moment I arrived in Kuwait, Lieutenant General David McKiernan, before he left, and then Lieutenant General R. Steven Whitcomb after he arrived—because General McKiernan was leaving very shortly after I arrived— General Petraeus, Major General Gary Speer, the deputy CG at CFLCC [Coalition Forces Land Component Command], they all said, 'How can we make you successful? What do you need?' There was a lot more trepidation back . . . at FORSCOM, at United States Army Reserve Command (USARC), and at the Department of the Army (DA)-level where there was a feeling of, 'How can you think of using institutional training division soldiers? All you get with those are drill sergeants and platform instructors who have no collective training experience.' I think there was also a certain amount of 'not invented here' resistance.[31]

LTG Helmly confirmed the resistance:

> Because we were doing something different that had never been done before, it got to be very difficult. I can't remember the number of people who kept telling me we couldn't do certain things; that [the 98th Division] was only a TDA organization and wasn't meant to do what we were proposing. One of the reasons I was voted Mr. Congeniality in the Pentagon was that I said, 'Screw you! I've got my orders and we're going to do it, goddamn it.' And we did it. It was hard but that's what you get paid for. By the way, the people who actually did the 'Lord's work' here—General Sherlock and the entire 98th—I never had one problem with them. They were all for it. They wanted

to do it. It was all the institutional pieces like the USARC staff . . . , it was all these other people.[32]

Despite the opposition, neither of the division's two higher headquarters ever seem to have proposed an alternative option to using a DIVIT to support MNSTC-I. The staffs were against it for a host of reasons, but largely because they perceived that the 98th's reservists did not have the right skill sets to be advisors—and that opposition was extant despite the fact that in excess of 50 percent of the personnel already performing as ASTs were Army reservists.[33] Whether or not Sherlock could overcome the combined opposition of the USARC and FORSCOM staffs would be contingent on what the survey team developed in the MNSTC-I requirements assessment and how well that assessment fit what the 98th Division could provide.

Notes

1. COL Bradford Parsons, telephone interview by author, Headquarters, 98th Division (IT), Rochester, NY, 3 November 2006, 1. Parsons had been asked to come to the division headquarters in Rochester to be part of the planning cell. He arrived on 18 June, the day of the Cody brief, and stood up the TOC 3 days later.

2. LTC James DiRisio, e-mail to author, Subject: 98th Division in Iraq, 9 January 2007.

3. Ibid.

4. LTC James DiRisio, telephone interview by author, Combat Studies Institute, Fort Leavenworth, KS, 9 January 2007.

5. Ibid. Todd Arnold also explained that some of the foot dragging on the part of the full-time staff was because their counterpart at the USARC was telling them the 98th Division would never get the mission and that BG Sherlock was wasting everybody's time. The full-time staffers apparently believed this and thus were reluctant to spend much time working on issues associated with the mission.

6. Ibid.

7. Ibid.

8. COL Robert Catalanotti, interview by author, Headquarters, 98th Division (IT), Rochester, NY, 3 November 2006, 2.

9. LTC James DiRisio, interview by author, Headquarters, 98th Division (IT), Rochester, NY, 3 November 2006, 2.

10. Ibid.

11. COL Sean Ryan, interview by author, Joint Center for International Security Force Assistance, Fort Leavenworth, KS, 21 December 2006, 3; Multi-National Security Transition Command-Iraq, Fragmentary Order #15, Subject: Training Support Division Training Assessment, Baghdad, Iraq, Date/Time Group: 032100D June 2004.

12. COL Todd Arnold, interview by author, Headquarters, 98th Division (IT), Rochester, NY, 4 November 2006, 1.

13. *New York Times*, 9 July 2004, "Rochester: 3,600 Face Prospect of Iraq Duty," 6.

14. DiRisio interview, 3 November 2006, 3.

15. Parsons interview, 3 November 2006, 3.

16. Headquarters, Department of the Army, Alert Order, Subject: DA Alert Order #549-04, DAMO-ODM, Washington, DC, Date/Time Group: 161816Z July 2004.

17. *USA Today*, "Army Reserve chief says force was not well-prepared for terror war," 16 September 2004, available at http://www.usatoday.com/news/washington/2004-09-16-army-reserve_x.htm; accessed 3 November 2006.

18. MG James R. Helmly, telephone interview by author, Combat Studies Institute, Fort Leavenworth, KS, 2 December 2006, 10.

19. DiRisio, telephone interview, 9 January 2007.

20. Ryan interview, 21 December 2006, 8. Some soldiers in the 98th Division were critical of Robinson's actions in this regard, but the argument can be made that these officers and NCOs were not likely to be assets to the division and may not have been positive contributors to the mission.

21. Arnold interview, 4 November 2006, 6.

22. The Office of Security Transition was essentially the forerunner to MNSTC-I.

23. Headquarters, 98th Division (IT), PowerPoint Brief, "OPLAN 04-XX (FA-TRAC), Mission Analysis Brief" (Draft), 7 July 2004.

24. MAJ John Vernick, interview by author, Headquarters, 98th Division (IT), Rochester, NY, 5 November 2006, 4.

25. MAJ John Vernick, telephone interview by author, Combat Studies Institute, Fort Leavenworth, KS, 10 January 2007.

26. Vernick interview, 5 November 2006, 2.

27. Headquarters, 77th Regional Readiness Command, PowerPoint Brief, "Task Force Liberty Soldier Readiness Program After Action Report for 2d Battalion, 390th Regiment, 2d Brigade, 98th Division," 10–12 July 2004.

28. MAJ Paul Loncle, interview by author, Headquarters, 98th Division (IT), Rochester, NY, 4 November 2006, 1–2.

29. Arnold interview, 4 November 2006, 7.

30. COL Todd Arnold, e-mail to author, Subject: RE: 98th Division in Iraq, 8 January 2007.

31. BG Richard Sherlock, interview by author, Office, Chief of the Army Reserve, Pentagon, Washington, DC, 16 November 2006, 10.

32. Helmly telephone interview, 2 December 2006, 6.

33. Sherlock interview, 16 November 2006, 11.

Chapter 3

The Survey Team

This is the right answer—for this snapshot in time.

LTC Sean Ryan

COL Cipolla and the advanced party arrived at Baghdad International Airport (BIAP) on 4 July. The work of the advanced party and the follow-on survey team would determine the future of the FA-TRAC, and to a lesser degree, the future of the 98th Division's association with the effort to reinforce MNSTC-I in its mission to rebuild the Iraqi Army.

The mission of the advanced party was to acquire initial survey guidance from Petraeus and prepare for the arrival of the survey team in terms of lodging, vehicles, phones, computers, and visit schedules. The party met with Petraeus on 5 July. In that meeting Cipolla recalled that Petraeus' main emphasis was on the creation of 39 Advisor Support Teams (AST) to replace those already deployed with the first three divisions of the new Iraqi Army.[1] The task seemed straightforward enough, though it would prove to be the most difficult task the division had to accomplish.

The following day, Cipolla went to meet with BG James Schwitters, the commanding general of CMATT to get his assessment. Cipolla recollected that Schwitters asked a number of questions regarding the differences between a DIVIT, a TSD, and a Reserve Readiness Command. Schwitters then proceeded to reinforce to Cipolla what the survey team needed to do while in Iraq. At this point it was becoming clear to Cipolla this was not just a training mission. He remembered Schwitters told him the ASTs were not really trainers, but that their jobs were "teaching, coaching, and mentoring. . . . General Schwitters always stressed those three things." The party's next stop was a command and control cell at Taji Military Base northwest of Baghdad. There, the officer in charge explained the cell's mission in supporting the ASTs, who and what the ASTs really were, and how the cell performed its job. It turned out to be the very job Cipolla would hold after the 98th deployed.[2]

As the advanced party gathered information on the situation in Iraq and the evolving requirements from MNSTC-I, Cipolla began sending reports back to the division headquarters at Rochester. First, Cipolla had been presented with five task areas that related to the MNSTC-I and CMATT missions that he relayed back to Sherlock. Figure 4 identifies the five task areas.

Task Area 1: Identify and institute professional development training with a timeline of events (2005 through 2008).

Task Area 2: Advise and support Joint Iraqi Forces for operations and training—staff exercises, mission essential task list (METL) development, yearly training guidance development, and yearly training calendar development.

Task Area 3: Integrate the Iraqi National Guard into the Iraqi Army—similar to a "One Army Concept."

Task Area 4: Develop senior-level Army staff capabilities— Combined Staff (Operations) and Joint Staff (Administration and Logistics).

Task Area 5: Provide Advisory Support Teams for the Iraqi Army.

Figure 4. Task areas identified by the advanced party.

Additionally, he sent back the observations that significantly changed the original planning assumptions (see figure 5).

1. Command and control requirements were smaller than anticipated due to theater structure in place (i.e., CMATT HQ).

2. Basic training requirements needed to support the Iraqi Army were smaller than anticipated.

3. The complexities of training a national army in the multi-ethnic and multi-tribal Iraqi culture had been underestimated.

4. The complexities of training through interpreters had been underestimated.

5. The structure of the Iraqi Army was still being refined, thus their training requirements and priorities would continue to shift to match the emerging requirements of the theater of operations.[3]

Figure 5. COL Cipolla's observations relayed to division headquarters.

In short, the original concept of an FA-TRAC headed by the 98th Division was fast becoming irrelevant—CMATT already occupied that position; the training aspect of the mission was about to be deemphasized; and the advisory aspect of the mission was about to become much more apparent as an emerging requirement.

Meanwhile, the survey team arrived in Iraq on 24 July after a 2-day stopover in Kuwait. On his arrival in Baghdad, Sherlock had an idea of what he (and many other Iroquois Warriors as well) thought the 98th Division's main task would be if it was to get the go ahead for the mission. He recalled, "We believed it would take a structure for an organization to flesh out the FA-TRAC concept, because the original mission we were given by Generals Cody and Helmly was to look at going over and *performing all the training for the regular army, essentially consuming what was then the CMATT mission* [emphasis added]."[4] After a very short time in country, Sherlock and the survey team confirmed Cipolla's initial reports. Seeing the command and control infrastructure that MNSTC-I already had in place, his original idea was now radically changed. As he later reflected on the situation, Sherlock stated: ". . . because you had a

Figure 6. BG Richard Sherlock, Assistant Division Commander, 98th Division, and later CG, Iraqi Advisor Group.

CMATT, a CPATT [Coalition Police Assistance Training Team], a joint headquarters AST, and a MNSTC-I staff already with a skeletal structure, instead of trying to supplant one of those organizations with a plug-in structure, we found it [would be] most efficient if we were to augment the existing structure and see where we could draw from our skill sets to flush out the rest of the organization."[5]

The FA-TRAC, at least as originally conceived, was now essentially dead (though the term would be used intermittently until well into the division's tour in Iraq). Nevertheless, there was still the task to determine what MNSTC-I and its subordinate commands needed, and Sherlock and his team set out to do just that. Tony Morales recalled that Sherlock:

> . . . broke down the survey team into two to three groups of individuals to go out to various camps and to interview Marines and Army advisors who were already in that role and learn their mission . . . we didn't have a script, we didn't have any questions written down. We put that together after being with General Sherlock and him asking what do we need to do.[6]

Over the next 8 days, the group interviewed Petraeus and Schwitters and their principal staffs; BG William J. Troy, Chief of Staff of the Multi-National Corps-Iraq (MNC-I); MG Peter Chiarelli, CG of the 1st Cavalry Division; and 37 advisors from 18 different ASTs.[7]

From Petraeus, the survey team received, among other things, one piece of pointed guidance—there was no need for the 98th Division headquarters to come to Iraq. CMATT was already in place; therefore, there was no need for the division commander or the flag to deploy.[8] Petraeus also indicated that his priority was to get his staff vacancies filled with people possessing the right skill sets. The MNSTC-I staff was operating at about 30-percent strength and he needed people as quickly as possible to fill positions and get the headquarters functioning properly.[9]

From Schwitters, who was in the position the CG of the FA-TRAC would have filled, the team received additional guidance. Regarding his interview with the team, Schwitters stated he emphasized the need to have ASTs that were cohesive and "familiar with each other." He believed team-work was critical to the success of advisor teams. He also made the remark that only about one-third of the current AST members were effective in working with their Iraqi units. Ryan recalled asking the general about what had been done to prepare them for their duties as ASTs. "Nothing" was Schwitters' response.[10] Ryan further explained:

[Schwitters] was very frustrated with the inability of the advisor support teams, or military transition teams (MiTTs) as they were later called, because only about a third of those teams were effective. The truth of the matter was that [nothing had been done] to prepare them to be effective—and [Schwitters] agreed with that. That led to an outgrowth of [the survey team] role, which was to develop an initial training package that would prepare them to be effective.[11]

Thus, one of the additional tasks the team had to tackle was to develop a training plan that, should the 98th Division get the mission to deploy, would better prepare those soldiers slated for advisor duties. As will be seen, the result of this effort was to later cause much friction between the 98th Division staff and the First Army G3.

The survey team also visited Chiarelli and ASTs that were working for the 1st Cavalry Division training the Iraqi National Guard (ING) to get a feel for what training and logistical support those personnel believed was needed for the advisor mission. The ASTs informed the survey team they were critically short of almost everything advisors needed in the way of equipment and supplies. From this discussion, the team began to develop a standardized set of equipment for ASTs that included two up-armored high-mobility multipurpose wheeled vehicles (HMMWVs) and two vehicle-mounted crew-served weapons (M2 .50-caliber machine gun, Mark-19 grenade launcher, or M240 machine gun) per team, M4 assault rifles with scopes, and AN/PVS-14 night vision devices.[12]

Additionally, the advisors told the team that incoming AST personnel needed specific training before they assumed the advisor mission. The recommended training included live-fire exercises in convoy training and forced-entry into buildings, communications training on the new generation of Single Channel Ground and Airborne Radio System (SINCGARS) radios, and cultural awareness training.[13] If it had been murky before, it was now crystal clear to Sherlock and his team (though it would not be to those to be assigned as advisors) that those soldiers assigned as advisors would not be *training* the Iraqi Army, but would be directly involved in working with Iraqi units in combat situations.

The team spent the better part of 2 weeks accumulating data with which they would build the requirements assessment. Once Sherlock and his team had gathered their findings, they met with COL Peter A. Henry, the MNSTC-I chief of staff, who provided them with the various manning documents and personnel requests that had been developed to support MNSTC-I. Henry also authorized LTC Craig Vest, the MNSTC-I J1 and his deputy, Lt. Col. Brian Kelly, US Air Force, to assist the team in developing the consolidated personnel requirements for the command. The team analyzed MNSTC-I's two existing Joint Manning Documents (JMDs) and three or four different requests for forces (RFF). Each document was thoroughly scrutinized to eliminate duplicate or unnecessary positions. The survey team also added a number of other requirements not yet thought of or requested by the MNSTC-I staff. Among the latter were positions to support an officer and NCO education effort for the Iraqi Army and a modest training capability for selected military occupational specialties (MOS). The existing AST Command and Control (C2) Cell at Taji was recommended to be increased to 21 people, and a convoy escort platoon that the J3 wanted to provide convoys with a security force was to be increased to two platoons.[14]

Using the information collected, the survey team then developed a list that incorporated all known personnel, logistics, and training requirements. All this information was integrated into a single comprehensive document entitled the Requirements Assessment that Sherlock and his team briefed to Petraeus on 6 August.[15] The assessment, among other things, called for about 730 soldiers to meet MNSTC-I's personnel requirements. About 310 of these soldiers were to be assigned as advisors.

Petraeus approved the assessment and authorized Sherlock to begin coordination with USARC, FORSCOM, and the Army G3 for approval. The first step was to inform the Army's force provider, FORSCOM, what MNSTC-I's requirements were. Previously, Sherlock and his team had conducted several video-teleconference (VTC) briefings with FORSCOM and USARC to let them know what was transpiring with the survey. However, MG Charles Wilson, the USARC Deputy CG and gatekeeper between the Army Reserve and FORSCOM, did not want to be briefed via VTC. He wanted to be briefed in person, as did MG Julian H. Burns, Jr., the FORSCOM G3. Thus, Sherlock and Ryan boarded a plane at BIAP on 7 August and headed for Georgia.

Arriving in Atlanta the following day, Sherlock and Ryan joined MG Robinson, COL Parsons, and LTC Arnold at USARC headquarters at Fort McPherson. About 15 minutes into Sherlock and Ryan's presenta- tion to Wilson and members of the USARC staff, a soldier entered the room and said, "Sir, it's time." At that point, Wilson, his CXO, and his sergeant major departed to promote a soldier and left the brief to two of his staff officers, COL David Lowry, the USARC G3, and COL William Hamilton, the USARC G7. Near the end of the brief, Wilson returned and merely reiterated the litany of concerns the USARC staff had expressed all summer. One-by-one the leaders of the 98th Division addressed each point with answers designed to counter the arguments and reinforce the idea that a DIVIT could meet MNSTC-I's requirements. Still dubious and without providing any positive word of support, Wilson gave his approval for the brief to be presented to FORSCOM. As a parting shot, Wilson told Robinson and his party that the FA-TRAC mission was only an additional duty—the division would still have to meet the requirements of its FY 2005 TASS, IET, and PD missions.[16]

The party of Iroquois Warriors next traveled across the post to FORSCOM headquarters where they briefed MG Burns. Ryan remembered that Burns was also doubtful of the idea of using a training division to reinforce MNSTC-I; however, he was primarily interested in the bottom line of what it was going to take to meet MNSTC-I's needs. "I just want somebody to tell me what the right answer is," Burns said before the brief. Ryan responded, "Sir, here's our recommendation" and proceeded along with Sherlock to brief the assessment. Once again, the two countered each of the concerns brought up by the FORSCOM G3. In contrast to Wilson, Burns' reaction to the arguments was one of growing encouragement. Brad Parsons recollected that initially, Burns,

> . . . was very aligned with what [Wilson] was thinking. But as the briefing and mission got articulated and he felt more comfortable with the plan . . . his big stumbling block was how much training would be required of the Reserve Component to get validated to be shipped to go overseas. That was his big concern—and to make certain we had enough training to prepare every soldier to be able to handle the mission over there.[17]

On conclusion of the briefing, Ryan recommended to Burns, "Sir, this is the right answer for this snapshot in time. Give us the authority to do it." Burns responded with words to the effect of, "Okay. I like it. Go with it," and gave his approval for the idea.[18] Sherlock and Ryan were soon on their way to Washington to convince the final decision makers there.

The following day, Sherlock and Ryan briefed LTG Helmly and Ms. Kathryn Condon, the Army's Deputy G3 in the Pentagon. Both gave their blessing to the assessment and to the idea of a training division supplying MNSTC-I's needs for personnel. The only question now was which division would support the mission. There had never been a formal decision on which unit would go, and there were people in the USARC who specifically did not want the 98th Division to get the mission.[19] In reality of course, that choice had already been made. The staff of the 98th Division in Rochester had been scrambling to develop various courses of action, plans, and battle rosters; identify deploying personnel; and acquire the necessary information needed from numerous sources to fill the holes in each. The final decision was pro forma.

When reflecting on the selection of which unit would go, Helmly recalled, "The most capable force at the time was the 98th Division. It was more ready. It was, frankly, just sharper. [When] we got the warning orders from DA and FORSCOM . . . I nominated the 98th."[20] Now, after 86 years, the 98th Division, or at least pieces of it, was about to get its first taste of combat.

Notes

1. BG Frank Cipolla, telephone interview by author, Combat Studies Institute, Fort Leavenworth, KS, 20 November 2006, 2–3.

2. Ibid., 3.

3. Headquarters, Multi-National Security Transition Command-Iraq, Support Unit, "Requirements Assessment," 3 August 2004, 3.

4. BG Richard Sherlock, interview by author, Office, Chief of the Army Reserve, Pentagon, Washington, DC, 16 November 2006, 2.

5. Ibid.

6. LTC Antonio Morales, telephone interview by author, Combat Studies Institute, Fort Leavenworth, KS, 16 January 2007, 1.

7. "Requirements Assessment," 3–4.

8. Sherlock interview, 16 November 2006, 5.

9. COL Sean Ryan, interview by author, Joint Center for International Security Force Assistance, Fort Leavenworth, KS, 21 December 2006, 4.

10. MG James Schwitters, telephone interview by author, Combat Studies Institute, Fort Leavenworth, KS, 13 December 2006, 1; Ryan interview, 21 December 2006, 4.

11. Ryan interview, 21 December 2006, 4.

12. LTC Jody Daniels, interview by author, Combat Studies Institute, Fort Leavenworth, KS, 20 December 2006, 4.

13. Morales telephone interview, 16 January 2007, 1.

14. Daniels interview, 20 December 2006, 2–3.

15. "Requirements Assessment," 3.

16. COL Bradford Parsons, telephone interview by author, Headquarters, 98th Division (IT), Rochester, NY, 17 January 2007, 10.

17. Ibid., 9.

18. Ibid.

19. Ibid. According to COL Ryan, Ms. Condon was present for purely informational purposes.

20. MG James R. Helmly, telephone interview by author, Combat Studies Institute, Fort Leavenworth, KS, 2 December 2006, 2.

Chapter 4

Mobilization and Training

They were doing the best they could.

COL Robert Catalanotti

The final decision to use the 98th Division to support MNSTC-I immediately made its way to the division headquarters in Rochester. Everybody expected the mobilization (mob) order from DA to arrive at any minute for time was believed to be of the essence. The training of the Iraqi Army was a priority mission in Iraq. The Bush administration wanted to get the Iraqi Army trained so it could provide security for the new democracy, therefore allowing Central Command to start drawing down American forces in the theater. Thus, the MNSTC-I mission was arguably the most important game in town. However, MNSTC-I and its subordinate headquarters were all severely undermanned and handicapped in effectively progressing toward meeting their mission objectives. Additionally, the rotation date for many of the initial advisors brought over by CMATT was quickly approaching, which would further deplete many of the already understrength ASTs.

Before the Iroquois Warriors could assume their missions in Iraq, most of them had to go through the mobilization process, complete a post-mobilization training package at a CONUS mobilization site, complete an advanced training package in Kuwait, and process through the Taji Military Training Base (TMTB). None of this could start until a mobilization order was issued. Nevertheless, despite the stated importance of the mission, it would take almost another month before DA issued the order.

The delay was a mixed blessing. While MNSTC-I desired to have the Iroquois Warriors in Iraq as soon as possible, various agencies stateside (USARC and FORSCOM), apparently still reluctant to support the decision to send the 98th, appeared to drag their feet. This delay gave other agencies that were unprepared to support the mobilization of the division (including the First United States Army, the agency responsible to train and validate the deployment of the Iroquois Warriors) time to finalize solutions to problems that had arisen earlier in the summer. From the First Army standpoint, the primary issues revolved around postmobilization training; specifically, where it would happen, what would be trained, and how long it would take to conduct the training. In addition, the 98th Division's own TOC and staff had only recently received the approved Requirements Assessment and still had to finalize assigning "faces to spaces" and getting enough qualified personnel to meet all of MNSTC-I's personnel requirements. Though the G1 staff had wrestled with battle rosters all summer trying to identify who would go, the delay would give them time to address final manning problems.

Manning the Battle Rosters

The primary task now confronting MAJ Vernick, the mobilization officer, was finding enough deployable and qualified personnel to fill all the slots on the consolidated MNSTC-I manning requirements provided by the survey team.[1] On the surface, it seemed rather easy—the division had over 3,000 soldiers from which Vernick could choose to fill about 730 slots. However, the task was not that simple. A number of variables came into play that rapidly reduced the pool of soldiers from which to select. First, as a training division, the 98th Division possessed a much higher percentage of officers, and especially field grade officers, when compared to the number of enlisted personnel in a comparable TOE-type organization. The requirements for enlisted personnel on the JMD were a higher percentage than the division possessed. Therefore, although the division had many officers, most were not needed because they could not be slotted against enlisted positions.

Another issue was that while the division had a number of drill sergeants, most of whom were MOS 11B (infantryman), the need in the enlisted positions was for noncombat arms MOSs. A training division has a relatively low number of enlisted personnel in logistics, administration, signal, maintenance, and other noncombat arms MOSs. Further, given the potential combat nature of the mission, females were barred from serving as advisors and a few other select positions. These constraints created further shortfalls. Thus, the division was forced to send requests to the USARC to find about 200 soldiers in the Reserve system, either from other Reserve units or from the IRR, to man slots in the 98th's battle roster that could not be filled from within.

In addition, the division G1 staff had to select personnel to fill the advisor slots. Given what was now understood to be a combat role, Sherlock had sent back specific instructions on how to select people for those positions based on what the survey team had learned from advisors in Iraq. MG Robinson consolidated and promulgated the criteria in a memorandum and issued it on 19 August (see figure 7). Furthermore, each potential advisor had to volunteer and submit a packet with a recent photo (in BDU), a medical fitness certification, a recent APFT scorecard, a biography, a security clearance, and a memorandum from the soldier's brigade

- **Personal Traits**:

  —Commitment to successful mission accomplishment
  —Experience
  —Physical toughness
  —Coolness under pressure

- **Competencies**:

  —"Train the Trainer" mentality (train yourself out of a job)
  —Ability to discern "ground truth"
  —Communications
  —Ability to establish rapport and maintain relationships
  —Sound grasp of planning and training management
  —Sound grasp of the diplomatic and political context
  —Ability to train using a translator

- **Other Requirements**:

  —Cultural sensitivity and awareness of current events in CENTCOM area of operations
  —Ability to adapt, improvise, overcome
  —Ability to work within a small group operating in an austere base of operations
  —Minimum APFT score of 220
  —Ability to be diplomatic under extreme stress
  —Ability to operate in a tactical environment while maintaining excellent situational awareness

Figure 7. Advisor selection criteria.

commander endorsed by the first general officer in the chain of command recommending the person for the AST mission.[2]

The process laid out by Robinson seemed to be thorough. COL Parsons recalled,

> We screened the soldiers we took on the AST mission. We really looked at their Army physical fitness test scores to judge their overall physical conditioning and see who would possibly struggle in that type of environment. We were very cognizant of the health conditions of our soldiers, their background and experience, and we did a really good job choosing who would get into the AST mission.[3]

However, there was, perhaps, a flaw in the process. MAJ Matthew Jones, a former Marine and a full-time staff operations and training officer with the division headquarters, had recently served a stint as an advisor to the Afghanistan Army. He believed the process skimmed over a key criterion:

> The one critical element that was really missing from the process was that, if you don't want to be there [in Iraq], don't be there as an advisor. Be there as a staff person or something else. So much of what you do as an advisor can easily be road-blocked by the reality of being in Iraq and you can easily get frustrated if you don't want to be there. It shows so transparently to the Iraqis. They know if you don't want to be there. In a heartbeat, they know if you don't believe in the mission. They also know if you're going to get easily sidetracked and road-blocked. And if you are, you're not much use as an advisor.[4]

He went on to explain that although many soldiers did volunteer to be advisors, it was largely due to the misunderstanding that the mission was training in nature and not advisory. When people began to realize they would actually be accompanying Iraqi units on combat missions, among some volunteers the desire to "be there" waned dramatically.[5]

As August wore on, the TOC staff identified advisors and filled the battle rosters with what appeared to be the best-qualified personnel. As the rosters solidified, Vernick coordinated with the USARC to get that headquarters to develop Derivative Unit Identification Codes (DUIC) so personnel could be assigned against them and mobilization orders could be prepared. Typically, Army personnel deploy as part of a unit under a Unit Identification Code (UIC). Vernick's preferred method was to transfer all personnel out of several of the division's subordinate units and reassign deploying personnel to those units based on the mission they were to perform in Iraq. However, the USARC G7, one of the key opponents to using a DIVIT for the MNSTC-I mission, barred this course of action and directed the 98th Division to deploy its personnel under DUICs, a kind of subunit UIC. Failing to get permission from the USARC to deploy using several UICs, Vernick pushed for establishing only seven DUICs based on the soldiers' latest arrival date (LAD) as requested by MNSTC-I, to simplify management and tracking of deploying personnel. When the USARC provided the DUICs, they did so based on the UICs to which the deploying soldiers were actually assigned. Therefore, when Vernick received the list from the USARC, it contained about 125 DUICs. Some had only one soldier assigned and many had less than five. This made for an administrative nightmare that would plague division personnel managers at Rochester as well as those in Iraq throughout the entire deployment.[6]

The DUIC issue was only one of several areas where it seemed the USARC was making life difficult for the division. Todd Arnold had a number of dealings with that headquarters during this period. He later stated:

> The thing that didn't go so well was coordination with USARC. There was a lot of resistance to the 98th Division or just to the plan itself for whatever reason. Perhaps because it was something out of the norm or it took too many people out of the regular mobilization feeder track for other missions. I think we could have coordinated that better. And quite frankly, I don't think it was our mission. I think it was USARC that should have stood up and supported us in being mobilized. Once they got on board, reluctantly in some areas, they were great in supporting us. But there was that lag of 2 months where it was very difficult to get a lot of USARC assistance.[7]

To help Arnold resolve premobilization issues and manage the deployment, the rear CP cell was nominally activated on 7 August to assume the responsibilities of the TOC. COL Parsons, LTC Semler, MAJ DiRisio, and other members of the TOC had volunteered or had been selected to fill deployment positions and had to start getting ready to go; therefore, there was a need to replace the TOC with a permanent control cell that would remain behind.

LTC Richard F. Monczynski, the division's deputy G3, was put in charge of the rear CP. Monczynski and about 10 other personnel were brought on active duty to operate the cell. These soldiers were sent to Camp Atterbury, Indiana, for 2 weeks in early September to go through the mobilization process, and were then brought back to the division headquarters in Rochester. Monczynski's team officially took the reins from the TOC on 18 September.[8]

The Battle Over Predeployment Training

Another fortunate aspect of the mobilization delay was it provided time to address a major challenge that encompassed virtually every command involved in this venture—the battle over the predeployment training plan. The disagreements between the division and the First Army actually began earlier in the summer. The main issues centered on where the training would take place, what would be trained, and how long the training would take. The first point of friction was solved somewhat by default.

The 98th Division desired to conduct its predeployment training at Fort Dix, New Jersey. The division's personnel were familiar with that post due to its basic training, TASS, and RC training functions. Besides, it was close to home. Fort Dix, however, was currently being used by the units of the 42d Division that were also to deploy to Iraq. The focus of the First Army training team there was to get the 42d Division headquarters ready to go.[9]

The division's alternate choice was Camp Shelby, Mississippi, but that installation was occupied. The 278th Armored Cavalry Regiment from the Tennessee National Guard was there undergoing its predeployment training. The focus of the First Army training team there was to get the 278th ready to go. That unit was stretching Camp Shelby's resources to the limit. There was no room there for the 98th.[10]

First Army wanted the division to undergo its training at Camp Atterbury. Some considered the post's training resources to be rather limited, but it only had to accommodate approximately 450 Iroquois Warriors for about 3 months and not all at one time. Moreover, it was available.

The other issues were concerned with training content and time. In mid-July, as Parsons and the TOC were going through their mission analysis, they assumed the training required to satisfy the emerging advisor requirement would be met by the same training plan used to prepare the advisors embedded with the Afghanistan National Army (ANA). Matt Jones was aware of that training due to his previous experience as an advisor in Afghanistan. "I knew the folks who replaced us in Afghanistan had built a training package, so I contacted the guys who were over there so they could send us that package . . . and that's what we proposed to use in preparation for Iraq," he explained.[11]

That plan called for 36 training days at the mobilization training site. To address MNSTC-I's desired LAD for the advisor teams and Sherlock's directive to try and cull the training to get troops to Iraq in the shortest possible time without sacrificing readiness, LTC Ryan developed a training plan that estimated the ASTs needed only 28 days of training at the Atterbury mob site.[12] (See figure 8.) Even with the proposed shorter timeline, it was going to take 70 days from mobilization until the first advisor arrived in Kuwait, much less arrived at his assigned Iraqi unit.

COL Al Jones, the First Army G3, on the other hand, wanted the Iroquois Warriors to go through the First Army's standard security force Program of Instruction (POI)—the same POI used to train the artillery units serving as military police units in Iraq. In addition, he took the position that the 98th Division troops would be trained on all the training

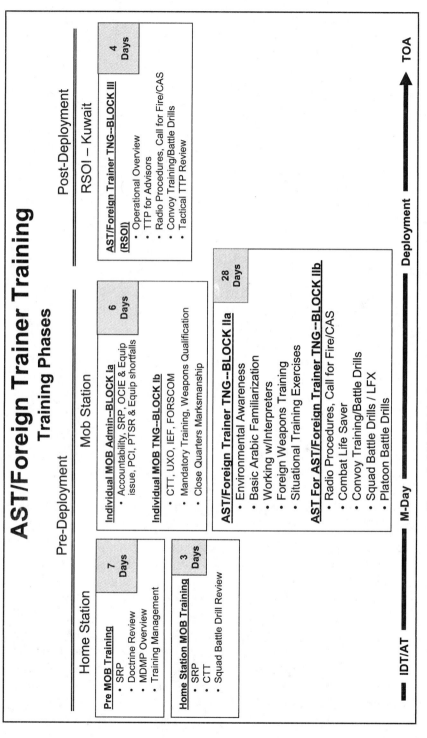

Figure 8. 98th Division's predeployment training plan.

tasks required by DA and CENTCOM for units deploying to Iraq. These included the "40 plus 9" tasks and drills directed by DA, the standard Army driver's training course, 40 hours of language training, and the full range of instruction for weapons qualification.[13]

CENTCOM also required the Iroquois Warriors to go through the standard Theater Specific Individual Readiness Training (TSIRT), the Theater Specific Leader Training, a defensive live fire exercise (LFX), a convoy situational training exercise (STX), and a convoy LFX required of all units deploying into theater. In addition, a change to FORSCOM's basic training guidance for all units deploying to Iraq after 20 September directed several additional tasks to include training on battle command systems, code of conduct, and cultural awareness.[14] Thus, these requirements were not based on COL Jones' training whims. The requirements were directed by various headquarters whose authority in the matters was beyond First Army's ability to change, even if that command wanted to do so.

In contrast to the division plan, the myriad additional tasks First Army had to address in preparing the soldiers of the 98th Division for employment in Iraq resulted in a solution requiring 44 training days. That plan extended the earliest arrival time for ASTs in Kuwait to 86 days, which amounted to almost one-quarter of the year that each AST soldier was expected to serve on active duty. The First Army training plan would delay the advisor team linkup with its assigned Iraqi unit by another 2 weeks. (See figure 9.)

The battle between First Army and the 98th Division lasted all summer. In numerous phone conferences, VTCs, and face-to-face meetings at the USARC and elsewhere, each side made its arguments to support its position. Matt Jones, who had been working closely with Parsons during this period, recalled that the division and First Army "fought over [these issues] for about 40 days. . . . We were just wasting time."[15]

About mid-August, LTC Morales, with the survey team in Iraq, entered the debate by providing new information via SIPRNET on training that could be provided in Kuwait. Once back in Baghdad after the briefings in Atlanta and Washington, Sherlock had pulled the survey team together to tell them about what had transpired and to let them know the mission was on. He also gave them additional guidance on actions needed to prepare for the reception of the division's soldiers.[16] There was pressure to get the division's soldiers to Iraq as soon as possible so Sherlock had been thinking of various ways to shorten the time it would take to get boots on the ground. One way was to shorten the postmobilization training period in CONUS.

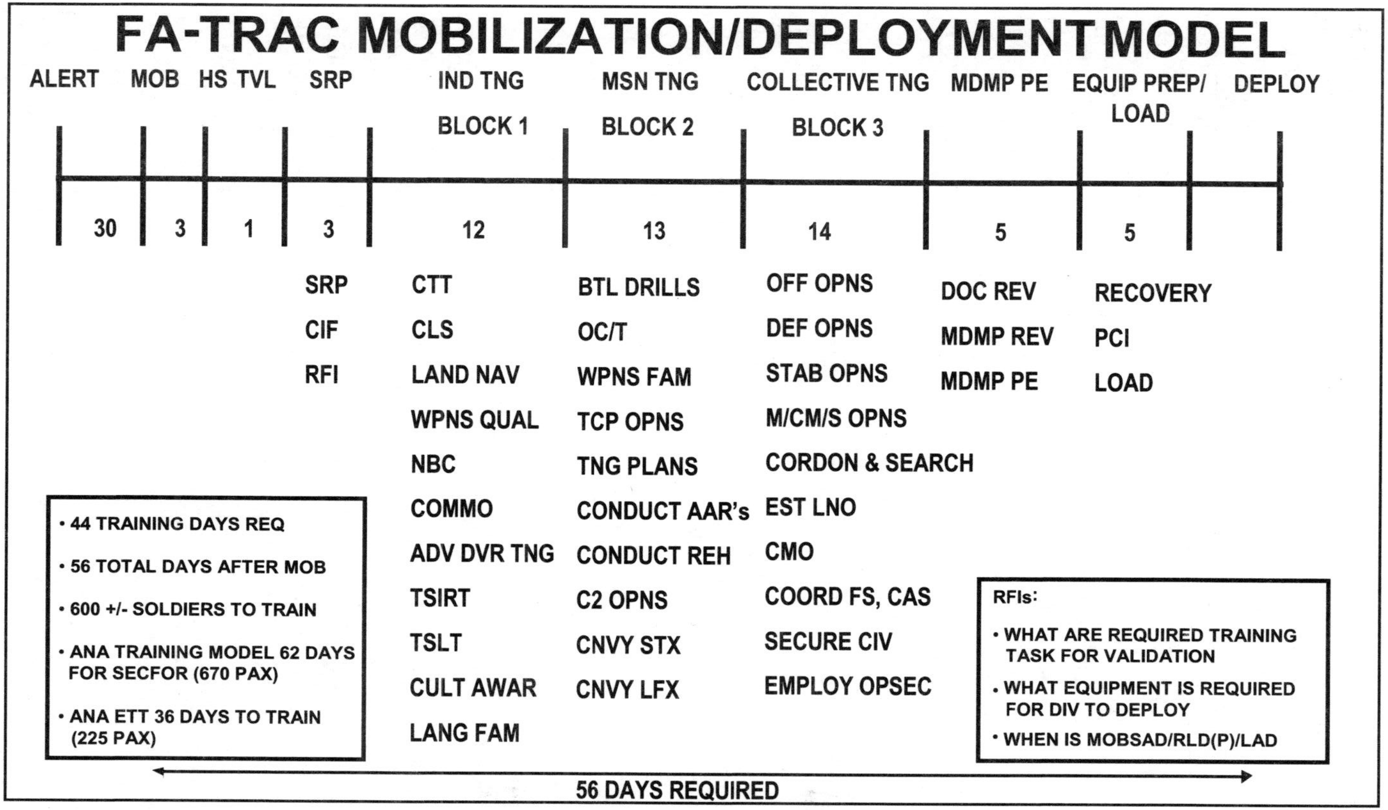

FA-TRAC MOBILIZATION/DEPLOYMENT MODEL

ALERT	MOB	HS	TVL	SRP	IND TNG BLOCK 1	MSN TNG BLOCK 2	COLLECTIVE TNG BLOCK 3	MDMP PE	EQUIP PREP/ DEPLOY LOAD
30	3	1		3	12	13	14	5	5

SRP	BLOCK 1	BLOCK 2	BLOCK 3	MDMP PE	EQUIP PREP
SRP	CTT	BTL DRILLS	OFF OPNS	DOC REV	RECOVERY
CIF	CLS	OC/T	DEF OPNS	MDMP REV	PCI
RFI	LAND NAV	WPNS FAM	STAB OPNS	MDMP PE	LOAD
	WPNS QUAL	TCP OPNS	M/CM/S OPNS		
	NBC	TNG PLANS	CORDON & SEARCH		
	COMMO	CONDUCT AAR's	EST LNO		
	ADV DVR TNG	CONDUCT REH	CMO		
	TSIRT	C2 OPNS	COORD FS, CAS		
	TSLT	CNVY STX	SECURE CIV		
	CULT AWAR	CNVY LFX	EMPLOY OPSEC		
	LANG FAM				

56 DAYS REQUIRED

- 44 TRAINING DAYS REQ
- 56 TOTAL DAYS AFTER MOB
- 600 +/- SOLDIERS TO TRAIN
- ANA TRAINING MODEL 62 DAYS FOR SECFOR (670 PAX)
- ANA ETT 36 DAYS TO TRAIN (225 PAX)

RFIs:
- WHAT ARE REQUIRED TRAINING TASK FOR VALIDATION
- WHAT EQUIPMENT IS REQUIRED FOR DIV TO DEPLOY
- WHEN IS MOBSAD/RLD(P)/LAD

Figure 9. First Army's predeployment training plan.

Sherlock had discovered training opportunities in Kuwait that might be used to validate the troops on required tasks rather than completing the training stateside. The training could also make up some training shortfalls identified by the existing ASTs during the survey. Morales recalled that after the meeting Sherlock said, "Tony, come on over here. After talking with Sean Ryan, I need you to go to Kuwait because we've got this mission. Go down to Kuwait and start to assess what's there in terms of training, training areas, and support." In particular, Sherlock specified he wanted realistic convoy training, communications training, and cultural awareness training if it could be coordinated. Soon after his meeting with Sherlock, Morales and Master Sergeant (MSG) John Compitello, G4 maintenance NCO, were on their way to Kuwait to find out what additional training might be available there. They were told to coordinate with CFLCC to determine reception, staging, onward movement, and integration (RSOI) requirements for bringing the division's elements into theater.[17]

In Kuwait, Morales met with COL Mike Milano, the CFLCC C3. Milano provided Morales with the basic details he needed to develop the division RSOI plan. Milano informed Morales that a US contractor in Kuwait had the capability to put the Iroquois Warriors through each of the training requirements that Sherlock had specified except for cultural awareness. In addition to those tasks, Morales coordinated for weapons training on ranges, live-fire forced entry into buildings, and training on the Blue Force Tracker (BFT) system, which few if any members of the 98th Division had ever seen much less trained on.[18] All of these findings were sent back to Parsons at Rochester for inclusion in the division's version of the predeployment training plan.

The information provided by Morales on the training available in Kuwait only added fuel to the fire. Furthermore, MNSTC-I (through the MNF-I) supported the 98th Division's position saying the training provided in Kuwait would preclude the necessity of many training events being insisted on by First Army for deployment validation. The implication was that the division's ASTs and other elements could be validated on those tasks in Kuwait.[19]

Little of this seemed to move First Army, primarily because its hands were tied. The G3 insisted the 98th Division was going to go through the entire training package required for deploying units. The only progress the 98th Division seemed to make was getting the First Army to shorten the timeline by 2 days for a total of 42 training days. Finally, about 18 August, the issues of location, content, and length of training were presented to LTG Russell Honoré, the First Army CG, for a decision. Honoré decided in favor of his staff on all counts.[20] The Iroquois Warriors failed in their efforts to shorten the deployment timeline, but the delay in the decision was to have repercussions on the training conducted at Camp Atterbury.

Mobilization

On 3 September, the mobilization order finally arrived at the division headquarters. Monczynski at the rear CP received the order and notified MG Robinson and other key members of the staff. By this time, Vernick had organized deploying personnel into eight mobilization groups (later expanded by three small groups in December 2004 and March 2005) based on the two mobilization training sites and when the groups would attend training. In general, those personnel going to the MNSTC-I, CMATT, and CPATT staffs and those going to support the C2 Cell were sent to Fort Bliss. Those troops slotted as ASTs and trainers on the BCT, OES, NCOES, and MOS training teams were sent to Camp Atterbury. Oddly, the convoy security team was sent to Fort Bliss. Jim DiRisio explained, "because of expediency we assumed some risk and sent them through the CRC instead" to get them to Iraq sooner.[21]

After many days and sometimes nights, the battle rosters Vernick had scrubbed, rescrubbed, and scrubbed again took final form. In his communications with the USARC staff while struggling to finalize the deployment lists, Vernick had been told to expect that upwards of 30 percent of the division's soldiers identified for deployment would fall out of the process for various reasons—physical problems, financial problems, security issues—based on the average for Reserve units since the USARC had been tracking activations after 9-11. When the dust settled and the figures came in, the 98th Division experienced a less than 10 percent fallout rate. "I think that shocked USARC," Vernick happily recalled.[22]

One of the issues to plague the 98th Division was that it was not going to mobilize and deploy as a unit, but as individual soldiers that would act as fillers in relatively small teams or as individuals based on MNSTC-I's requirements. Moreover, the urgency of MNSTC-I's situation demanded that certain fillers, such as those slated for the headquarters, get there as quickly as possible. Therefore, mobilization of the division's soldiers in one big package was not feasible. Sean Ryan explained:

> . . . to get the 98th alerted, mobilized, trained, and deployed we needed 2 months or more. Well, that wasn't acceptable so we broke the 98th into packages. We had the staff sections that were going straight into the MNSTC-I, CMATT, and CPATT staffs go through the

CRC and they were expedited. Then, the ones who would be more in harm's way—who would be conducting training and operations with the Iraqis—would go through the full training package, which ultimately was done at Camp Atterbury, Indiana. We piecemealed the 98th in because of the urgency of getting MNSTC-I filled, which led to the mindset that they were individual augmentees as opposed to a unit solution.[23]

To meet MNSTC-I's requirements and the 98th's own unique circumstances, Vernick had developed a total of eight mobilization groups and determined their departure dates for Fort Bliss and Camp Atterbury based on the mobilization order (figure 10).

Mob Group	Location	Departure Date	No. of Personnel
CRC-1	Fort Bliss	11 September	64
Mob-1	Camp Atterbury	11 September	123
CRC-1.5	Fort Bliss	25 September	18
Mob-1.5	Camp Atterbury	25 September	5
CRC-2	Fort Bliss	10 October	131
Mob-2	Camp Atterbury	6 October	174
CRC-3	Fort Bliss	16 October	62
Mob-3	Camp Atterbury	20 October	139[24]

Figure 10. Division mobilization groups.

Of course, in the first two mobilization groups were most of the initial 200 or so volunteers who had waived their right to the 30-day delay. Those going to Fort Bliss would complete the standard processing and training most individual replacements experienced before going to Iraq or Afghanistan. The training primarily consisted of CTT and the nine required premobilization battle drills. In short, the CRC process at Fort Bliss was mature, efficient, and relatively smooth. Few Iroquois Warriors experienced any problems at Fort Bliss. The training at Camp Atterbury, as it turned out, was to possess few of these traits, at least from the perspective of those who received the training.

Camp Atterbury

Camp Atterbury, located just outside Edinburg in southern Indiana, had been established in 1942 as a training cantonment for an infantry division. It had also served as a prisoner of war camp for German and Italian soldiers, and later as a demobilization center at the end of the war. It had not seen much use since then except to support the summer training of the Indiana National Guard. It was reopened in February 2003 primarily to support the mobilization of RC units and soldiers participating in the GWOT.[25]

As mentioned, Camp Atterbury was not the division's first choice. Nor was it the choice of LTG Helmly:

> I didn't feel Camp Atterbury was equipped or organized to do [what was needed for the 98th Division]. . . . Camp Atterbury simply needed a lot of capabilities that I didn't feel were resident, but that decision was made and we sent the 98th there. I argued against it, but it was done anyway. It wasn't one of those things, though, that we couldn't make work regardless of the shortcomings.[26]

COL Charles "Gus" Stafford, the commander of the 3d Brigade, 85th Division (TS), and the man who would eventually get the mission to train the troops of the 98th Division at Camp Atterbury, disagreed with that assessment. His opinion was:

> The 98th Division and its initial role in going over as ASTs was focused on the basic combat training piece of the mission with new recruits to the Iraqi Army. With that in mind, their principal tasks were focused on soldierization skills, weapons qualification and the initial forming of units as individuals and squads—no higher than platoon level. Camp Atterbury, being a platform to train units up to the battalion level, had sufficient assets to do that training.[27]

Interestingly, Stafford's belief that the 98th Division was "focused on the basic combat training piece of the mission with new recruits to the Iraqi Army" reveals a fundamental misinterpretation of the mission common to many people before the 98th Division's advisors arrived in theater. This impression was also common to his trainers who, in turn, reinforced it to the advisors. Many of the advisors were already of the mistaken belief that they were still going to be in a *training* role, not an *advisory* one, while in Iraq. The idea that the division's soldiers were going over to train the Iraqi Army helps explain some of the training conducted for the Iroquois Warriors while they were in Indiana.

Whether Atterbury was or was not the best option, the late decision in choosing the location and the content of the training had a negative impact on the experience for the Iroquois Warriors. Stafford acknowledged that his brigade was not assigned the mission until about 20 August, only 3 weeks before the first mobilization group arrived from Rochester. In that period, he had to design and coordinate a viable training package that met the First Army requirements and have his trainers ready to start operations shortly after the troops' arrival. The concern, and perhaps frustration, registered by Stafford with the late notice is palpable in a message he sent to the 85th Division G3 on 24 August. He wrote, "98th Division Train-up: When? By who? With what resources? I know we aren't deploying folks to the war zone inside a 5-week lock-in, are we? Having said that, if it's ours, then tell us when it needs to be done, and we'll make it happen. . . ."[28]

Making it happen was no mean feat. The 98th Division contingent was an add-on to the 3d Brigade's already crowded training schedule. Although Camp Atterbury was relatively empty when the first mobilization group arrived in September, the 3d Brigade had numerous other units scheduled for training soon after. Within the next month, the population of the post would swell to over 4,000 soldiers in training from four Army Reserve and National Guard engineer battalions and several other smaller units. All of these units would be competing for ranges and resources with the 98th Division, especially mobs 2 and 3, which arrived in October.[29]

Committed to providing a good training package to the soldiers of the 98th, Stafford and his staff went to work designing the plan and squeezing it into the existing schedule. To his advantage, Stafford's 3d Brigade was well acquainted with Camp Atterbury. The post had been the brigade's primary training site since well before 9-11. The 3d Brigade's primary mission was to develop, conduct, and evaluate lane training for Guard and Reserve units throughout Ohio, Indiana, and Michigan. Its primary customers, however, had been units of the Indiana National Guard's 38th Infantry Division and the division's 76th Infantry Brigade. The 3d Brigade had been mobilized after 9-11 to help reactivate Atterbury as a mobilization training site for RC units deploying to support the GWOT, and so Stafford and his troops had a good idea of what it took to get units through the validation process for deployment.[30] Still, with such short notice, it would take a great deal of effort to ensure his people were ready to begin training when the Iroquois Warriors began to arrive on 11 September 2004.

COL Catalanotti was already at Camp Atterbury. MG Robinson had contacted him in August and asked him to go to Indiana and assume the position of Commander of Troops for the 98th Division contingent going through training there. Catalanotti arrived on Labor Day, 6 September, and immediately began coordination with Stafford on the training program.

He recalled that from the beginning, the relationship between his staff and those on the installation was solid:

> There were really three chains of command. There was the 98th internal chain of command, which all the soldiers and their layers of leadership were accountable to, namely to me. There was the Camp Atterbury garrison structure, which had the billets, food, transportation, and all the equipment. And then there was the 85th Division (Training Support) that provided the training and the ultimate certification. The good news was that we three colonels [Catalanotti, Stafford, and the garrison commander] came together very nicely with our staffs. As a result, we were able to get four-plus increments through Atterbury swiftly with certification in 39 to 45 days, with all the equipment resources and all the personnel issues, from medical to operational readiness, taken care of.[31]

Though Catalanotti's opinion that the Camp Atterbury experience was good for him and his staff, for the Iroquois Warriors who began to arrive shortly thereafter, the impressions went downhill. The subsequent disgruntlement of the trainees would focus on four main areas: their treatment, the experience and knowledge of the trainers, the quality and content of the training, and the inefficient use of time.

There's an old Army saying that "Soldiers aren't happy unless they're complaining." There is truth in that statement, and anyone who has been a leader in the Army knows that that statement can be as true for officers and NCOs as it is for private soldiers. Given the nature of the missions they had been assigned to perform, the majority of the 98th Division personnel sent to Indiana were officers and senior NCOs. The genesis of their unhappiness may have been the fact that they were at Camp Atterbury. According to Gus Stafford,

> One of the problems in this entire mobilization process that we've been going through has been the desire on the part of the Army Reserve and the Army National Guard to follow a model that says, 'We will train. We will mobilize. We will deploy.' That's an endstate we're seeking as we move toward the Army Force Generation (ARFORGEN) model. However, in the experience of the 98th Division, that was not the case. With the 98th Division, we mobilized them, we trained them, and we deployed. Because of their desire to quickly mobilize and get to theater, it

was a constant battle to explain to them that they had to go through certain training before they could get into theater.[32]

He went on to explain,

> There are insufficient days in the current model for the Army Reserve and National Guard to bring a unit up to the level of proficiency required at the collective level simply using . . . 39 days [annually]. . . . In spite of the fact that we were doing the right thing by providing the training opportunity that they otherwise couldn't have gotten during their normal drill weekends and annual training periods, there was still a feeling on the part of the Reserve and Guard folks going through the mobilization process that somehow the active force was looking down on them, that they were less prepared, and that's why we were doing what we were doing. And that, by being less prepared, we were somehow challenging their professionalism. I would say, though, that nothing could be further from the truth. We were simply focused on giving them the training they needed to best prepare them for combat in Iraq.[33]

In retrospect, few, if any, of the Iroquois Warriors who went through the training at Atterbury would deny the training was necessary, and most would chalk up any griping as fulfilling the old saw about soldiers' complaints. What they would argue with, perhaps, was the way some of the administrative aspects of the training were conducted. For example, a number of them resented being treated like privates. MAJ Scott McConnell, a staff officer in the division G3 section and slated to be on an AST, related:

> The whole experience there from start to finish was taking master sergeants, captains, majors, and lieutenant colonels and putting them into the private-going-through-basic-training mindset. They put us in formation and accounted for every minute of our days. We slept in barracks. We were locked down, couldn't leave post. We were put through a training program and weren't utilized as anything but students going lockstep through this training.[34]

MAJ Paul Loncle, division budget officer and assigned to work on the OES team, agreed. "I was kidding with my friends. I said, 'I'm an E3/O4—I'm treated like a private first class and I'm paid as a major,'" he recalled. "You look at who's going [through the training]. In the OES we're talking majors and lieutenant colonels. You have a lot of people here who know how to lead and we've proven it through our military careers."[35] The implication was that these senior soldiers did not need to be marched around like privates in basic training.

However elementary the environment, there were reasons for such actions. COL Stafford explained:

> From the Training Support Brigade side, we put huge emphasis on forming cohesive teams. We tried to billet, train, and eat in [AST] team organization so they would get to know each other's strengths and weaknesses. We fought against letting folks 'do their own thing' since many of these teams formed at the mobilization station. We encouraged them to form internal chains of command and to define roles and missions within their teams. The 98th Division leadership fought hard to keep this same rigor in maintaining accountability and validation records management. No one went anywhere by themselves. [In addition,] Camp Atterbury has long had a requirement for squad-sized elements to move in formation due to the congested road networks and number of units mobilizing at any time . . . we could have over 4,000 soldiers in over 30 different units training at one time on everything from infantry tactics to heavy engineer equipment to heavy equipment transports. Marching was a safety issue, not a haze.[36]

Still, for those soldiers in the group who were drill sergeants, to be treated like basic trainees must have been particularly galling. Despite the perceived basic training atmosphere, however aggravating it may have been, the majority of those leaders going through the Atterbury experience basically accepted it as the price of being there and focused on what they needed to learn from those who had been selected to train them.

The majority of the trainers at Camp Atterbury were soldiers of Stafford's own 3d Brigade. The 85th Division was a multicomponent training support division, meaning that its brigades and battalions were a mixture of Regular Army and Army Reserve soldiers. Most of the reservists were assigned to the division's multiple battalions. The 3d Brigade consisted of seven training support battalions and a contractor cell. The contractor cell provided training on the Arabic language and culture, Combat Life Saver (CLS) training, and role players for various simulated exercises. Stafford's trainers had developed various training scenarios that used these role players (many of whom were Iraqi ex-patriots) as Iraqi civilians, soldiers, and insurgents to put units in as realistic situations as possible.

The rest of the brigade consisted of one logistics support, one engineer, two infantry, and three combat service support training support battalions. These battalions typically consisted of a number of lane training teams. These teams could be composed of branch-specific trainers, such as infantry, engineer, or transportation, or they could be multifunctional. For example, a logistics lane team possessed quartermaster, transportation, and medical personnel to train and grade multifunctional units such as division support battalions. Likewise, these lane training teams could function as observer/controllers (O/C) for external evaluations of units during AT.

What the lane grading teams were not designed to do was to conduct weapons training and qualification. To assist the 3d Brigade with those tasks, Stafford acquired a number of soldiers from the Indiana National Guard's 76th Infantry Brigade, who would be responsible for training and validating the 98th Division's troops on individual weapons qualification and with training on, and familiarity with, crew-served weapons.[37]

The problem with the trainers, from the standpoint of the Iroquois Warriors, was that the situation seemed to be the "blind leading the blind." Many of the trainers were reservists too. Additionally, from the beginning it seemed to the trainees that their trainers were ill-prepared to execute the training due to their short preparation time and unfamiliarity of some of the tasks. "Since we weren't programmed into the deployment, we were kind of thrown onto the TSDs," Matt Jones recalled. "They were overwhelmed. They didn't know we were coming until about 15 to 20 days before we arrived, so they were scrambling. I don't think there was a really good understanding of what the mission was going to be and there was no training plan that was really focused on the mission."[38]

The lack of preparation time and the perceived lack of combat experience led to negative impressions of the trainers themselves. Loncle felt that "the trainers we had at Atterbury weren't necessarily the best ones." LTC Douglas Shipman, S3 for the 98th Division's 1st Brigade in Providence and soon to be the deputy senior advisor to the Iraqi 3d Division AST team, explained that the trainers "gave it the old college try, but these were people who had never been to Iraq teaching us about improvised explosive devices (IEDs) and things like that. It was very difficult for them to be credible." Staff Sergeant (SSG) Brian Charnock, a drill sergeant with the 1st Battalion, 390th Regiment, a basic training unit from Buffalo, New York, agreed. "A lot of them had no experience in country. They were basically drill sergeants like us who did the same jobs we do. . . . There were a few who gave us a lot of insight, those who had actually gone to Iraq or Afghanistan, and they were obviously the more valuable trainers. Otherwise, though, it was just one Reserve soldier teaching another Reserve soldier. . . ." Perhaps the most charitable in his view was COL Catalanotti: "Your best trainers are the ones who've experienced Iraq. Well, we were the first division to go through there, so there wasn't a whole lot of experience with their trainers. They were doing the best they could."[39]

The professionalism of the trainers was questioned as well. The soldiers of the 98th Division were trainers and instructors themselves, so any flaw in the presentation, whether it was technique or, more importantly, facts, was quickly detected. It also added to any friction existing between trainers and trainees. Looking back at the situation, Loncle recollected:

> . . . a lot of the [trainers], we know, just got the info wrong and we learned real early that it just wasn't worth bringing it up to them. They just got way too defensive. So later on we would get everybody back together and say, 'Okay, this is what they put out, but let me tell you—this is how it really is, just so you don't get any false ideas.' We just tried not to step on any toes and cause any trouble. It was more like, 'Hey, those of you who know that what they're putting out is wrong, don't call them on the carpet. If you have a problem with them, take it up the chain outside and don't bring it up here in front of the whole class.'[40]

The late mission assignment also affected the 3d Brigade's ability to issue training schedules in a timely manner so troops could plan to fill any holes in the schedule with supplementary training. The Army standard is to publish training schedules 6 weeks out. In theory, the training schedules for all 6 weeks should have been available on arrival. But as MAJ Roger Swartwood, slated to be on the AST for the Iraqi 1st Division, recalled, "the information flow became discouraging at times, trying to find out what we were doing 2 or 3 days in advance so we could maybe plan for some of the training we were trying to do as a team." He added, "We would have liked to have had at least a week out training schedule, but we had only a 2-day type thing. We knew what we were going to do today and then they gave us an idea of what we would be doing the next day, but that was it."[41]

Compounding the frustration of the Iroquois Warriors was the content and quality of the training. One of the early events on the training schedule was a 40-hour block of training on cultural awareness. Jody Daniels remembered that the survey team's guidance on this block of instruction had been very specific. She stated, "We specifically requested that the language training not be done as a 40-hour week but as 2 hours a day every day for 4 weeks or whatever. We wanted it spread out over time so they actually had a better chance of learning a few things about the language, rather than trying to get immersed in it in 5 days. We knew that just wasn't going to take."[42] Matt Jones explained, "We had 5 [straight] days of Arabic, and they even tried to teach us how to write Arabic. . . . They put us in the officer's club where there was no air conditioning. . . . It was ridiculous." Moreover, the Civil Affairs officer assigned to give the country study briefing had never been to Iraq, which further strained credibility.[43]

Following that less than effective experience, the Iroquois Warriors then entered individual skills training. For many, this was as demoralizing as trying to learn Arabic in 5 days. Scott McConnell, who like many Iroquois Warriors, had completed most of the "40 plus 9" tasks at his Reserve Center during the summer now had to do them all over again. Sergeant First Class (SFC) Dennis Ewing, another drill sergeant with the 1st Battalion, 390th Regiment, remarked that the trainers "were spending a lot of time on common tasks that we do every year. We're different from other units that may not do common tasks as often as we do. We do them every weekend so it was a waste of time for us."[44]

The CTT training was followed by weapons training that Ewing described as minimal. For example, there was no training on any of the common foreign weapons that advisors might encounter in Iraq such as the AK-47 with which Iraqi Army units were equipped. Additionally, Ewing felt that more time should have been spent on crew-served weapons, and everybody should have had the opportunity to get the training. During that block, "Only two people on each team were sent to [the training on] each crew-served weapon," Ewing said. COL Parsons, when reviewing the training at Atterbury agreed. He believed the major flaw in the training plan was there had not been more training on crew-served weapons.[45]

The training on the newer, high-tech pieces of equipment the Iroquois Warriors would be working with in Iraq was equally lacking. Similar to the crew-served weapons training, only one person per advisor team was sent to gain experience with the new Blue Force Tracker (BFT) system. No practical exercises were conducted; the training was no more than a brief familiarity session with the piece of equipment. Each of the soldiers sent to the training was then expected to train his team on the BFT once they were issued the item in Iraq. Training on SINCGARS radios was conducted with older versions of the system that were not widely used in Iraq and was limited to just a small number of people. As a result, Ewing recalled that when the advisors arrived in country "there were senior NCOs and officers who didn't know how to operate a radio. That's the wrong time to have to figure that out."[46]

Figure 11. Iroquois Warriors practice clearing a house at Camp Atterbury.

One block of training at Camp Atterbury that was almost universally praised was the CLS training. McConnell believe that the CLS training "was the most effective of all the things there."[47] Perhaps the real possibility of casualties in Iraq made the training seem to be all that much more important.

On conclusion of the individual-level tasks, the training shifted to collective tasks. These blocks included offensive and defensive tasks such as cordon and search missions; planning, coordinating, and conducting fire support and close-air support; civil-military operations; and convoy security operations. These events received higher praise from the Iroquois Warriors, but even they came in for some criticism. In a postdeployment series of interviews with members of the division, it was the convoy training that seemed to be the most memorable part of the Atterbury experience, and therefore garnered the most comments. Catalanotti explained the basic problem with the convoy block.

> They [the 3d Brigade trainers] tried very hard academically [to conduct the training] by the training doctrine. Training doctrine can only go so far, though. You can study

the driver's education booklet and take your driver's test, but to understand how to drive you need to get out there on the road. Early on, those running convoy exercises did not [reflect the] Iraq experience; they were running them from a training doctrine standpoint.[48]

The 3d Brigade trainers were teaching a purely doctrinal approach to conducting convoy security operations and not techniques that were reflective of the situation in Iraq. COL Stafford explained, ". . . the tactics, techniques and procedures (TTPs) were a hedgehog principle. Every soldier in the vehicle would point his weapon out of the vehicle to show an aggressive presence and be able to return fire, because the primary threat was insurgents with small arms and rocket-propelled grenades (RPGs)." This technique was being used because in the summer and fall of 2004, according to Stafford, the insurgents were still primarily using ambush as a means to intercept, destroy, or delay convoys rather than IEDs. LTC Shipman, however, countered this with the comment that the convoy scenario trained at Atterbury "was not consistent with the current threat situation [that existed] when we got into country."[49]

The HMMWVs that were used for training at Atterbury were the soft-skinned version and the technique of having weapons pointed out the window so one could immediately return fire was the proper one if the threat was a traditional ambush against such vehicles. The ASTs deploying to Iraq were to be equipped with the up-armored HMMWV and the emerging threat was from IEDs. In such a scenario, the best technique was to keep the shrapnel-proof glass rolled up and drive through an ambush. Moreover, having the windows up in the event of an IED explosion would further protect the soldier from death or injury. Though the correct equipment might not have been available at Atterbury, conceptually the technique could have been trained. Despite any shortcomings revealed in the training, in a posttraining after action report (AAR) prepared by personnel of the division, the convoy live-fire exercise conducted by the 3d Brigade was rated as "excellent."[50]

For those soldiers at Camp Atterbury assigned to ASTs, the training they expected to teach them "how" to be advisors was a further disappointment. When asked about the advisor-specific training he received during his stay at Camp Atterbury, Roger Swartwood responded, "I can't remember getting any." Shipman generally supported that assessment. He said, "We strongly recommended that we get more training on being an advisor . . . but I don't think the training was set up to accommodate that."[51] In short, advisor-specific training was not provided. But there was a potential, albeit only partial, remedy to the problem.

The approximately 42 days spent at Camp Atterbury by the various mobilization groups of the 98th Division were not overly busy. In fact, Shipman described the experience as having "2 weeks of training crammed into 5."[52] Thus, there was sufficient time to undertake hip-pocket training if one knew when time would be available. Along with conducting additional training, there was time to conduct further research on the advisor mission if one was so inclined. Some members of the 98th Division attempted to perform these actions in their spare time. Scott McConnell remembered that Matt Jones used his spare time to train his team: "Matt Jones had been in Afghanistan in this role and so he really knew what was going to be expected of him. He went the extra mile and did training above and beyond the official curriculum, after hours, and they were doing different tactics and techniques that he thought were going to be appropriate for a battalion AST—and he had almost the entire team together there with him."[53]

Others used their spare time wisely as well. MAJ Jeffrey Tennyson, assigned to an AST for the 3d Iraqi Division, also conducted training after duty hours with his team. "What my team ended up training on were things we felt were the highest risks—things like room clearing and first aid," Tennyson explained. "We all went through Combat Life Saver and, as a follow-up, we just kept practicing what we learned. We made a huge list of tasks, broke them down, and then prioritized what we wanted to train on first. I also brought a little bit of stuff on IEDs from my work at Fort Leonard Wood."[54]

In an effort that is truly reflective of the times, Swartwood conducted a great deal of research on-line looking for information on ASTs. "I got a lot of it from the Internet," he recalled.[55] Shipman confirms that the Internet was probably the best means of determining what an advisor was and what one did:

> . . . a couple weeks out from mobilization, we found a website about advisor support teams that someone had set up. One of our noncommissioned officers found it accidentally through a Google search and e-mailed it to us—and you know, there was more information on that website than we had received from anybody up to that point. It was kind of humorous that the Army's official system hadn't really provided the information that we needed.[56]

COL Edward P. Castle, the division G6, was slotted on the battle rosters to be the commandant of the OES/MOS school. He and most of his personnel were in the division's second mobilization group (Mob-2) to go through Camp Atterbury. During their spare time he pulled his team together to do some brainstorming on how the team would perform its mission. His team also "concentrated on getting documentation around the particular branch [we] were going to train in, just to have some kind of information when we went over there—field manuals, training manuals or any kind of a document; lesson plans from different schoolhouses," he recalled. "We did a lot of e-mailing and a lot of burning CDs to get documentation. That's what we did to get ready as a team."[57]

The major portion of the division's troops accomplished very little with their spare time, however. McConnell later revealed, "There were maybe two or three out of the eight or so [advisor support] teams that actually took it upon themselves to do that extracurricular training. The rest of the brigade, division, and some of the battalion teams just went through the curriculum and that was all."[58]

Overall, the training experience at Camp Atterbury drew mixed reviews from members of the 98th Division. One officer described it as ". . . horrible . . . a complete waste. . . ." Another said it was "marginal." SFC Ewing reflected that the training "wasn't even close to what we needed."[59] Others gave a more positive assessment and were probably closer to reality. They tended to characterize the quality of the training as varied. Castle may have expressed it best when he said,

> Some of it was good and some, unfortunately, wasn't. I think the biggest disappointment with Atterbury's training was that a lot of it was left up to us. There were portions of the day where they said, 'Well, this is mission-specific or up to the team you're with to decide.' But since we knew very little about our mission, it was kind of hard to develop what it was that we wanted to train on.[60]

Tennyson further addressed the challenge of that task, at least as it related to those slotted for the AST mission: "It was like we were trying to train for a mission in a black box. We were shaking it, holding it up, and trying to guess what was in that black box."[61]

Unfortunately, some of the members of the 98th Division were not even attempting to do that. In all fairness to the 3d Brigade trainers, if the training experience was considered inadequate by some Iroquois Warriors and did not prepare them as well as they thought it should have, the fault in part may be due to their own failure to take advantage of the time and opportunities they did have to build on their level of readiness. It is clear that at least some of them did, but others did not.

Ever the optimist, Catalanotti gave the 3d Brigade trainers the highest marks. "For the resources they had, they did a good job," he remarked. "Some of the more common skills [tasks] . . . they did very well on. . . . Medical readiness and Combat Life Saving, the whole biological and chemical piece, they did well on too."[62]

Gus Stafford acknowledged that the training might not have been as good as it should have been, but his reasons for why differed from the Iroquois Warriors. He believed the major shortfall was the inability of the training package to develop a sense of teamwork. He thought the number of days available in the plan to conduct the training was too short, and the number of tasks that had to be trained and validated precluded adequate time to develop teamwork among the 98th Division elements, especially the ASTs. "We did not build enough of an employment exercise with training vignettes and lanes to hammer home their ability to operate as teams," he reflected.[63]

Stafford understood the frustration expressed by many of the 98th's soldiers who went through the training at Camp Atterbury. Regarding the basic marksmanship and CTT training, for example, he wrote, "Since the 98th Division (IT) was manned with individual training experts, there is little wonder that they felt we were wasting their time as we trained, practiced, and tested them on the very tasks they said they already knew."[64] Most of the training was conducted, not because there was any belief that the Iroquois Warriors were not trained, but simply because the training was required by a higher authority.

Stafford did take issue regarding the level of experience of his trainers, however. He explained, for example, that the unit that conducted the convoy training for the 98th Division, the 1st Battalion, 335th Regiment, was composed almost exclusively of combat veterans who had served in either Iraq or Afghanistan.[65] They were indeed soldiers who could, and did, impart their knowledge and experience in combat operations in the GWOT. Charnock acknowledged as much in comments regarding those who had been in Iraq or Afghanistan, and their value as trainers.

Arguably the most glaring shortfall of the Atterbury experience was the lack of training that focused on actual advisor duties and responsibilities. This was not the fault of the 3d Brigade, but perhaps the fault of the Army as an institution. Sean Ryan recalled that during one of the many meetings between the 98th Division and First Army to discuss the training plan, COL Jones, the G3, "gave a great soliloquy on the fact that this was really a Special Forces Foreign Internal Defense mission and the institutional Army didn't have the ability to train advisors . . . [and] he was absolutely correct."[66] The reality, however, was that Special Forces (SF) units were already stretched thin with multiple missions, recovering from recent missions, or preparing to go on other missions, and that included the SF groups in the National Guard. There were no SF units available for training the Iraqi Special Forces (ISF) and the Army had to look elsewhere to satisfy the advisor requirements, as it had often done in past conflicts. Additionally, because the conventional Army has not performed advisor missions on a routine basis, it has never developed a basis for training advisors, nor has it even adopted a basic doctrine for advisor missions for conventional forces. Thus, there were no (and to date are no) tasks, conditions, and standards available with which the 3d Brigade could have trained the ASTs of the 98th Division on advisor-specific responsibilities.

Boots on the Ground—Kuwait

At about the mid-point of Mob-1's training at Camp Atterbury, CRC-1 from Fort Bliss arrived at the BIAP just west of the city on 22 September. Just 2 weeks after the receipt of the mobilization order, the 98th Division had boots on the ground ready to go to work for MNSTC-I. Consisting of just over 60 soldiers, the majority of CRC-1 was assigned to MNSTC-I's J-Staff. After processing through BIAP, these soldiers arrived at their various places of duty, mostly at the MNSTC-I or CMATT headquarters in Baghdad where they would spend 10 to 11 months of their active duty tour. This group would be followed by four more groups about every 2 weeks until all troops slated on the JMD for the command's various staffs were in country.

At about the same time the third Atterbury mobilization group began assembling at home stations in mid-October to travel to Indiana, the first mobilization group at Camp Atterbury was preparing to depart for Kuwait. On 17 October, Mob-1 took off from Indianapolis and headed for Rhein Main Air Base near Frankfurt, Germany. After a stop there, the plane flew to Kuwait where it landed at the Kuwait City International Airport. There to greet them were Sean Ryan and Tony Morales. Once the troops were off the plane, the two colonels took turns briefing them on the plan for their stay in Kuwait and various aspects of the local environment, to include security and the potential for heat casualties. Ryan explained, "One of the things we briefed them on was heat. They just left Rochester, New York, and they're now in Kuwait. It's 116 degrees, so we told them the impor-tance of drinking water all the time and not skipping meals. We told them about slowing the tempo down to where they could sustain and get through the training." After the briefs, the troops were loaded into buses and taken to a tent cantonment at Camp Virginia for their next phase of training.[67]

Camp Virginia was located in the desert about 50 kilometers due west of Kuwait City. LTC Daniel Christian, slated to be the brigade advisor for the 3d Brigade, 5th Iraqi Division, generously described the camp and its surrounding environment as austere. He noted, "There was certainly a heightened situational awareness [among us] as we were getting ready to go north at that point."[68]

Unlike Camp Atterbury, the training that the Iroquois Warriors were to receive in Kuwait was almost universally praised. The package at Camp Virginia consisted of training in close quarters combat using the "glass house" technique, training on AK-47s (to include field stripping and firing the weapon), training on crew-served weapons—on which everybody had the chance to train, and a realistic live-fire convoy training exercise.

In contrast to Camp Atterbury, contractors employed by Military Professional Resources Incorporated (MPRI) conducted the training in Kuwait. All were ex-military, and many were former SF soldiers. Paul Loncle's assessment of these teams was, "They were really good."[69]

Most of the training in Kuwait was conducted at the Udairi Ranges about 40 kilometers north of Camp Virginia and most of it revolved around combat operations and substantive live-fire exercises. "It opened my eyes," Charnock recalled. "The training in Kuwait was to the standard I would have expected going into country. It was pretty good."[70]

Figure 12. Members of the 98th Division (IT) undergo AK-47 familiarization training in Kuwait before deploying to Taji, Iraq, in October 2004.

As in Indiana, the convoy training seemed to be the highlight of the training experience in Kuwait. One of the key factors in the quality of the experience was, for the first time, the Iroquois Warriors were trained in up-armored HMMWVs. These heavy vehicles provided a different driving experience than the canvas-top models at Camp Atterbury, especially in the sandy terrain of the Middle East. In addition, some were equipped with the M2 .50-caliber heavy machine gun in a ring mount on the top, as well as the BFT system that proved to be so rare in Indiana. In some cases, the HMMWVs mounted no crew-served weapon. In those instances, a soldier was posted in the hatch and used his rifle to simulate the missing weapon. The training was conducted over a 3-day period at Udairi and concluded with a live-fire convoy exercise.[71]

While considered a major improvement over the Atterbury experience, the training at Camp Virginia was not without flaw. The convoy technique taught by the MPRI instructors was more or less the same as what had been taught at Camp Atterbury—the "hedgehog" principle with windows down and weapons pointed outward. Scott McConnell recalled:

> Some of those tactics we didn't end up using in theater anyway, things like marking IEDs with stuff you throw out of the vehicle. Mostly the tactics were pretty consistent and the only drawback was that it was all based on us having our own convoy. [When] we're going to run a convoy of 25 vehicles [in Iraq] . . . they're all going to be Americans. In reality, if it was an all-American convoy, it was maybe three or four vehicles with small teams. If it was any bigger than that, it was because we were part of running an Iraqi convoy. When we got there, we had to train Iraqis, communicate with Iraqis, and do all that as part of their convoy—and we never touched on any of that during our training.[72]

McConnell's last comment highlights the fact that there was no AST-specific training provided at Camp Virginia either. Swartwood and other AST leaders continued to send requests up through their chains of command to provide training, or at least information, on AST duties and responsibilities, but to no avail.[73]

One of the challenges anticipated by the division's planners was that their troops would need time to acclimatize on arrival in Kuwait. Daniels explained that the survey team had deliberately planned to make acclimatization a part of the Kuwait experience:

When you're in a training environment in the United States, you are very typically on e-mail, on cell phones, and very connected to your family and friends and your normal lifestyle. We figured if we could pause in Kuwait, do some training and get immersed in what it was like to be in 110-degree days with body armor, not attached to a cell phone and not having all those lifelines before they actually went up into a more combat-like environment, it would be very helpful. . . . It was very conscious. We needed to stop and do more training in the desert environment, in the vehicles, and Kuwait was a good place do that.[74]

Despite the planning and despite his initial warnings to the troops on their arrival, Ryan recalled that "not 2 days [went] by and we had the first heat casualty. Then we had two more heat casualties. The first one was a female colonel who had skipped three meals."[75]

Another problem facing the Iroquois Warriors that had been anticipated by the survey team, but was not yet apparent to the troops, was that some of them would end up changing jobs once they arrived in theater. Christian encountered this situation soon after his arrival: ". . . my original mission requirement was to be the officer in charge of an engineer schoolhouse and I would have had three majors working for me. When I arrived in Kuwait, though, within 24 hours we were notified that that mission was really up in the air and no one was sure if it was going to occur."[76] It did not. This kind of situation was to become more prevalent once the troops arrived in Iraq.

About 29 October, Mob-1 boarded C-130s at Kuwait International Airport and flew into BIAP. (The rest of the mob groups transited through the training in Kuwait between mid-October to mid-December.) The following day, the troops were transported by bus to the Taji Military Training Base (TMTB), located about 20 kilometers northwest of Baghdad. Before Operation IRAQI FREEDOM (OIF) in 2003, Taji had been the headquarters of the Republican Guard's Al-Medina Armored Division and possessed extensive tank repair facilities. Therefore, the camp was a lucrative target and had been heavily damaged in Operation DESERT FOX in 1997 and again during OIF. A few new facilities had been built and much of the damage had been repaired by the CPA before the Iroquois Warriors arrived, though the damage to many areas was still very much in evidence.[77]

The TMTB was divided into two sections: the US side, which housed the aviation brigade of the 1st Cavalry Division, and the Iraqi side, where various Iraqi Army units and training facilities as well as the C2 Cell for

CMATT's ASTs were located. At Taji, the Iroquois Warriors were billeted in "The Green Hotel," a two-story, metal and corrugated tin building that had originally been painted green. McConnell described the experience of a stay there: "I think [it had] corrugated tin floors as well. Every time somebody walked down between the bunks, it echoed through the building, one end to the other. They crammed us all into these buildings with just enough room for you to stick your legs between the bunks. It was pretty tight quarters and pretty friendly, so to speak, for the time we were there."[78]

The primary activities for the Iroquois Warriors at Taji were theater in-processing, familiarization with the Iraqi culture, and preparing for movement to their place of duty. The in-processing was accomplished by 98th Division personnel from the J-Staff at MNSTC-I and by the AST C2 Cell for those troops being assigned as advisors. As part of the reception, BG Schwitters typically talked to each arriving group and related the expectations of them as part of the MNSTC-I and CMATT team.[79] The in-processing was followed by cultural awareness training.

The cultural awareness training consisted of almost 2 days of briefings on the Iraqi culture, the Arab mindset, the history of Iraq, and "why things work the way they do in Iraq."[80] The training, perhaps better described as indoctrination, was provided by Dr. Chin, a man who seemed to be a character out of a James Bond movie. When asked about Dr. Chin's first name in an interview, Matt Jones responded:

> He didn't officially have one. He was a scary guy. He was Delta Force's psychiatrist/psychologist or Jedi mind master or something like that. Anyway, that was the best training we received the entire time. Dr. Chin gave a 3-hour breakdown of the history of Iraq so you could understand some of these cultural issues and the implications of some of the decisions that had been made. I wish we had had that on day one. He was such a clear presenter. He made it easy to understand why certain things were going on and it was very helpful.[81]

Dr. Chin's presentation was widely regarded by the Iroquois Warriors as one of the best, if not the best, block of instruction in their whole training experience prior to assuming their missions. Chin's presentation was Schwitters' idea. Schwitters had worked with Chin on previous occasions in the Special Operations community. The general had recognized that Chin was uniquely capable of performing this kind of training and had him contracted to come to Taji to do it.[82]

The training at Taji completed the process to prepare the advisors, and any other 98th Division soldiers slated to work directly with the ISF to perform their mission. Now it was a matter of moving to their assigned places of duty and going to work—or so it seemed.

Even while the troops were at Camp Atterbury, mounting evidence indicated there would be turbulence in assignments and duties when they finally arrived in Iraq. Soldiers designated to be advisors had been slotted against specific ASTs going to specific Iraqi units. On his arrival at Camp Atterbury, Swartwood learned he was assigned as the team leader for the 1st Battalion, 1st Brigade, 1st Iraqi Army Division. "When I put my stuff down on my bunk, they had my name over my bunk with '1st Battalion Team Leader' written on it," he recalled.[83] Unfortunately, for many, those assignments were about to change.

LTC Daniels, who had been sent over on the survey team to function as the operations liaison officer, had actually been functioning as the personnel officer. She had sent numerous messages back to both the TOC at Rochester and to Camp Atterbury attempting to explain that there was no way to ensure the ASTs currently designated for a given Iraqi unit would actually end up going to that unit. Therefore, the AST designations assigned at Atterbury really meant nothing, but apparently that word had not filtered down to the advisors.[84]

The problem lay in the AST situation the survey team found when they conducted their assessment during the summer. Daniels explained that due to the rapid expansion of the AST requirement in the winter and spring of 2004 and the lack of adequate staffing at CMATT, nobody knew exactly where the ASTs were, how many there were, and what their rotation dates were:

> Part of what I was doing, while the plan was being approved, was spending a significant number of hours with a warrant officer in the J1. He and I kept turning over rocks and finding ASTs. We came up with who was really in country and where they were. We found ASTs that had been reassigned to other missions. We also found people who had come in on other missions that had terminated and later became ASTs. We found records of people who never made it into country but were reported to be there. One guy had broken his leg at Fort Benning and never got on the plane, but he was being reported as physically being in Iraq. It was a nightmare trying to find out who was actually there, when they showed up and what their

365 [i.e., rotation date] was. We had to find out what their orders said, how long they could stay, and whether we needed to get them an extension. We basically had to sort out where all these people were.[85]

To compound the problem, the existing advisors were from numerous different CONUS and United States Army Europe (USAREUR) commands and were assigned on orders for varying lengths of time. Some were in Iraq on as short as 60-day orders, others as long as 1 year and many in-between, and all were due to rotate at different times. "That's why," Shipman recalled, "if I was signed up as a 3d Division [advisor] but the current 3d Division [advisor] didn't leave for another 2 months, they could put me in 5th Division. That made sense once you got on the ground, but nobody understood that back home so we were a little irate."[86]

Additionally, some advisors had different rotation dates than others on the same team, thereby creating vacancies that had to be filled by individuals rather than by an entire cohesive team. Thus, the battle handoff between the 98th Division ASTs and the existing teams was not going to be a clean, one-for-one swap on a given date.

The upshot was that some 98th Division ASTs were no longer going to be assigned to their originally designated Iraqi units. Others would have to be broken up to fill individual slots on short-handed ASTs. The resulting reshuffling of team assignments to Iraqi units and the breaking up and rebuilding of others caused a great deal of frustration among the troops. " . . . there were a few touchy days there," Matt Jones recalled. "There were a lot of very upset people because it made absolutely no sense in the world to do that. All these teams had worked together all through training and now they were just going to blow them apart and send them to different units."[87]

Both Schwitters and Sherlock were directly involved in many of these changes, which at first seems a bit odd when one considers Schwitters' own desire to build well-trained, cohesive ASTs. His belief was that to be most effective, CMATT needed "to have teams that know themselves well, that have been functioning together as a team for some time, and that are well functioning small groups."[88] But Schwitters understood that given the situation with the original ASTs, it just was not possible to smoothly transition to the 98th Division's replacement teams.

In reality, it made sense to make such changes, although to many of the incoming advisors it did not seem so at the time. What seemed to be arbitrary reassignments to some were for the most part rational and calculated, especially now that the advisor situation was becoming clearer. Shipman explained:

Our senior leader, who was COL Sanford Holman, had input into the decision-making process, as did COL Bradford Parsons who was the 5th Division [AST] leader. It wasn't done in a vacuum entirely. We had a couple people pulled off our division team and put in other assignments. Those were good decisions, actually. We had a major who was going to be the S3 advisor but ended up being the senior battalion advisor—and that was the right place for him. He was a former enlisted Ranger Battalion guy. He needed to be out there helping the Iraqis shoot bad guys, not pushing papers and answering e-mails at division.[89]

Valid or not, the changes added to the frustration and uncertainty felt by many of the advisors.

Another jolt to the advisors was that on the day the first teams arrived at Taji two of the battalion ASTs headed to the Iraqi 5th Division were informed they would immediately be convoyed out to their Iraqi units to begin the transition with the existing ASTs. Word spread that these two battalions were soon to enter combat operations at Fallujah (with the 6th Battalion) and Samarra (with the 7th Battalion). As McConnell described it, "That was a huge shock to all of us . . . at that time [we] still thought the whole Iraqi Army was in a garrison training mode. So it really opened our eyes."[90]

While those two teams were made aware of their assignments and the status of their Iraqi units, other teams were, perhaps unavoidably, kept in the dark. Tennyson, who would be one of the lucky ones whose team was untouched by the advisor shuffling, stated he and the others on his team "knew we'd be going to Al Kasik but we didn't know what battalion we'd be assigned to or what they were doing. We didn't know if they were going to be in training, fully operational, or just forming up." As it turned out, they would not get the answers until they physically arrived at Al Kasik.[91]

The frustration and uncertainty caused by assignment changes and lack of concrete mission information was by no means limited to the ASTs. Others experienced similar problems. COL Castle's OES/MOS school began to fall apart as his people were pulled for other assignments. Christian, a part of the cell responsible for developing the engineer OES recalled, "The original cadre was supposed to be three majors, but it ended up being another major and myself. But [even] that folded and it ended up just being me."[92]

Jim DiRisio, who had been slated to be an operations officer in the division's AST C2 Cell at Taji, had been delayed in Kuwait by a severe foot infection. When he finally arrived at Phoenix Base, he was informed that Sherlock had recommended him and three other officers to interview for a job as BG Schwitters' executive officer (XO). The JMD called for an active duty combat arms officer in that position, but such an animal had apparently not made it through the replacement pipeline to CMATT yet, so the 98th was asked to offer up a few possible candidates. DiRisio ended up with the job, but at the expense of the C2 Cell.[93]

Once it was definite that a given advisor team or staff replacement assignment was finalized, the next hurtle was getting there. For those assigned to jobs on the MNSTC-I or CMATT staffs in Baghdad, it was relatively simple, though potentially dangerous. Those soldiers had to ride in armored "Rhino" buses along the IED-infested Highway 1 out of Taji and into the International Zone (IZ) or "Green Zone" in the city. Though dangerous, the process of getting troops to the Green Zone was easy when compared to those who were going to places like Al Kasik, Numaniyah, and Kirkush.

Between mid-September and mid-December, the mobilization groups from Fort Bliss and Camp Atterbury filtered into BIAP and Taji, in-processed, and made their way to their duty locations in Iraq. Throughout the fall of 2004, the MNSTC-I, CMATT, and CPATT staffs grew and became more functional as each wave of Iroquois Warriors arrived to go to work. The AST C2 Cell in Taji became exclusively 98th Division soldiers. The ASTs transitioned with the outgoing teams. These, however, were not the only missions for which the Iroquois Warriors would assume responsibility for in Iraq. There were numerous others. How well they would perform those missions over the next 9 to 10 months though, remained to be seen.

Notes

1.   According to COL Sean Ryan, the JMD represented only one portion of the overall requirement. To get support from the Joint Staff and HQDA, MNSTC-I had to gain approval to waive the formal RFF and JMD processes to consolidate the requirement.

2.   Headquarters, 98th Division, Memorandum, AFRC-TNY-CMD, Subject: Identification and Selection of Advisor Support Teams (ASTs) in Support of Operation Iraqi Freedom for Soldiers Outside of the 98th Division, 19 August 2004.

3.   COL Bradford Parsons, telephone interview by author, Headquarters, 98th Division (IT), Rochester, NY, 3 November 2006, 3.

4.   MAJ Matthew Jones, interview by author, Headquarters, 98th Division (IT), Rochester, NY, 4 November 2006, 5.

5.   Ibid., MAJ Matthew Jones, e-mail to author, 21 March 2007, Subject: RE: Question About Advisors.

6.   MAJ John Vernick, interview by author, Headquarters, 98th Division (IT), Rochester, NY, 5 November 2006, 2–3. To make matters worse, as people arrived at Fort Bliss the 98th Division received word that MNSTC-I wanted those individuals to go through training at Camp Atterbury based on the jobs they were to do in Iraq. Headquarters, First Army cut new orders for them that "split" their DUICs creating sub-DUICs that had to be tracked as well. The only person with that detailed information was Vernick, who became more a focal point for management of the 98th Division's personnel than even the gaining command as he had the most accurate data.

7.   COL Todd Arnold, interview by author, Headquarters, 98th Division (IT), Rochester, NY 4 November 2006, 6.

8.   LTC Richard F. Monczynski, telephone interview by author, Combat Studies Institute, Fort Leavenworth, KS, 18 January 2007, 2.

9.   COL Charles A. "Gus" Stafford, telephone interview by author, Combat Studies Institute, Fort Leavenworth, KS, 8 December 2006, 2.

10.   Ibid.

11.   Jones interview, 4 November 2006, 4.

12.   Headquarters, 98th Division, PowerPoint Brief, "The Foreign Army Training Command Proposed Timeline and Operational Concepts," 8 July 2004; Jones interview, 4 November 2006, 4.

13.   COL Charles A. "Gus" Stafford, e-mail to author, Subject: Training Requirements, 6:38 p.m., 30 March 2007. Stafford recalled the marksmanship blocks were Pre-Marksmanship Instruction, Maintenance, Zero, Day, Night, and NBC qualification tables. "All soldiers went through M-9 and M-16 qualification. A smaller number followed the process on the M60, M2, and M249. This process took 3 to 4 days and nights based on refires and range scheduling. We also provided opportunity ranges to give more of the soldiers familiarization on automatic weapons," he recalled.

14.   Headquarters, US Army FORSCOM, Message, XX Sep 04, Subject:

Change 4 to Training Guidance for Follow-on Forces Deploying ISO Operation IRAQI FREEDOM.

15. Jones interview, 4 November 2006, 3–4.

16. LTC Antonio Morales, interview by author, Combat Studies Institute, Fort Leavenworth, KS, 30 January 2007, 6.

17. Ibid.

18. Ibid.

19. Stafford telephone interview, 8 December 2006, 3.

20. Briefing, "The Foreign Army Training Command Proposed Timeline and Operational Concepts," 8 July 2004; Jones interview, 4 November 2006, 4.

21. LTC James DiRisio, interview by author, Headquarters, 98th Division (IT), Rochester, NY, 3 November 2006, 4. LTC Jody Daniels, one of the people working the JMD requirements for the survey team, later explained that the MNSTC-I J4 office actually developed the requirement for the convoy security team and had included it in the request for logistics personnel who would perform base support functions. It was not initially clear to the survey team that the convoy team was essentially a security unit rolled into the logistics request. The survey team eventually figured that out, and the fact that the convoy team was really a J3 asset, not a J4 asset. By the time that was realized, the convoy team had already been slated to go to Fort Bliss and it was too late to change the mobilization flow.

22. Vernick interview, 5 November 2006, 9.

23. COL Sean Ryan, interview by author, Joint Center for International Security Force Assistance, Fort Leavenworth, KS, 21 December 2006, 6.

24. Headquarters, 98th Division, PowerPoint Brief, "Information Brief, 98th Division (IT) FA-TRAC and TY04/TY05 Missions," 2 October 2004, 7. Three additional small mob groups would be mobilized and sent over in December 2004 and March 2005. These soldiers were either additional troops mobilized to replace others who were KIA, WIA, sick or sent home on emergency leave or other reasons, or were to fill additional requirements identified later by MNSTC-I.

25. Timothy J. Hansen and Jocene D. Preston, ed. *An Encounter with History: The 98th Division and the Global War on Terrorism: 2001–2005* (Washington, DC: Government Printing Office, 2006), 67.

26. MG James R. Helmly, telephone interview by author, Combat Studies Institute, Fort Leavenworth, KS, 2 December 2006, 8.

27. Stafford telephone interview, 8 December 2006, 2.

28. COL Charles A. "Gus" Stafford, e-mail to author, Subject: 98th Division (IT) Documents 5, Attachment: Subject: FW: New Guy Stuff, 19 January 2007. This e-mail contained a string of e-mails that were between Stafford and COL William J. Mushrush, the 85th Division G3. The difficult planning environment facing Stafford and his brigade is evident in the messages.

29. Headquarters, 3d Brigade, 85th Division (TS), Master Training Schedule, September–December 2004.

30. Stafford telephone interview, 8 December 2006, 1.

31. COL Robert Catalanotti, interview by author, Headquarters, 98th Division (IT), Rochester, NY, 3 November 2006, 2–3.

32. Stafford telephone interview, 8 December 2006, 3.

33. Ibid., 5.

34. MAJ Scott McConnell, telephone interview by author, Combat Studies Institute, Fort Leavenworth, KS, 12 December 2006, 2.

35. MAJ Paul Loncle, interview by author, Headquarters, 98th Division (IT), Rochester, NY, 4 November 2006, 2.

36. COL Charles A. "Gus" Stafford, e-mail to author, Subject: RE: 98th Division (IT) 3d Brigade Organization (Unclassified), 23 January 2007.

37. Ibid.

38. Jones interview, 4 November 2006, 4.

39. Loncle interview, 4 November 2006, 2; COL Douglas Shipman, interview by author, Headquarters, 98th Division (IT), Rochester, NY, 3 November 2006, 3; SSG Brian D. Charnock, interview by author, Headquarters, 98th Division (IT), Rochester, NY, 4 November 2006, 2; Catalanotti interview, 3 November 2006, 3.

40. Loncle interview, 4 November 2006, 2.

41. MAJ Roger Swartwood, interview by author, Headquarters, 98th Division (IT), Rochester, NY, 3 November 2006, 3.

42. COL Jody Daniels, interview by author, Combat Studies Institute, Fort Leavenworth, KS, 20 December 2006, 5. Stafford explained that the division's request for spreading out the training was not simply ignored. The problem was a contracting issue over which he had no influence. The contract provided for three instructors to conduct the training over a 5-day period.

43. Daniels interview, 20 December 2006, 5; Jones interview, 4 November 2006, 4.

44. SFC Dennis Ewing, interview by author, Headquarters, 98th Division (IT), Rochester, NY, 4 November 2006, 2.

45. Ewing interview, 4 November 2006, 2; Parsons telephone interview, 3 November 2006, 3.

46. Ewing interview, 4 November 2006, 2.

47. McConnell interview, 12 December 2006, 3.

48. Catalanotti interview, 3 November 2006, 4.

49. Stafford telephone interview, 8 December 2006, 4; Shipman interview, 3 November 2006, 3.

50. SFC Andrew T. Brown, After Action Report, Subject: 98th Division AST Mobilization at Atterbury, IN, undated, 3.

51. Swartwood interview, 3 November 2006, 4; Shipman interview, 3 November 2006, 3.

52. Shipman interview, 3 November 2006, 3.

53. McConnell interview, 12 December 2006, 3.

54. MAJ Jeffrey E. Tennyson, interview by author, Headquarters, 98th Division (IT), Rochester, NY, 3 November 2006, 3.

55. Swartwood interview, 3 November 2006, 2.

56. Shipman interview, 3 November 2006, 1.

57. COL Edward P. Castle, interview by author, Headquarters, 98th Division (IT), Rochester, NY, 5 November 2006, 3.

58. McConnell interview, 12 December 2006, 3.

59. Jones interview, 4 November 2006, 4; McConnell interview, 12 December 2006, 3; Ewing interview, 4 November 2006, 2.

60. Castle interview, 5 November 2006, 2.

61. Tennyson interview, 3 November 2006, 3.

62. Catalanotti interview, 3 November 2006, 4.

63. Stafford telephone interview, 8 December 2006, 8. Stafford was not satisfied with the training plan used to validate the 98th Division. Contrary to the news reports in 2006 that implied there was no effort to improve training at Camp Atterbury after the 98th Division's stay there, Stafford made great efforts to improve the training plan for the 80th Division, which would take over the advisor mission from the 98th in 2005. He and that division's assistant division commander, BG John P. McLaren, Jr., traveled to Iraq in May 2005 to see first hand what the conditions were on the ground. That experience enabled Stafford to significantly revamp the training package at Atterbury to address the needs of the 80th Division's advisors.

64. Stafford e-mail, Subject: Training Requirements, 6:38 p.m., 30 March 2007.

65. COL Charles A. "Gus" Stafford, telephone interview by author, Combat Studies Institute, Fort Leavenworth, KS, 28 March 2007.

66. Ryan interview, 21 December 2006, 9.

67. Ibid., 5.

68. LTC Daniel Christian, interview by author, 98th Division Headquarters, Rochester, NY, 3 November 2006, 2. Christian arrived in Kuwait with Mob-2.

69. Loncle interview, 4 November 2006, 3.

70. Charnock interview, 4 November 2006, 2.

71. McConnell interview, 12 December 2006, 4; Jones interview, 4 November 2006, 5.

72. McConnell interview, 12 December 2006, 4.

73. Swartwood interview, 3 November 2006, 5. In a 29 March 2007 e-mail, Swartwood stated he was referring to the 98th Division's command element at Camp Atterbury. "More than once we were told that the situation (as to where and even what we would be doing) was fluid and to 'be flexible.' I do not know if the requests went any higher than my immediate commander or above the 98th Div."

74. Daniels interview, 20 December 2006, 5.

75. Ryan interview, 21 December 2006, 11.

76. Christian interview, 3 November 2006, 1.

77. *Global Security*, "Al Taji Army Airfield/Al Taji Camp," available at http://www.globalsecurity.org/military/world/ iraq/ al-taji.htm, accessed 3 November 2006.

78. McConnell interview, 12 December 2006, 5.

79. BG Frank Cipolla, telephone interview by author, Combat Studies Institute, Fort Leavenworth, KS, 20 November 2006, 3.

80. Shipman interview, 3 November 2006, 4.

81. Jones interview, 4 November 2006, 6.

82. BG James Schwitters, telephone interview by author, Combat Studies Institute, Fort Leavenworth, KS, 13 December 2006, 2.

83. Swartwood interview, 3 November 2006, 4.

84. Daniels interview, 20 December 2006, 8.

85. Ibid., 7.

86. Shipman interview, 3 November 2006, 4.

87. Jones interview, 4 November 2006, 6.

88. Schwitters interview, 13 December 2006, 6.

89. Shipman interview, 3 November 2006, 4.

90. McConnell interview, 12 December 2006, 5.

91. Tennyson interview, 3 November 2006, 5.

92. Christian interview, 3 November 2006, 3.

93. DiRisio interview, 3 November 2006, 5.

Chapter 5

Staff and Training Team Operations

Then we were operating as an "Army of One."

COL Cipolla

If one were to ask an Iroquois Warrior who participated in the mission in 2004–2005, "What did the 98th Division do while it was over there?", he or she would likely give an answer along the lines of "A lot of things," and then provide a litany of missions that members of the division performed. If there is one word that describes the breadth of missions that soldiers of the 98th Division performed in Iraq it is "diverse," not only in terms of what missions they undertook, but also where they did them and with whom they did them.

Of course, the original question would be flawed, because technically the "division" did not go to Iraq. The division commander did not deploy, the flag stayed in Rochester, and the soldiers were sent over on orders bearing DUICs, not UICs. Indeed, the attitude on the part of the MNSTC-I and CMATT soldiers already in theater was not that the 98th Division was coming over to help; their view was, "Well he's just another filler from the Army Reserve," and technically they would be right. But that was not the view of the Iroquois Warriors. ". . . our intent was to be viewed as the 98th Division," John Vernick later said. "[If it were me,] I'd say, 'The 98th Division was deployed.'"[1] To some degree, that divergence of attitudes on the status of the division would color the relationships between the Regulars (whether they were Army, Marine, Air Force, or otherwise) and the reservists of the 98th Division for at least the initial period of the mission, and for some, the entire period.

The Mission

Regardless of the different views on the status of the division, few could argue with the diversity of the mission, especially when one considers the mission was only remotely related to those the division was doctrinally supposed to perform in wartime. In addition to manning the staffs at MNSTC-I, the training teams, the C2 Cell, and the advisor teams, members of the 98th Division would create or assume the responsibility for organizations and institutions that were not originally on the JMD. These would include ASTs for ING divisions, several Combat Service Support (CSS) unit ASTs, the Phoenix Academy, the Iraq Advisor Group (IAG), and some installation command and staff positions at various bases in Iraq. The Iroquois Warriors would perform these missions at locations from Tall Afar in the north to Basra in the south and numerous places in between (see figure 13), and they would perform them with Sunnis, Shi'as, Kurds, Marines, Airmen, Sailors, Australians, Brits, Poles, Salvadorans, and a host of American soldiers from a vast array of units from all three components.

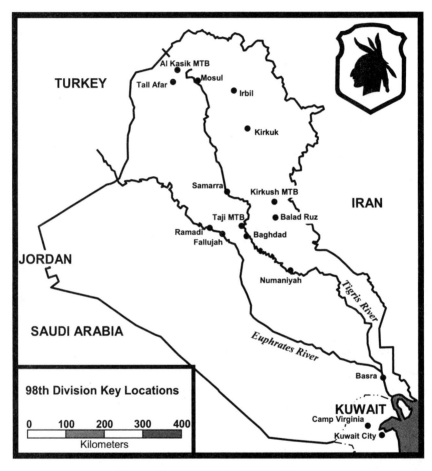

Figure 13. 98th Division key locations.

The Staffs

One of the largest groups of Iroquois Warriors deployed to Iraq was designated to fill various positions on the MNSTC-I, CMATT, and CPATT staffs. No less than 164 division soldiers were assigned to supplement these three headquarters.[2] The 98th's "fillers" brought those staffs from around 30-percent strength to something approaching 90 percent in a relatively short period of time.[3] Most of these soldiers' place of duty was in the Green Zone, though others were located at posts in Iraq, Kuwait, and Jordan. On the same compound as the MNSTC-I staff was the American Embassy and the headquarters for the MNF-I, both located in Saddam Hussein's former presidential palace. The compound was walled and secured by contract security guards, concertina wire, and other security measures. The area was considered relatively secure, although occasionally an insurgent would attempt to lob in a mortar shell from across the Euphrates River.[4]

The MNSTC-I and CMATT headquarters where the staffs actually worked was designated "Phoenix Base." It was a one-story former schoolhouse located near the Assassin's Gate about a mile from the presidential palace. The CMATT headquarters had originally been located in the palace, but as that command grew, it needed more room and so it too was moved to the school. When CMATT moved over from the palace, MNSTC-I allocated it one cramped classroom. As Jim DiRisio described it:

> We were literally in there elbow to elbow with our laptop computers. Any spare flat space we could put a laptop computer on we did. It was very close quarters, but it was air conditioned and we had generators, electricity. . . . We would have like 20 people crammed into this little classroom, yet there was a classroom next door to us the same size that had the [MNSTC-I] J7 staff, the engineers from MNSTC-I, and they only had like 5 guys in there.[5]

Those soldiers assigned to the CPATT staff were not colocated with the MNSTC-I as was the CMATT. The CPATT headquarters was located with the offices of the Ministry of the Interior (MOI) at Adnan Palace, which was in the Green Zone about a 5- to 10-minute drive from Phoenix Base. The working conditions for the soldiers in CPATT were comparable to the MNSTC-I and CMATT headquarters with two major differences. Established more recently than CMATT, the CPATT headquarters was not as far along in its organization, planning, and establishment of internal procedures as its military counterpart. Additionally, it was staffed with a very large percentage of civilian employees, which made the working environment at the same time more difficult and easier than at CMATT. Being on a newer staff, the CPATT soldiers ended up spending more of their time planning and developing procedures than implementing and adjusting existing plans.[6]

While the physical work environment at these headquarters was better than what most 98th Division soldiers experienced while they were in Iraq, the initial relations between the reservists and the active duty members of the various headquarters staffs were uncomfortable. Concerning the 98th Division soldiers sent to reinforce his command, Petraeus recalled, "We were happy to have them. We were just glad to get somebody over there to help us out—and the sooner the better."[7] Unfortunately, the CG's attitude did not seem to filter down to many on the staff. As Lawrence Kelly remembered it:

> We were not well received when we got there. . . . We had to deal with those prejudices, I'll say. It got so bad one time that I had a Marine Corps colonel tell me that when this was all done he was going to write a book and title it *Blame It on the 98th.* . . . I told him, 'When we got here, you had people all over this country. You didn't have any idea how much time they had boots on the ground and you didn't have any idea when people were leaving, what they were doing or anything else. We brought you 700 soldiers that you didn't have prior to us getting here. We filled the joint manning document, we filled CMATT, we did the police side of the house, we loaded people on the MNSTC-I staff, we did MOS training, the ASTs, and we did logistics support.' They could not have done without the 98th Division or another Reserve unit coming in and bringing that many bodies.[8]

The Marine colonel would later apologize for his remarks.

Chaplain (COL) J. Paul Womack, the 98th Division's command chaplain, recalled his introduction to CMATT in Baghdad shortly after his arrival in September. The chaplain was having breakfast in Saddam's palace when BG Sherlock walked up. Sherlock apparently wanted to warn Womack of the atmosphere in the CMATT headquarters and related to Womack an incident that transpired between him and a senior colonel on the staff. The general told Womack that at some point during his conversation with the colonel, this officer made an impassioned outburst to the effect of "Your division was told not to being any (expletive deleted) chaplains over here!" Womack explained that CMATT apparently had concerns that "military chaplains and chaplain assistants and their religious support responsibilities would translate into efforts to proselytize Iraqi military personnel." He then added, "Nothing, of course, could have been further from my mind. . . ."[9] Still, it was clearly an unnecessary and unprofessional remark on the part of a senior leader in that headquarters and would have been an extremely unlikely occurrence had Sherlock been a Regular Army general officer.

Frank Cipolla recalled that his initial reception was mixed at best:

> General Petraeus was great. Most of the colonels and below, though, wouldn't even talk to us because we were a Reserve unit—that is, until they found out what we could do; about a month later, they were much more receptive. But initially they didn't want to have anything to do with us. My first impression was, 'I thought we were an "Army of One" here.' Yet there were active component colonels who wouldn't even look at us.[10]

He further reflected that there was, at least initially, a perceived attitude that if anything went wrong, "it was the Reserves' fault."[11]

The initial "anti-RC bias" was detrimental to the efficiency of the staffs for a number of reasons, to include dampening the reservists' enthusiasm for shouldering the load. COL Daniels believed this led to an unwillingness of the regulars to trust the reservists with important staff actions. The obvious lack of trust for the reservists caused some regulars to take on "a greater load than they [could] handle, because they [would] not share or delegate responsibilities." She went on to remark that such actions could potentially lead to rapid exhaustion in a stressful combat environment.[12]

The apparent "we–they" attitude may have been exacerbated because the soldiers of the 98th Division felt they had deployed as a unit and desired to maintain that identity. A soldier who is worth his salt and who serves in a good outfit wants people to know he is a member of that unit. It is a point of pride. Esprit d' corps is one of those intangibles vital to a good unit, and the troops of the 98th Division had it. Thus, many desired to continue wearing their Iroquois Warrior patch, and the issue soon became a command-interest item. It was enough of a problem that Vernick, back in the TOC at Rochester, heard about it: "A lot of our soldiers would not take off the 98th Division patch. It was a real issue. A lot of those commands wanted them to take off that patch because they did not view them as 98th Division soldiers."[13]

Schwitters directed DiRisio, already working as the XO at CMATT, to prepare an information paper that described the regulatory requirements and proper wear of shoulder sleeve insignia. The paper, issued 20 October 2004, emphasized that "Soldiers in CMATT are not assigned to MNSTC-I as *units*, but rather as *individuals*" and went on to state that "Soldiers who are cross-leveled, assigned, attached, or augmenting deployed units . . . according to AR 670-1, 'Will wear the same SSI–FWTS worn by members of the deployed unit(s) to which attached or OPCON.'" Technically, the proper patch for the 98th Division soldiers was actually the CENTCOM patch, and so off came the Iroquois Warrior patch. "A lot of people out of protest still wore the 98th patch, though," DiRisio reflected, "and a lot of our people were in places that were so far from the flagpole that it didn't really matter what patch they were wearing."[14] Still, the incident did little to establish better relations on either side.

It appears that most of the prejudices and frustrations between regulars and reservists, perceived or otherwise, were relatively short-lived. As they settled in and began to work together, much of the mutual mistrust in capabilities and intents seemed to fade away. Cipolla recalled that after a month or two the relationships began to improve: "Their initial skepticism was eventually replaced by an attitude of care and concern. They witnessed what we were doing and realized that we were accomplishing the mission. It was at that point that things got a lot better. Then we were operating as an 'Army of One.'"[15] Even so, some 98th Division soldiers maintained that, in their environment anyway, the prejudices remained for the rest of the rotation.

The reception of the Iroquois Warriors by MNSTC-I's commanding general was generally regarded by the reservists as very positive. Petraeus had commanded the 101st Airborne Division during the march on Baghdad in March— April 2003. It was a command of which he was clearly proud and in which he had great confidence. In an interview in 2006, Petraeus expressed the idea that it would have been nice to have had the division headquarters come over to help him stand up the MNSTC-I operation. He knew that would not have been possible and the situation was such that he was going to have to make do with an ad hoc organization. As

Figure 14. LTG David H. Petraeus, commanding general of the MNSTC-I.

for the incoming reservists, he was indeed delighted to receive their help. His attitude toward the members of the division was apparent and was reciprocated by them. In postdeployment interviews, the Iroquois Warriors were unanimous in their praise of his leadership.

Of the 164 soldiers assigned to the three major headquarters, about 112 were assigned to the joint staff sections of Petraeus' MNSTC-I headquarters. Of this number, only four 98th Division soldiers were assigned to the J1. This seems to be a small contribution until one considers that there were only seven Army slots for the section on the JMD. The senior Iroquois in the section was MAJ Ann Pellien, who not only managed MNSTC-I's JMD personnel requirements and personnel support, but played a major role in tracking and managing the division's personnel in theater. This section would later assume the responsibility for acquiring additional personnel for MNSTC-I's ever-increasing requirements for ASTs as new Iraqi units were stood up and for the new Special Police Transition Teams (SPTT). It also mentored the Ministry of Defense's (MOD) personnel directorate and assisted it in developing policies on key personnel actions such as pay, promotion, and accountability.[16]

Like the J1, the J2 section possessed four 98th Division soldiers for the seven Army slots allocated. Initially run by a Reserve colonel (who was not from the 98th Division), its leadership would be turned over to Daniels in February 2005. The Iroquois Warriors in this section helped to develop the daily intelligence estimates for Petraeus, operated the Secure Compartmented Intelligence Facility (SCIF), and conducted the route analysis for the movement of Iraqi Army units into the Fallujah area for the major operations conducted there in November 2004. After Daniels took over, the J2 became deeply involved in developing intelligence training support to the Iraqi Army, in part by establishing an intelligence school at Taji.[17]

The J3 section was considered the "Coordination Hub" of the MNSTC-I headquarters. Of the 33 Army positions (from about 40 total) in the J3 on the JMD, 20 were filled by 98th Divisions soldiers. This section's mission was the "development, justification, prioritization, and implementation of projects to train, equip, and mentor" the ISF. As such, it coordinated the rest of the MNSTC-I staff to meet the command's mission requirements. Among other missions, it coordinated the development of the SPTTs and the operational transition between the 98th and its successors in the 80th Division.[18]

Not included in the J3 numbers but working directly for it was the J3's Convoy Security Team, commonly referred to as the "Rough Riders."

Consisting of about 40 soldiers, mostly from the 98th Division but including troops from other Reserve divisions and even a few Marines and a sailor or two, this outfit was essentially a small company consisting of two platoons. The division soldiers were a conglomerate of troops. " . . . they wanted combat-oriented infantrymen over [on the Convoy Security Team]," remarked Vernick, "but it ended up being a variety of MOSs."[19] Provided up-armored HMMWVs armed with crew-served weapons, the team's mission was to provide security to military convoys all over central Iraq. During its tour in country, elements of the Rough Riders conducted over 2,000 security missions. Elements of the team experienced a number of ambushes and IEDs from which they sustained a number of casualties, but it suffered no KIAs.[20]

MNSTC-I was authorized 128 personnel in the command's J4 section. Of this number, Iroquois Warriors filled 51 positions. This was clearly the largest group of division soldiers in the MNSTC-I headquarters. Arguably, the J4 section had the most complex and far-reaching mission. The J4 not only coordinated and managed the logistics operations for MNSTC-I and its subordinate commands, it also coordinated logistics support to the Iraqi MOD. During the year the division troops functioned in the section, the J4 was responsible for the delivery of 50,000 tons of supplies to the Iraqi Army and police units. It coordinated the shipment of 80,000 weapons and over 30 million rounds of ammunition. It acquired and issued all the equipment needed for the ASTs to include 550 up-armored HMMWVs, SINCGARS radios, BFTs, night vision goggles (NVGs), and a host of other items.[21]

The survey team operation in Kuwait under LTC Morales and MSG Compitello transitioned into positions on the J4 staff and became the J4's liaison team to CFLCC in addition to the RSOI functions (reinforced by four more Iroquois Warriors at Camp Virginia), which they maintained until all 98th Division troops were in country. As that operation closed down, another J4 RSOI cell opened operations at Camp Buehring to handle RSOI operations for new ASTs coming into country when MNSTC-I's mission expanded to cover the former ING divisions as well as the three initial Regular Army divisions. Additionally, the Iroquois Warriors in the J4 operated the Central Issue Facilities to support ASTs and Iraqi Army units at Taji, Al Kasik, Kirkush, and Numaniyah.[22]

The 98th Division filled five slots in the J6 section, which handled communications and automation systems for MNSTC-I. Like the other sections, it not only performed its mission for MNSTC-I, but accomplished tasks for the Iraqi MOD and MOI by "designing solutions to requirements, purchasing, and implementing radio and computer-based systems" for those agencies. This section coordinated the transfer of tens of thousands of radios and thousands of computers to the ISF, MOD, and MOI. Like the other sections, it mentored and developed its counterpart sections in the MOD and MOI.[23]

The 98th Division contributed 28 soldiers to the CPATT staff, to include COL Michael R. "Mike" Smith, who was assigned as the chief of staff and, as such, was the senior Iroquois Warrior in that command. His tour in Iraq would last for 18 months, extending through both the 98th and 80th Divisions' rotations and into that of the 108th Division in 2006. As mentioned before, the demand to fully organize this headquarters was not as great as it was for CMATT, thus the division reinforcements for CPATT arrived with the later mobilization groups.[24]

The majority of Iroquois Warriors, by far, were assigned to the CMATT headquarters and its subordinate elements. These included a number of diverse missions that included reinforcing (and in some instances commanding) base support commands; establishing and operating various OES, NCOES, and MOS training activities; and of course, the major effort, the manning of no less than 31 of the 39 ASTs in CMATT. In all, about 476 division soldiers were assigned to CMATT.

The commanding general of CMATT, BG Schwitters, was a former commander of the Delta Force, an organization with which he had a long-time affiliation. He had served in, or with, Delta for at least 11 of his over 25 years of service. One Iroquois Warrior described Schwitters as a "Southern gentleman," and indeed, he had been educated at the evangelical Christian school of LeTourneau University in Longview, Texas. While he was not as popular with many of

Figure 15. BG James Schwitters, commanding general of the CMATT.

the Iroquois Warriors as Petraeus, they considered him a dedicated, no-nonsense commander.[25]

For his part, Schwitters was not as happy, perhaps, to have the 98th Division soldiers on his staff as his boss, but it had nothing to do with the fact that they were reservists. "My initial impressions were mixed but did not revolve around any issues of it being a Reserve organization; rather, it was simply an issue of having the right folks in the right quantities with the right skills to do the mission," he recalled. "I just wanted people who could do the job."[26] Like many others, Schwitters was not convinced the incoming reservists possessed the requisite skill sets for the mission.

Twenty-four Iroquois Warriors were assigned to Schwitters' staff and headquarters. With only 58 people assigned to the headquarters, every staff section in CMATT had representatives from the division. Being colocated with the MNSTC-I headquarters, working at CMATT came with all the attendant advantages and disadvantages. While communication with the higher headquarters was extremely easy, being the subordinate headquarters at Phoenix Base ensured that priority for space and communications capabilities went to the MNSTC-I staff.

CMATT was a joint and combined command that, along with its basic mission, made it an interesting, though challenging, work environment. DiRisio explained:

> Everything you learned at CGSC about how a joint staff operates was pretty much thrown out the window at CMATT. Maybe I'm being a little facetious. There were certain things I learned at CGSC that were helpful. But where we were, the mission was so ambiguous and so evolving that we were very much a seat-of-the-pants type of organization—and that isn't a knock on the professionalism of anybody in CMATT. General Schwitters had been the commander of Delta Force before he came to this position. The chief of staff of CMATT was an active duty colonel—Fred Kienle—and he had been at Norfolk at Joint Forces Command when he was selected to go over. He was no schlep by any means as far as planning. We had competent people but the mission was very ambiguous, so we basically developed standard operating procedures for ourselves and evolved those over time. We also had four Australians [working] there. In fact, the main planner of the organization was an Australian engineer officer. We had active duty Air Force and Navy; we truly were

joint. If you looked at any given time in our little building, you'd see any number of different uniforms and people coming from different perspectives all trying to dig in and do the same thing.[27]

Much of the CMATT staff's efforts went to supporting the AST mission, especially the administration and logistics requirements, and the Iraqi Army. In a nutshell, the CMATT mission was to man, train, and equip the new Iraqi armed forces, which included air force and navy requirements though the latter were very small. That mission included recruiting Iraqi service personnel; however, none of the Iroquois Warriors were directly involved in the recruiting effort.

Base Support

One of the missions vital to the overall CMATT effort, but only peripherally associated with it, was the requirement to staff the installation commands of a number of military training bases important to the command's mission. One of the largest of these was the TMTB commanded by COL Catalanotti.

On completion of the training of mobilization groups going through Camp Atterbury, Catalanotti was notified he would deploy to Iraq to backfill Frank Cipolla, who was designated to return to Rochester as the OIC for the C2 Cell at Taji. Arriving at Baghdad in December, Catalanotti had been there only a few days when COL Henry approached him about becoming the base commander for Taji. "Absolutely," was Catalanotti's response. He then met with Schwitters to confirm the decision and was soon off to Taji to take command.[28]

Catalanotti took over command of TMTB from the temporary commander, a Marine major by the name of Gallagher, who had been attempting to keep it under control while operating with an almost nonexistent staff. The command at Taji included providing housing and life support for 15,000 Iraqi and 500 Coalition soldiers, and promised to get bigger. "They wanted to formally make Taji one of the largest military training bases," Catalanotti recollected. Thus he quickly began building an installation staff, developing a command structure, and formulating policies and procedures for the post. A few of the people he acquired for his staff were 98th Division personnel. As he described them, ". . . I had to take from here and there. I had an Air Force officer. I had a Navy corpsman for my medical staff. I had a couple individuals from the 75th Division (Training Support)."[29] His installation sergeant major, however, was Command Sergeant Major (CSM) Milton Newsome, who had been the CSM for the 6th Brigade back in Mattydale, New York.

In Catalanotti's opinion, the greatest challenge he faced was providing force protection and security for the post. The installation was surrounded by a series of guard towers. The first thing he went to work on was getting the Iraqi security force trained to man them. "I needed those guard towers . . . to be manned by soldiers who knew what to do, who knew the rules of engagement and how to fire a weapon," he recalled. Some of the other priority tasks that his new command trained for included force protection, reaction to incoming mortars and rockets, and triage procedures for wounded Iraqi soldiers and civilians.[30]

One of the key security problems Catalanotti and his staff faced was the East Gate. Newsome described that location:

> When I first got over there, we called the East Gate 'Dodge City' because you could drive down the highway and mortars would be lobbed at you. As people came into the base to work during the day, they were lined up like a shooting gallery and it was very bad. We closed the East Gate down and built the South Gate, which ran parallel to the American gate. That helped alleviate a lot of the tension and helped us protect the Iraqis.[31]

But even with the new South Gate, there were problems. "Taji had the largest entry control point in all of Iraq, and the volume of vehicles, soldiers, pedestrians, and workers coming into that base was enormous," Catalanotti said. ". . . the [South Gate] opened off Highway 1 and that was one of the most dangerous roads. I needed Iraqi security, contractors, and the American advisors at the gate, because you needed multiple echelons of people checking each other, and the ultimate group was the Americans checking everyone else. It was the only way it could be done."[32]

The control measures at the gate were indeed stringent. Corruption by the Iraqi guards was always a problem, and not necessarily because they were allowing the terrorists in. Most often it was because they wanted to take care of a friend, a fellow tribesman, or perhaps they had accepted a bribe. Catalanotti described some of the many other problems:

> Who was letting what in? Who was only being somewhat checked versus someone not getting checked at all? It was as silly as the ice cream man trying to get ice cream onto the base and yet his vehicle could only go so long in 130-degree weather. He would spend 4 hours sitting outside the gate before he could come through, and he would wind up bringing in melted ice cream. From issues like

that to severe issues like an Iraqi general who said we're not going to check him. Well, how did I know that someone wasn't holding that Iraqi general's wife hostage at his house until he came on the base and killed *me*? No matter how much that Iraqi general respected me, he would've had to make a decision: 'Do the insurgents kill my wife or do I kill you as the American colonel?' Needless to say, he got checked.[33]

The second major challenge for Catalanotti and Newsome was life support requirements. "How to get food into the base and keep the Iraqis fed, how to run the dining facilities, how to run the barracks, how to keep law and order among the different tribes that were in the force, [and] how to deal with hygiene and cleanliness. Trying to get 15,000 Iraqis fed in a reasonable way is very difficult," Catalanotti recalled. Part of providing life support for the post was building new support infrastructure or rebuilding that which had been previously destroyed or damaged. "Taji had been hit very hard . . . and there wasn't much left when we moved in," Catalanotti said. "Trying to put a training base in there required all the buildings to be restructured and refurbished. All the contractors, the security of the contractors, who was legit to come into the base—all that came under my responsibility."[34]

The third primary area of responsibility for Catalanotti was to support the training functions of the post. Taji was the headquarters for the Iraqi 1st Division, and home base for most of its subordinate units. As such, the installation had to provide the life and logistics support to that command and to the Iraqi Army NCO Academy located there. Late in February 2005, when the so-called "Phoenix Academy" was stood up to provide the final training for advisors coming into Iraq, Catalanotti assumed responsibility for supporting that school as well.[35] Newsome recalled that the Taji training functions were even more diverse: "We actually trained the Iraqi police department there too. In addition, we trained medical and supply there as well. We also had the transportation corps and the air corps. We had a lot of different training going on at Taji all at the same time. Plus, Taji was the largest logistical base in Iraq. . . ."[36]

In retrospect, Catalanotti was proud of what was accomplished at Taji. He had worked wonders at Taji, but did not do it without assistance. He commented, "I had a great relationship with General Schwitters. He gave me a lot of support. We were able to take a base from nothing to something very potent in 10 months. His support, MNSTC-I's support, and the support of my staff were all very important [to the end result]."[37]

There were at least six other bases that MNSTC-I controlled. One of the smaller ones was Forward Operating Base (FOB) Shield in Baghdad. This small compound was located near the MOI and the Baghdad police academy, and it housed the Transition and Assistance Support Center along with a mixture of corps-level support units. The post was the responsibility of MAJ Shauna Hauser of the 98th Division.

Hauser had originally deployed as a planner in the MNSTC-I J5 section. Her primary focus had been researching requirements and developing plans for CPATT and their efforts to train the various Iraqi police forces. About the end of January 2005, she was selected to be the base commander for FOB Shield, but as she described the job, "I was what you might call a 'base management officer.' Some people say 'base commander' but I had no authority over really anybody on the base. . . ."[38]

To assist in her mission, Hauser had one deputy, a Marine warrant officer, who functioned as her "staff." She controlled a contract security force that consisted of a dozen former British Special Air Service (SAS) soldiers who provided the leadership for the Fijian security guards that protected the compound. Beyond that, her control on the base was practically nil. "Because I didn't have direct control over one unit, it really came down to, 'Hey would you do this? Would you do that?' [in] trying to get the units to work as a team toward the betterment of the base," she remembered.[39]

The biggest headache Hauser faced was the ownership of the post. It was initially under MNC-I, but that command wanted to give it up and turn it over to the Iraqis. MNSTC-I, however, wanted the base due to its location near the MOI and the police academy and decided to retain it. The problem was that the post was dependent on MNC-I for support but, as Hauser explained,

> MNSTC-I wasn't set up to really support itself. It could support Iraqis, but could not support itself. So on some of the issues, like water for instance—that KBR [Kellogg, Brown, and Root] didn't provide—MNSTC-I would provide water for an interim period, but then the corps was like, 'Well, this isn't my base. Even though I have 60 percent of the soldiers living on it fall under me, it's not my base.' And so those were some of the issues that day to day, we had to work out, to make sure we had water, we had support, we just had stuff that sometimes we take for granted.[40]

Although not originally planned as part of the support package for the mission, the experiences of Catalanotti and Hauser illustrate some of the ways troops of the 98th Division were able to adapt to meet the challenges faced by the MNSTC-I. They also point out the range of responsibilities the Iroquois Warriors were asked to accomplish for which they were not specifically trained. However, one area the soldiers of the division were particularly suited to address was that of institutional training.

Figure 16. CPT Joe Burkhart demonstrates operation and assembly procedures to Iraqi soldiers.

The "Training Package"

The Iroquois Warriors played a major role in the effort to establish various training institutions for the Iraqi Army. That mission came under the purview of the so-called "Training Package" organization that was to be established at the TMTB. Not so much an organization per se as it was a group of related and loosely organized training and education teams, this element performed, at least in part, what was probably the closest thing to the 98th Division's original mission. Unlike the other elements sent to support MNSTC-I, the Training Package included no USAR filler personnel from outside the 98th Division. It consisted of 136 soldiers who were divided into four smaller elements: the MOS trainers (25 personnel), NCOES trainers (34 personnel), OES trainers (47 personnel), and the ING BCT team (30 personnel).[41]

The MOS training team, of which COL Castle was designated the commandant (as well as for the entire Training Package), was probably the most diverse organization in the group. It consisted of one large generic combat arms training team and six smaller MOS-specific teams that included engineer, signal, ordnance, medical, quartermaster, and maintenance instructors, almost all of whom were majors and lieutenant colonels.[42] These elements were not positions that MNSTC-I originally envisioned, but were believed by the survey team to be needed for training the Iraqi Army. Unfortunately, most of the personnel on these teams would be pulled away for other missions due to the exigencies of CMATT's ever-evolving situation. None of these teams would ultimately perform the actual missions they were sent to Iraq to perform. Castle described how it happened:

> When we first got to Taji, we still thought that [we were going to do the MOS training mission]. We were separated from the ASTs who were getting assigned out to units around the country. We stayed in Taji and just started working on developing POIs because that's what we thought we were going to be doing . . . folks would come to me and say, 'Hey, we need two people for this AST mission,' or 'We need two people for this staff position,' or 'We need somebody to go over here.' Little by little, folks were taken from my organization to a point where I think we just had a few engineer officers there who were working on the engineer POI.[43]

Castle's two deputies, LTC Lawrence Kelly and LTC Sean Sullivan, were OICs of the NCOES and OES teams, respectively. These two officers, however, were sent to Baghdad to work on the J-Staff soon after Mob-2 and 3's arrival in Iraq. Both officers, at least nominally, remained in charge of their respective teams, though these teams too, would suffer losses from personnel being pulled away for other missions.[44]

Though the instructors from these teams did not ultimately perform their intended missions, that does not mean they were idle or were mal-employed. Most still went on to achieve training successes with the Iraqi Army. The engineer MOS instruction team is a good example.

The engineer MOS team consisted of LTC Daniel Christian, MAJ Brian Miller, and MAJ Kevin Myers. These three went to work preparing a POI for the engineer MOS training. The problem was that no one at CMATT seemed to have any interest in the engineer MOS training (or for the whole MOS school mission for that matter) and it began to appear to Christian that they were wasting their time. "For the first 3 months, the three of us really tried to get interest, support, and funding for the school," Christian remembered. "It was a really difficult thing to do at that time, just to get the concept off the ground." Not one to be idle, Christian found other things to fill his time and skills as an engineer officer:

> While I was in Taji I took it as an opportunity to do force protection. We were on the Iraqi side and the footprint of the base was that it backed up against the forward refueling point for the 1st Cavalry Division. That perimeter was riddled with holes in the fence and things of that nature, so I assumed the responsibility as the engineer to do force protection for Taji and just started to move that down the road. I begged and borrowed for resources. I got some concertina wire and we really shored up that area pretty well before I left.[45]

For several weeks, Christian and Miller worked for Castle in laying the foundation for the establishment of an engineer school but it was apparently a frustrating experience. However, Christian ultimately found what he considered more useful employment. "I went to Phoenix Base in Baghdad, met up with COL Parsons and the other folks who were running the 5th Division, and pleaded my case," he explained. "I was going crazy with that mission in Taji and needed to do something else." Soon after this meeting he received orders to report to Numaniyah Military Training Base (NMTB) where he was assigned to replace an existing brigade advisor from the 91st Division (TS) whom Christian later described as "very much mentally on his way out."[46]

Meanwhile, Castle and Miller received a new mission—that of helping to develop the Iraqi Army's engineer force. It was a CMATT mission, like many others, that was created "on the fly." Before Christian had departed for Numaniyah, Castle had noted the disintegration of his school and decided to address the issue with CMATT:

> About 1 month into this I noticed that things were getting peeled away. I actually contacted BG Richard Sherlock and said, 'Sir, I'm not doing anything here. Is there something else I can do?' He called me down to Baghdad where I talked both to him and BG James Schwitters. Probably about a week into the trip to Baghdad, General Schwitters either saw or was told about a need to develop the Iraqi Army engineer force because they just didn't have anything; and since I was an engineer officer, it kind of fit. He

interviewed me for the job and that's when I got started. It didn't appear to me that it was a planned position, more of an opportunity that had come up.[47]

Castle returned to Taji, grabbed Christian and Miller and went to work, though he lost Christian soon after this effort started. The mission for the engineers now was not to develop an MOS course, but to help stand up and train a 200-man engineer battalion that would form the basis for the support troops of the Iraqi Army's engineer training center. In essence, Castle and Miller would be a two-man AST. As such, Castle worked with Brigadier General Marza, the engineer branch representative in the MOD responsible for engineer force development. These two officers worked hand-in-glove on organizational design, equipment quantities and specifications, and like issues in developing the vision for the future Iraqi Army engineer force. Meanwhile, MAJ Miller worked with Colonel Ali, the commander of the 1st Engineer Regiment (equivalent to a US battalion), in organizing, equipping, and training the first engineer unit.[48]

In working with Marza, Castle recalled that he sometimes had to advise "pretty hard." The engineers of the old Iraqi Army were largely trained as bridge units or mine laying units and a fair number of the officers and men from these old units were now in the new army. As is human nature, they desired to work on tasks with which they were familiar. "Well, what am I going to do if we don't do bridges?" he recalled some of them saying. With plenty of old Soviet-style bridging equipment sitting around, Marza was in agreement with their desires. However, Castle disagreed. There were more pressing needs for these engineer units, and Castle pushed hard to make him see the soundness of his position:

> We had a lot of discussions with General Marza and the engineers too, because General Marza wanted to have bridge companies and mine laying companies. I told him we needed to think about what will be the most important things about our mission, and it was really more around survivability and construction as to what they were looking for. We worked on the training to prepare those areas, so we didn't really talk about mine laying or bridges at all, even though they had some bridges still left over there that we could've used to do some training on: using the excavators that were there and then just basic masonry— we had equipment in for that; pipefitting and some other things they could use to refurbish some of their buildings so they could use them to either live in or work in. In a lot of the areas we went into to stand up these companies,

the buildings were there but everything else had been stripped out—wires, pipes—everything had been taken to use somewhere else.[49]

Ultimately, Castle's view won out.

Following through on Castle's vision, Miller worked with Colonel Ali to develop training on immediately useful engineer-specific tasks. In addition to the more routine training events such as marksmanship and drill, they included basic tasks in masonry, piping, and electrical wiring, as well as identification and reduction of IEDs and mines. They likewise arranged training on more advanced skills with engineer equipment. Castle was able to arrange for the transfer of excavators from the MOI to the Iraqi Army. At Taji, there were 28 new civilian versions of these power shovels sitting idle. He convinced the MOI they would be better utilized by the army and so they went to the 1st Engineers for use at the training center, and later two were issued to each division.[50]

Castle's work with Marza caused him to work closely with the MNSTC-I J5 section. In doing so he discovered several months into the effort that the MNSTC-I plan was to create an engineer regiment in each of the Iraqi divisions (which by now included the former ING divisions and two completely new divisions that were forming) for a total of eight new units. The 1st Engineer Regiment, which had just completed organizing and going through its basic and advanced training, would have to support this new initiative. Working with the MOD, Castle and Miller arranged to send 80 of the 1st Regiment's engineers to the United Arab Emirates (UAE) on C-130s to be trained by the German Army on additional engineer skills. On return from the UAE, these troops formed the core of the Iraqi Army's basic training unit that would help populate the new divisions with trained engineer troops.[51]

The engineer basic training unit at Taji would eventually go on to train one engineer company (which would eventually expand to form a regiment) for each of the existing Iraqi divisions that had not yet acquired one. Interestingly, the three ING divisions each possessed an explosive ordnance disposal (EOD) company, since that mission (the Iraqis had no Ordnance Corps at the time) was of higher priority than other missions for those units. The basic training unit ran the EOD companies through engineer training and eventually qualified them to perform basic engineer tasks. Significantly, it was an early success story of Iraqis training Iraqis.[52]

While the engineer team was at least employed in working with the Iraqi Army in its branch skills, such was not true for other members of the MOS training teams. The two officers on the ordnance team, for example, were sent to other duties that were not directly related to their branch. MAJ Theresa Baginski was pulled out of the MOS training team about mid-November and reassigned to be on the AST for the 1st Transportation Regiment headed by LTC McGrath (who himself had been originally slotted as an intelligence officer on the CMATT staff).[53]

Having been assigned to the MOS training team, Baginski had not received the same training at Camp Atterbury as had the other AST members. "We were all in the same situation—none of us were slotted to be [on an AST]," she explained. "There were times in Camp Atterbury, Indiana, when they divided us up and [the AST] people got this training [e.g., combat-related training] while the [MOS, NCOES, and OES] people tracked a different way or maybe skipped something."[54]

Though reassignment to do a job for which she had little preparatory training was disconcerting, Baginski felt that being the first AST assigned to the regiment was a distinct advantage. She believed the team was very lucky "because we were there from the very beginning. Because of that, we didn't have to overcome a lot of, 'Well, the Americans before did it this way.' The Iraqis didn't have a lot of experience to go off or didn't have expectations of how it would be because we were the first Americans with whom they had worked."[55]

In spite of the fact that being on the first AST had its advantages, it did not mean the team was free from problems. When they arrived at the unit, there were only 50 soldiers and 30 old Russian-made trucks. The assigned regimental commander had not yet arrived, and the acting commander was busy creating new problems. Baginski explained:

> We had issues because the Iraqis weren't prepared to address some of the soldiers' basic needs, like getting them paid. The soldiers wanted to go home and wanted to take their pay home with them. At one point early on the Iraqi soldiers decided they were going to go home no matter what, they mobbed together and demanded to go on leave . . . they just got that attitude and said, 'You're not going to pay me? I don't have to stay here. I'm allowed to go home on leave.' The acting commander, the Iraqi colonel, just got very angry because he wasn't used to an army where soldiers even dared to speak out. So he told them they were all lazy and undisciplined. His insults were what really provoked that situation. Soon after that, the Ministry of Defense provided us with a colonel who would be the regimental commander.[56]

The new commander, Colonel Ea'ad, turned out to be a fine commander and things began to run much smoother. He had 24 years of service in the old army and was experienced and skillful at leading and training men. His interaction with his American advisors minimized many of the problems they and the unit faced. One of the issues that was potentially a significant problem was that Baginski, and CPT Stacy O'Keefe, another advisor on the team, were female.

This issue had raised its head originally when assigning the first groups of Iroquois Warriors to the ASTs—no women were assigned to those teams due to the perception that Iraqi soldiers, steeped in the traditions of a male-dominated Arab culture, would refuse to listen to female advisors. The acting commander, to his credit, quashed any notion in his troops that they would be allowed to cause trouble for Baginski and O'Keefe. Baginski remembered that the acting commander had "pulled all the soldiers into a room and told them there would be absolutely no disrespect shown to American females, that they would treat us with the respect that's due a Muslim woman and that was that." It was a sentiment the permanent commander reinforced, and the two women experienced no problems with the Iraqi troops. Baginski's recollection was that it was quite the opposite: "In fact, I think they sometimes turned to us more than the men because they knew we were going to follow through and take care of them. They didn't have clothing; they didn't have anything. At the very beginning, I was the one carrying around the box with all the medicine in it. We did everything for them." That positive relationship even extended to the rest of the AST: "They became very loyal to the Americans from the beginning because we took care of them. The soldiers had more faith and trust in the Americans that we were going to protect them than they did in their chain of command, originally. That was something we had to get around later."[57]

Another aspect of this unit that made the advisor-unit relationship go smoother was the nature of the soldiers themselves. Baginski described them and why their mission may have been a breeze compared to many others:

> Our soldiers were primarily Shi'a and they were much older than the typical infantry battalion soldier. Many of our soldiers had previous transportation experience in the Iraqi Army. . . . They knew how to drive and maintain vehicles. We still had to do a lot of training, but our training focused more on convoy operations and convoy defense. We started off initially putting together our training schedules, thinking we were going to have to do the

training, but then within a week we realized that that was not going to work. The Iraqis needed to train the Iraqis. So we started the train-the-trainer concept very early on, which took away the language barrier issues. We put the people who had the expertise up front right away and that just made things move along quicker.[58]

Around the end of January, McGrath was ordered to move to Numaniyah to stand up a new AST for the 2d Transportation Regiment. Leadership of the AST for the 1st Regiment was passed to Baginski. She did not miss a stride and continued to develop the training plan for the regiment. There was no specific template for CMATT's ASTs to take their units through a collective training cycle. Each AST was free to develop its own methods, tasks, and schedule. Baginski described how her AST conducted its business:

We went through stages. Everything that we were doing, I worked directly with Colonel Ea'ad on. We met and talked daily. We worked daily moving the regiment further along toward independency. I found myself advising him on all facets of the operation and constantly reminding him that the officers needed to take care of their soldiers and develop NCO/officer relations. So, on a daily basis, I asked him if he went out and checked training, if he made sure he knew what his people were doing. I asked him, 'Do you know how your soldiers are living? Have you talked to your soldiers?' We worked to empower the first sergeants, which was something that had not happened. We established training meetings—initially daily meetings where they brought in their staff and the company commanders—to hold the commanders responsible for knowing their people and knowing what was going on. We would demonstrate to them the importance of planning in advance. The Iraqis didn't want to plan anything out. They didn't seem to have the concept of planning so we worked really heavily on that. We started out initially doing the training and getting the companies trained up. We started at that level. We had an advisor for each of the Iraqi company commanders who worked directly with them in planning, training, and executing training. That ultimately led to us running convoy missions, and that company advisor would go through all phases of planning the convoy operation. Initially the US advisor planned it more than the Iraqis. Eventually, though, it transitioned over to where the advisors were just supervising and out there being mentors and guides to the Iraqis, because we wanted the Iraqi company-level officers to execute on their own. We started out doing everything at the company level because they didn't have any staff. It was the commander, an executive officer, and the company commanders.[59]

The fact that there was no staff was another challenge Baginski had to overcome. She remembered that she and Ea'ad had to fight with the MOD directly to get the officers they needed. "The commander and I went to the MOD on a couple different occasions to talk to the Iraqi leadership and tell them we needed more officers. We couldn't build a battalion without a staff, so he and I took two or three trips to Baghdad to do that." Eventually the staff officers began to dribble in, which increased the capabilities and efficiency of the regiment. "Our focus initially was mainly on the command side of the house, both at the company and battalion level," she explained. "But as we progressed and started running missions and started filtering in more officers, then we shifted responsibilities so we were training up more of the staff side of the house."[60]

By this time the unit was actually running convoy missions for the Iraqi Army, but they were limited in distance, scope, and complexity. To increase the skill-level and value of the unit to the overall war effort, Baginski and Ea'ad opened communications with the 1st Corps Support Command (COSCOM) in late February to coordinate missions. Three months later, in May, control of the regiment was formally transferred to the COSCOM for assignment of missions. The COSCOM wanted the Iraqi unit validated before assigning it primary missions and so directed that the 46th Corps Support Group send over a team to train and certify the regiment. Baginski recalled that the 46th Group "came in and developed a program of instruction and brought in a team of about 30 NCOs who were assigned to train each of the companies to conduct convoy operations. They went through a very intensive train up. . . . The training ended with a convoy live-fire operation . . . and upon completion of the exercise they started to run missions."[61]

The job of Baginski's team was not over, however. Her team was now nine strong with the addition of advisors from a different USAR training division in February. It was now equipped with four up-armored HMMWVs, each with a crew-served weapon mounted on the top. Therefore, she insisted that each convoy from the regiment be escorted by two of the team's vehicles as additional security and to provide the commander with feedback on how the operation went. These missions were not without risk, of course, as Baginski described:

> . . . we had a few incidents. One of our missions was going to Ramadi and an improvised explosive device (IED) went off right after Captain O'Keefe's Humvee went by. She was the convoy commander of that mission. One of her convoys also took gunfire and an Iraqi passenger was shot in the leg. We were transporting troops that day and we had to pull into Abu Ghraib to get him medical support. On another occasion, I was on a mission and we were going into Baghdad. We were coming around one of the traffic circles and started taking fire from the left, but the Iraqis took care of that one.

She went on to add that, "We never lost an Iraqi, though, and none of the Iraqi soldiers or our American team members were ever shot. We had absolutely no combat injuries on any of our missions."[62] Looking back on the experience of her time in Iraq, Baginski was clearly proud of the efforts of her team and that of her advised unit. She said:

> I'm very, very positive about how the 1st Motor Transportation Regiment went from literally nothing to the point where they were effectively running missions when I left there. There were some fights along the way on how independent the Iraqis needed to be. But we got to that phase where they were planning the missions; they had the staff piece in place and were actually executing the missions. We were not quite at the point where they could go out on their own without our help, but a lot of that was due to limitations within country. They didn't have a system in place where they could call for support if they were being attacked and they didn't have a system for medical evacuations in place either. They didn't have long-range radios yet. When I left, we were still working on that. We were trying out a couple different things. But when we left, they were more than capable.[63]

The MOS training team was not the only organization to see a significant shift in its organization and the missions that its assigned personnel actually performed. Another was the OES team. MAJ Loncle described the team's mission as more or less "running the Iraqi West Point. We each would have been assigned as professors or instructors in certain areas. We would have all gone to one or two military academy type places and then students would have come to us." The plan was to run modified courses that included a Platoon Leaders Course, Company Commanders Course, an Operations and Training Course, and an Administration/Logistics Course, among others. However, the team members discovered soon after their arrival that the mission was scrubbed. Loncle remembered that instead of running schools the team was " . . . going to be broken into mobile training teams and they would be farming us out to each of the area commands to support them."[64]

Part of the reason this change transpired was that several countries in the North Atlantic Treaty Organization (NATO) had volunteered to take over officer training for the Iraqi Army. Once that mission was taken, the OES team had no function. "What are we going to do with these people?" was CMATT's response, Loncle recalled. It was left up to the 47 members of the team to figure it out. Loncle continued, "We had to work out who we were and what we could do. . . . We were given very general limitations. They didn't want us to all become ASTs and go running out playing battle. We had to still stay in that realm." That "realm" was the business of officer development and education. What was decided was to build about 9 five-man OES mobile training teams (MTT). Loncle described the team's parameters:

> Each team had to be able to teach skills from basic, advanced, Command and General Staff College (CGSC), all the way up the line depending on where our students were. We basically did collective staff training. . . . We were doing more formal classes. As you go through the officer education, if they needed to start down at the basic level, we had to be able to step in there. As our students progressed, we would ramp it up toward Combined Arms and Services Staff School (CAS3)/Intermediate Level Education (ILE)-level training as necessary.[65]

The MTTs were sent to teach at numerous locations to include the Kurdish Military Academy, the Iraqi Military Academy, and the various military training bases. The experience of each team was varied, but Loncle's team OES MTT #4 gives one a good idea of what these teams accomplished.

LTC Mark Truhan was the OIC of MTT #4, and reported to his nominal chief, Sean Sullivan at CMATT. In addition to Loncle, there were three other officers on the team. The team's first mission was to work with ING units at FOB War Horse in Ba'qubah. The team was transported to

War Horse and dumped off with their baggage in the middle of the post, then their escorts departed, "because they wanted to get home before it got dark," Loncle recalled. No one on the post knew the team was coming. Having no vehicles, the two lieutenant colonels on the team sought the TOC of the 3d Brigade, 1st Infantry Division (Mechanized), the owners of the installation, and informed the command of their presence. Thus, this team rapidly learned a lesson that many other Iroquois Warriors would come to understand about working for CMATT in Iraq—CMATT personnel were largely at the mercy of the American operational units of MNC-I when it came to life support. Sometimes it was good, and sometimes it was not.

For MTT #4, things happened to turn out well. Loncle described the reception: "Hats off to the first sergeant of Headquarters and Headquarters Company (HHC) of the 3d Brigade, 1st ID who adopted us. He came with a truck, picked up all our gear and put us into a transient tent for one night. By the next night, then, we had containerized housing units to live in, so they reacted very quickly and took care of us."[66]

Not only was the housing relatively decent for the team, the post boasted other luxuries. War Horse had a large Army and Air Force Exchange Service (AAFES)-run Post Exchange (PX) where they could buy just about anything they needed for maintaining something close to a US lifestyle. It also possessed a large dining facility that was considered quite good for the quality of its meals.[67]

One drawback to War Horse, at least in the way of convenience for the team, was that, like Taji, it was split into two areas—the US side and the Iraqi side—and the team was billeted on the US side. This was problematic for a team with no transportation. " . . . the students came to us as opposed to us going to see them. That was difficult," Loncle recollected. It was difficult because the students had to be searched and processed through the security entrance each time they attended training on the US side of the compound.[68]

The team coordinated with the four-man AST provided by the 3d Brigade to work with the four ING battalions located near the post. "Hey, this is what we can do," Loncle recalled telling them. "I have to say that the 3d Brigade really did a great job supporting us. They were quite receptive and happy to get us. We hooked up with their team and integrated in."[69]

The Iraqi units—the 204th, 205th, and 206th ING Battalions—were all part of the newly formed 32d Brigade, 5th Iraqi Division.[70] Each was in varying states of training, experience, and readiness. The team went to work training the battalion staffs. Each staff received an initial overview training package of staff roles, responsibilities, and procedures.

The presentations were a challenge because they all had to be conducted through interpreters. Loncle explained the process:

> The hardest working people in Iraq are the interpreters, and we were blessed with having two very, very good interpreters who worked with us when we were at FOB War Horse. We'd write our lesson plans in English and submit them to the translator team they had there. We did everything on PowerPoint but it was all dual language, so half the slide was in English and the other half was in Arabic. As such, whoever was looking at it could follow in whatever language they were comfortable in. We practiced our classes with the interpreters to make sure they were comfortable with the material. It was slow but you learned how to do it. Even though you don't understand their language, you learned how to read body language. You could tell if the students were picking up the lesson or if they weren't quite sure what you were going over. You almost had to do it by body language. You could tell what parts they understood by their questions, because they would start asking really intelligent, pointed questions. It's almost an art but with practice you got more comfortable. We were just blessed with really good interpreters.

Loncle also emphasized, "Initially it was tough, though."[71]

Soon after the team began their work with the 32d Brigade, the pace of the effort slowed, then stopped due to the upcoming January elections. The ING units were needed to provide polling place guards and other security. Additionally, the 1st Division had been extended on its tour in country to cover the elections, then almost immediately after began leaving as the 3d ID came in to replace it. It was at about that time the team's focus shifted. "We were on the back burner until 3d ID landed and got up to speed," Loncle explained. "Somewhere during the 3d ID's mobilization process, they were informed that they would have to form these military transition teams [MiTT—ASTs were redesignated as MiTTs in January 2005] to work with the Iraqi Army and that it was going to be one of the highest priority missions while they were there."[72] The notification to the 3d ID that they would have to provide MiTTs for the ING came very late in the division's mobilization. The staff had no time to form and train the teams before deployment, so the teams were organized once they arrived in country. Thus, the MTT #4 switched its efforts, for the time being, to training the new MiTTs for the 3d ID.[73]

Initially, the team provided a 3-day orientation and train-up to the MiTTs during which it provided the new advisors with CDs and DVDs full of lesson plans and other training aids. This was followed by another 3 weeks of more practical work. Loncle recalled that the most valuable service to the 3d ID MiTTs was probably orienting them to their ING charges: " . . .we had already established rapport with the Iraqi staffs. They knew us, so we could help the 3d ID assess them and tell them, 'All right, this is where your battalion is at; this is what they're strong at and this is what they're weak at.'"[74]

In early April, MTT #4 was transferred to the Kirkush Military Training Base (KMTB) to work with the 5th Iraqi Division staff and the staff of its 3d Brigade. At KMTB, the team was billeted on the Iraqi side, which eliminated the security hassles. "It was way better for us because now we lived on the Iraqi side of the post with the ASTs and every day I could go see my students," Loncle remembered. "I didn't have to bring them on the American FOB or arrange for a convoy in support to get me to them. Now we were with them." Additionally, the team was able to acquire the use of several vehicles for transportation. Futhermore, the US side, FOB Caldwell, still possessed most of the comforts that the team had come to enjoy at War Horse.[75]

At KMTB, MTT #4 worked closely with COL Parsons, the senior advisor to the 5th Division. In fact, Parsons was in large part responsible for the transfer of the team to Kirkush. He discovered that his NCO advisors had limited experience at brigade and division level staff work and needed someone to help with that effort. MTT #4 filled that bill perfectly. For the next several months, the team continued to work for Parsons and helped bring that division to higher levels of capability. In reflecting on his time there, Loncle explained his definition of success when working with the Iraqis: "Was it hard? Yeah. I lived for what I called 'the days the light bulbs went on.' We'd be up teaching something and I'd know they weren't getting it, and then finally the light bulbs would come on—they had gotten it and you could see it."[76]

Unlike the MOS and OES teams, the NCOES and ING BCT teams actually performed the tasks they were sent over to do. Like the OES team, the NCOES team was to set up and operate a sort of NCO academy and run courses that included a Squad Leaders Course, a Platoon Sergeants Course, an Advanced Platoon Sergeants Course, a First Sergeants Course, and a Supply/Maintenance Course.[77] This team actually ran these courses at the Kirkush NCO Academy.

The ING BCT team, consisting of 30 drill sergeants, was developed to assist the MOD in expanding the Iraqi National Guard to six divisions. Initially, Coalition maneuver units were responsible for running the basic training for the Iraqi National Guard at six different regional training centers located at Mosul, Tikrit, Habbaniyah, Taji, Al Kut, and Talil. The ING BCT team was brought in to assist Iraqi drill sergeants develop the skills needed to assume the mission, to put an Iraqi face on the training, and eventually to release the Coalition units for other missions. Teams of Iroquois Warrior drill sergeants were sent to each of the regional training centers where they taught their newly minted Iraqi drill sergeants in a train-the-trainer fashion.[78]

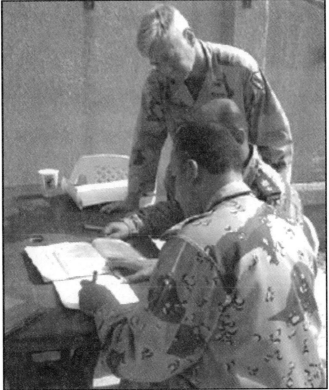

Figure 17. LTC George Crowell conducts logistics training with two Iraqi officers as part of the "Co-Op" program.

The 98th Division soldiers who served on the MNSTC-I, CMATT, and CPATT staffs helped bring a level of efficiency and accomplishment to those headquarters that would have been much later in realization had the Iroquois Warriors not shown up when they did. They filled those staffs with officers and NCOs who, on arrival, went to work helping to create and establish operating procedures for a new headquarters that possessed what was arguably the most important mission in Iraq. The soldiers on the many training teams also contributed by assisting the Iraqi Army establish viable training and logistics support institutions of its own and by helping to create or improve specialized combat support and combat service support organizations.

While the missions assigned to the Iroquois Warriors who worked on the various staffs and training teams were diverse, that of the ASTs was singular: teach, coach, and mentor the Iraqi Army to enable it to take the lead in combat operations. Nevertheless, it was a varied mission in terms of location, activities, level of readiness, and number of Iraqi units the soldiers advised. Those varieties made the AST mission the largest single effort of the division in Iraq—and the most dangerous.

Notes

1. MAJ John Vernick, interview by author, Headquarters, 98th Division (IT), Rochester, NY, 5 November 2006, 3.

2. Headquarters, 98th Division, PowerPoint Brief, "Information Brief, 98th Division (IT) FA-TRAC and TY04/TY05 Missions," 2 October 2004, 7. All numbers provided in this chapter regarding the personnel strength contributed to each section of MNSTC-I, CMAAT, and CPATT are derived from this briefing. The numbers reflect all 98th Division personnel contributions including those from other commands who deployed as part of the division's mobilization groups.

3. BG Richard Sherlock, interview by author, Office, Chief of the Army Reserve, Pentagon, Washington, DC, 16 November 2006, 5.

4. LTC James DiRisio, interview by author, Headquarters, 98th Division (IT), Rochester, NY, 3 November 2006, 10.

5. Ibid.

6. LTC James DiRisio, e-mail to author, Subject: CPATT, 26 January 2007.

7. LTG David H. Petraeus, interview by author, Headquarters, Combined Arms Center, Fort Leavenworth, KS, 11 December 2006, 6.

8. COL Lawrence Kelly, telephone interview by author, Combat Studies Institute, Fort Leavenworth, KS, 15 December 2006, 7.

9. Chaplain (COL) J. Paul Womack, written response to author's queries, 31 January 2007, 2.

10. BG Frank Cipolla, telephone interview by author, Combat Studies Institute, Fort Leavenworth, KS, 20 November 2006, 4.

11. Ibid.

12. COL Jody Daniels, e-mail to author, Subject: RE: Your Interview Transcript, 16 March 2007, 4:33 p.m.

13. Vernick interview, 5 November 2006, 3.

14. Headquarters, Coalition Military Assistance Training Team, Information Paper, "Subject: Authorization and Wear of Shoulder Sleeve Insignia (SSI) for US Army Personnel Belonging to the Coalition Military Assistance Training Team (CMATT)," 20 October 2004, 2. The information paper was also sent to the rear CP at Rochester to ensure that deploying soldiers understood they would have to remove their division patches once they arrived in country; DiRisio interview, 3 November 2006.

15. Cipolla telephone interview, 20 November 2006, 4.

16. Timothy J. Hansen and Jocene D. Preston, ed. *An Encounter with History: The 98th Division and the Global War on Terrorism: 2001–2005* (Washington, DC: Government Printing Office, 2006), 98–99.

17. Ibid., 100–01.

18. Ibid., 103–04.

19. Vernick interview, 5 November 2006, 8.

20. Hansen and Preston, *Encounter with History*, 105–06.

21. Ibid., 86.

22. Ibid., 87–89.

23. Ibid., 107–09.

24. DiRisio interview, 3 November 2006, 11.

25. Army Knowledge On-line, General Officer Management Office website, BG James Schwitters; COL Jody Daniels described BG Schwitters as such in a telephone conversation with the author in December 2006.

26. BG James Schwitters, telephone interview by author, Combat Studies Institute, Fort Leavenworth, KS, 13 December 2006, 1–2.

27. DiRisio interview, 3 November 2006, 5–6.

28. COL Robert Catalanotti, interview by author, Headquarters, 98th Division (IT), Rochester, NY, 3 November 2006, 5.

29. Ibid.; LTC James DiRisio, e-mail to author, Subject: RE: Taji BSU Commander Before Catalanotti, 29 March 2007, 1:50 p.m.

30. Catalanotti interview, 3 November 2006, 5.

31. CSM Milton Newsome, interview by author, Headquarters, 98th Division (IT), Rochester, NY, 3 November 2006, 3.

32. Catalanotti interview, 3 November 2006, 8.

33. Ibid.

34. Ibid., 6.

35. Ibid., 6–7.

36. Newsome interview, 3 November 2006, 3.

37. Catalanotti interview, 3 November 2006, 6.

38. MAJ Shauna Hauser, interview by John McCool, Operational Leadership Experience Project, Combat Studies Institute, Fort Leavenworth, KS, 29 November 2005, 2.

39. Ibid., 10.

40. Ibid., 12.

41. Headquarters, Multi-National Security Transition Command-Iraq, Support Unit, "Requirements Assessment," Enclosure 4, "Army Support to MNSTC-I Requirement," 3 August 2004, 10–13.

42. Ibid.

43. COL Edward P. Castle, interview by author, Headquarters, 98th Division (IT), Rochester, NY, 5 November 2005, 3.

44. Kelly and Sullivan had both been on the survey team and so were already in Iraq when the mobilization groups with their teams arrived.

45. LTC Daniel Christian, interview by author, 98th Division Headquarters, Rochester, NY, 3 November 2006, 2, 4.

46. Ibid., 3–4.

47. Castle interview, 5 November 2005, 4.

48. Ibid.

49. Ibid., 6.

50. Ibid., 5.

51. Ibid.

52. Ibid., 5–7. Incidentally, LTC Sean Sullivan was the action officer at CMATT who arranged the contract for the ING EOD companies to receive EOD training near Basra.

53. LTC Theresa Baginski, telephone interview by author, Headquarters, 98th Division (IT), Rochester, NY, 5 November 2005, 1.

54. Ibid., 2.

55. Ibid.

56. Ibid.

57. Ibid., 3.

58. Ibid., 2–3.

59. Ibid., 3.

60. Ibid., 3–4.

61. Ibid., 4.

62. Ibid., 6–7.

63. Ibid., 6.

64. MAJ Paul Loncle, interview by author, Headquarters, 98th Division (IT), Rochester, NY, 4 November 2006, 3; "Information Brief, 98th DIV (IT) FA-TRAC and TY04/TY05 Missions," 2 October 2004, 13.

65. Loncle interview, 4 November 2006, 4.

66. Ibid., 7.

67. Ibid., 8.

68. Ibid., 4.

69. Ibid.

70. Designations of Iraqi units referred to in this work use those assigned at the time the 98th Division ASTs took over the mission. The Iraqi Army units underwent several major reorganizations and redesignations between January and May 2005. See appendix C for a conversion chart that details the before and after designations.

71. Loncle interview, 4 November 2006, 4–5.

72. Ibid., 5.

73. Ibid.

74. Ibid.

75. Ibid., 4, 8. The team lost LTC Truhan at this point. He was transferred to Rustamiyah to work with the Iraqi Military Academy.

76. Ibid., 8.

77. "Information Brief, 98th DIV (IT) FA-TRAC and TY04/TY05 Missions," 2 October 2004, 13.

78. Ibid., 16; Headquarters, Coalition Military Assistance Transition Team, PowerPoint Brief, "CMATT JMD Staff Brief," undated, 5.

Chapter 6

The Advisor Mission

... we were pretty happy with the turnaround.

SFC Ewing

The largest, and arguably most important, mission the Iroquois Warriors performed in Iraq was that of advising Iraqi Army units. Approximately 335 of the soldiers who deployed as part of the 98th Division's package to support the MNSTC-I (which included the C2 Cell) were assigned to perform this mission. The number of soldiers who participated as advisors is actually somewhat larger when one considers there were at least 20 or more soldiers mobilized and deployed as fillers to replace advisors who were killed, wounded, or for some other reason left one of the ASTs. There were still others, as previously stated, who were later reassigned as advisors to unplanned ASTs once they were in Iraq.

The primary components of the 98th Division's AST mission in Iraq consisted of the C2 Cell (which underwent several mission changes) and over 30 advisor teams who worked primarily with the 1st, 3d, and 5th Iraqi Divisions, although as described, a few worked with Iraqi Army engineer and logistics units too. Though these troops had a single focus to their mission, their experiences were easily more diverse—and hazardous—than any other team of Iroquois Warriors sent to Iraq.

The Command and Control (C2) Cell

In the original planning for this mission, the AST C2 Cell was intended to function as the Headquarters, 98th Division (Forward). As such, it would have been MG Robinson's headquarters element that controlled the RSOI of division elements coming into theater, and then the FA-TRAC headquarters to provide the planning, administration, and logistics support to those elements for the duration of the mission. Once it was discovered that CMATT existed, the C2 Cell's mission rapidly evolved into something less than originally envisioned, although the responsibilities remained substantial.

Officially, the cell's mission statement was "Coordinate all administrative, logistical, reporting, and liaison functions for Advisor Support Teams (AST) and CG CMATT, CJTF-7." Functionally, it was a little more involved than the statement leads one to believe. The cell's RSOI function came to include the reception of those non-98th Division advisors identified to deploy and support the expansion of the Iraqi Army, which occurred in January 2005 when the ING was integrated into the Regular Army and two additional divisions were created. This task included the operation of the Green Hotel, the issue of AST supplies and equipment at Taji, the coordination of transportation of the advisors to the location of their respective Iraqi units, the coordination of the transfer of team equipment between incoming and outgoing teams, and the retrograde of the old teams to Taji. Part of the cell was located in Kuwait to help in these tasks. In addition, the C2 Cell was the node to which all ASTs sent their monthly Unit Personnel Reports, daily Personnel Status Reports, AARs, and other data. In turn, the cell would forward this information to the CMATT operations section.[1]

COL Cipolla, OIC of the C2 Cell at Taji, assumed responsibility for that mission in September. LTC Joseph Friedman was assigned as Cipolla's operations officer, but due to the immediate supply and deployment requirements after his arrival at Taji, he ended up doing much of the logistics work in the cell. Initially his primary task was to go to the BIAP to meet the mobilization groups. "Every week I was in BIAP meeting and greeting a new group coming in and escorting them by Chinook to Taji, getting them in the Green Hotel, getting them bedded down with meals in their bellies and pots to piss in," he recalled.[2]

Friedman discovered the cell had inherited a lot of supplies and equipment waiting to be issued to the ASTs:

> Almost nothing had been distributed to the ASTs. They had team boxes which contained all the stuff they would need to work as an AST—not TA-50 or weaponry, but just stuff . . . whatever they felt they wanted in a team box—and those hadn't even been distributed; they were still in Taji. A lot of these ASTs were already in their field environments and thus had to convoy back to Taji to pick up their team boxes. We had tons of stuff in a warehouse on the other side of Taji that hadn't been distributed and there wasn't any plan as to who was going to get what. It was just, 'Here's a whole bunch of stuff for your ASTs.' There were night vision goggles (NVG), but they were old and worthless—5Cs maybe. They gave us a bunch of batteries, but you'd need a whole lot of batteries to equip these guys. There was also soap, field vests, and all this stuff was in this big barn-like warehouse on Taji.[3]

Fortunately for the deploying 98th Division ASTs, they would have the opportunity to acquire most of their supplies before they deployed to their duty locations; however, many of the up-armored HMMWVs would not arrive until around the beginning of January 2005.

The Advisor Support Teams

As described, there was confusion among the advisors as to what the teams were really going to be doing. Most advisors had concluded, at least initially, that they would train their assigned Iraqi unit in basic tasks on a safe compound. Few had the idea they would be advising their units on combat missions.

The actual mission of the ASTs was to teach, coach, and mentor their Iraqi units. In theory, these units were to have completed basic training at about the time the ASTs arrived, so there would be minimal training requirements. On completion of the basic training, the assigned leaders of the battalion (Iraqi officers and NCOs) would consolidate with their trainees and soon after be declared operational. The 98th's ASTs, once they relieved the existing advisors, were to merely coach and mentor the leaders of those units as they prepared for and conducted actual operations. Of course by the US Army's standards, these Iraqi battalions would be no where near ready for combat operations, but the pressing need to "put an Iraqi face" on the security efforts in Iraq, especially before the upcoming January elections, ensured that these units would be employed in such operations well before they were truly prepared.

By the MNSTC-I JMD, organizationally the ASTs were to consist of the following personnel:

- Division AST (10 Advisors):

Position	Rank	Branch/MOS
Team Leader	COL	Combat Arms
Staff Advisor	LTC	Combat Arms
Staff Advisor	MAJ	Branch Immaterial
Staff Advisor	CPT	Branch Immaterial
Staff Advisor	CPT	Branch Immaterial
Advisor/Team NCOIC	SGM	MOS Immaterial
NCO Staff Advisor	SSG-MSG	Combat Arms
NCO Staff Advisor	SSG-MSG	Combat Arms
NCO Staff Advisor	SSG-MSG	MOS Immaterial
NCO Staff Advisor	SSG-MSG	MOS Immaterial

- Brigade AST (10 Advisors):

Position	Rank	Branch/MOS
Team Leader	LTC	Combat Arms
Staff Advisor	MAJ	Combat Arms
Staff Advisor	MAJ	Branch Immaterial
Staff Advisor	CPT	Combat Arms
Staff Advisor	CPT	Branch Immaterial
Advisor/Team NCOIC	SFC-MSG	Combat Arms
NCO Staff Advisor	SSG-SFC	Combat Arms
NCO Staff Advisor	SSG-SFC	Combat Arms
NCO Staff Advisor	SSG-SFC	MOS Immaterial
NCO Staff Advisor	SSG-SFC	MOS Immaterial

- Battalion AST (10 Advisors):

Position	Rank	Branch/MOS
Team Leader	MAJ	Combat Arms
Advisor	CPT	Combat Arms
Advisor	CPT	Branch Immaterial
Advisor/Team NCOIC	SFC-MSG	Combat Arms
NCO Advisor	SSG	Combat Arms
NCO Advisor	SSG	Combat Arms
NCO Advisor	SSG	Combat Arms
NCO Advisor	SSG	Combat Arms
NCO Advisor	SSG	MOS Immaterial
NCO Advisor	SSG	MOS Immaterial[4]

Within the teams, each was organized by its OIC in ways that seemed to best suit the needs of the Iraqi unit advised. Depending on what level the unit was at in terms of training often determined where the focus was for the advisors. In some cases, advisors were habitually assigned down to the companies to work on small unit tactics. In others, the OIC kept his team at battalion level to train the staff and sent advisors out with companies as needed.

The 98th Division's teams were fully manned to meet the requirements of the JMD. Each team was to be equipped with two up-armored HMMWVs, each with a mounted crew-served weapon (M2 .50-caliber heavy machine gun, M240 7.62-mm machine gun, or a Mark 19 grenade launcher), one or two SINCGARS radios, and a BFT system per vehicle. In addition, the team was to be issued a basic load of ammunition and the materials and supplies issued as part of the team box. What these soldiers soon discovered, however, was the manning and equipping documents that specified the ideal package for an AST did not match the existing conditions on the ground.

The units the ASTs were originally deployed to advise were the three Iraqi Regular Army divisions—the 1st, 3d, and 5th—consisting of 3 division headquarters, 9 brigade headquarters, and 27 battalions. Therefore, this mission required 39 ASTs. Of these, Marines were responsible for advising one division headquarters, two brigade headquarters, and five battalions, all in the 1st Division. Additionally, the Australian Army retained responsibility for two brigade headquarters and six battalions, all in the 3d Division.[5] Thus, the 98th Division was originally responsible for the remaining 23 ASTs, which included 13 ASTs in the 5th Division, 5 ASTs in the 1st Division, and 5 ASTs in the 3d Division.

That number increased to 31 teams by October, when the Australians dropped out of the mission. The Australian government's rules of engagement (ROE) for its troops in Iraq stated they would not participate in combat operations; therefore, once the Iraqi units they were advising finished their basic training, the Australians considered their mission completed. They would not go with the Iraqis beyond the garrison fence. That left the 98th Division to fill the void and caused further turmoil over mission and team changes when the division's personnel arrived at Taji.[6]

The Iraqi 1st Division headquarters was located at Taji, as were its subordinate brigades. The 1st Division was originally designated as the Iraqi Intervention Force (IIF) and trained counterinsurgency operations. Originally, the MOD intended this force to be employed anywhere it was needed throughout Iraq, though ultimately it would be employed as a standard infantry unit. The 3d Division, less two battalions, was located at the Al Kasik Military Training Base (AKMTB) about 50 miles northwest of Mosul. Its initial mission was to be the security force for northern areas of Iraq and guard the Syria-Iraq border. The 5th Division, less the 3d and 9th Brigades, was located at the Kirkush Military Training Base (KMTB) east of Baghdad and was responsible for the southern part of Iraq. The 3d Brigade was located at Numaniyah, and the 9th Brigade existed on paper only.

The existing ASTs working with these divisions were a conglomerate of personnel from the US and Australian Armed Forces. Though many of the American advisors were Marines, most were from one of the three US Army components, and primarily from the Army Reserve. There was a smattering of people from the National Guard and Regular Army, but most seem to have been from the USAR's 75th, 91st, and 95th Training Divisions. One team was made up entirely from Regular Army observer/

controllers (O/C) from the Combat Maneuver Training Center (CMTC) at Hohenfels, Germany. Many felt O/Cs were the best example of a perfect fit for the advisor job.[7] Most ASTs, on the other hand, were entirely ad hoc organizations composed of personnel who showed up in Iraq, were pooled together at the last minute, and sent off to advise an Iraqi unit. Some had received at least minimal levels of training to prepare them for the mission; others had received only the individual skills refresher training such as that at Fort Bliss. Some wanted to be there, others did not; therefore, their success with training the Iraqi units was just as mixed as their overall composition. Thus, the advisors the Iroquois Warriors were replacing were a curious mixture of military personnel with varying levels of training, experience, competence, and ability to perform the AST mission. In fact, Schwitters had earlier estimated that only about a third of the ASTs then assigned were effective in their duties.[8]

The next task for the ASTs was to link up with their respective Iraqi units. The plan was for the teams to load all their ammunition, supplies, and equipment in their HMMWVs and convoy to their respective duty locations. However, none of the crew-served weapons were yet available and, with the exception of the ASTs in Fallujah, neither were the vehicles. Friedman remembered that the existing ASTs "were out there in Toyota pickups with M16s and that was all they had. It was a while before up-armored Humvees, Blue Force Trackers, M4s and other weaponry came [in]."[9] All the items were on order, but most had yet to make their way through the supply system to Taji. As a result, the C2 Cell had to find another way to get the teams to their field locations.

For a few of the ASTs, members of the teams they were replacing, who were anxious to be replaced, showed up at Taji to pick up their replacements and get them to their new home. For most, however, that option was not feasible. Most AST duty stations were too far from Taji to make it convenient for the old advisors to drive over and pick up their replacements, especially for those up north at Al Kasik. Therefore, the best option was to fly.

Fortunately, the aviation brigade of the 1st Cavalry Division was nearby and amenable to help, for which Cipolla was grateful: "We did a lot of wheeling and dealing when it came to requesting Blackhawks because we were not really on the top of the priority list. If it wasn't for the 1st Cavalry Division, we would have had problems. They did me a lot of favors when it came to getting the troops out into the field."[10]

Once at their respective places of duty, the advisors were to link up with the existing team and conduct a "right seat ride," or officially, the

Relief in Place/Transfer of Authority (RIPTOA) process. Ideally, this event consisted of an orientation by the existing team members with their individual replacements to teach them how to do the job, show them where various facilities and training areas were, and, most importantly, introduce them to the Iraqi leaders from the unit they were to advise, coach, and mentor. The new team members would watch the old advisors perform their tasks for a week followed by a week where the new advisors took charge while the old advisors mentored them. Trying to coordinate this event was problematic for a variety of reasons. Sherlock explained one of them:

> . . . in many cases, our ASTs in the September/October 2004 timeframe were being met at the aircraft by their outgoing counterparts who were simultaneously throwing their bags on the aircraft saying, 'See ya. Your barracks are over there, have a good time. Oh by the way, the name of your counterpart is . . .,' whatever. In some cases, we had to go back and get them from the airfield, take them back into their quarters and do a very rudimentary RIPTOA with the teams we replaced.[11]

The "right seat ride" experience encountered by the Iroquois Warriors varied between poor to excellent, depending on the dedication of the outgoing team. Doug Shipman recalled that the outgoing AST for the Iraqi 3d Division headquarters was not helpful.

> I don't think the incoming people felt like the outgoing people had much to contribute. It was like, 'Here are your computers, here are your desks, here are the people, here are your interpreters, and this is the state of the training so far. See you later. . . .' It was only a matter of 2 or 3 days.[12]

Scott McConnell's team replaced the division staff AST for the 5th Division. His experience was better, but still not great. "I spent the first 5 days following him [the outgoing advisor] around and he did all the introductions," he remembered. "I got hooked up with e-mail and points of contact in Baghdad. The next 5 days he followed me around with less and less interest in what we were doing and more interest in packing bags and getting out of Dodge."[13]

In some cases, the outgoing ASTs were very good about preparing their replacements to assume the mission. Matt Jones recollected, "The guys we replaced did a phenomenal job. They did everything they possibly could to set us up for success. . . . Logistically they did everything they could for us. When we got there, they knew what we were going to need and they had already gotten it for us. We were very appreciative."[14]

SSG Charnock, assigned to the 1st Division, related how important the outgoing AST was to the integration process with the Iraqi unit as well. He explained that the RIPTOA process—

> . . . really helped establish trust to have the Iraqis see us with the guys they'd been working with for the last 8 months. They realized that we weren't just new faces but could be trusted as well. I think my American counterpart, whom I was replacing, gave the Iraqis some assurances about me and that helped a lot. Instead of starting from zero, maybe I started at two out of ten with the Iraqis.[15]

At the same time the Iroquois Warrior ASTs were conducting their right seat rides, they were also discovering just how Spartan the living conditions were for advisors. Though part of MNSTC-I's charter was to provide logistics support to the Iraqi Army—it was not set up to support the ASTs assigned to it. Thus, there was a tacit agreement between MNSTC-I and MNC-I that the Coalition Major Subordinate Commands (MSC) would provide life support to the advisors. In theory, this was a workable solution; in practice, often it was not.

First, there was not always a Coalition unit colocated at posts with the ASTs. For example, there were no Coalition units at Numaniyah where the ASTs for the 9th Brigade, 5th Division were stationed. Christian, the engineer who had successfully wrangled an AST assignment to leave Taji and the OES team, described the life support situation there:

> Numaniyah is 125 kilometers southeast of Baghdad and borders the Al Kut-Baghdad Road. The forward operating base is 9 square miles. There are about 40 ASTs with 10 to 12 people each and at various times as many as 15,000 Iraqis. It was all Iraqi run. There were no other Americans or American support. In fact, our higher headquarters was the Poles and they were located in Diwaniyah, about 180 klicks [kilometers] south of us. Needless to say, it was really a different world. All they served was Iraqi food and it was a very austere environment. Power was up and down every day. Internet didn't exist. TV didn't exist. We really had no idea what was going on in the outside world. For all intents and purposes, we were in the middle of Iraq on our own, doing what we needed to do. It was a big shock for me. While I was in Taji, we had everything.

There was a Burger King and a Cinnabon. We went from that to pretty much having nothing.[16]

In the case of Numaniyah, CMATT had arranged to support those ASTs through contracts. "We had life support contract arrangements set up that supported both the Iraqi Army and the advisors embedded there. When they needed things that only the Coalition could provide, we either had it delivered or they developed their own convoys and went up to Taji to get that stuff," Schwitters explained.[17]

Another problem arose with the Coalition units themselves. The ASTs with the 5th Division at KMTB were reliant on the New York National Guard's 42d "Rainbow" Division as their Coalition support unit. Parsons, the senior division advisor, recalled, "We would have to constantly plead our case to get support from the 42d. It was made available to us, but it was not without a great deal of wailing and gnashing of teeth to get things going. This was true not only for our support, but also to get support for the Iraqi forces."[18] In other words, the level of support provided to the ASTs (and the Iraqis) was directly proportional to the willingness of the supporting unit to provide it, and that was usually directly related to the commanding officer's view of that responsibility. If the local commander was not particularly interested in helping, the ASTs would often go without. Some commanders took that responsibility seriously and supported the ASTs in their area of operations (AO) as well as they could. Life support for those advisors tended to be significantly better than for those whose US counterpart unit commander did not view that responsibility with importance.

Availability of food and water seems to have been rarely, if ever, a problem for the ASTs, although the quality of the food was sometimes a matter of comment. At Kirkush, Charnock recalled that his Iraqis had hot food delivered to them and the advisors often ate with their charges:

> They were happy to have us. In fact, they wanted us to eat their food. You would only eat so much of it, though, because of the way they served it and the cleanliness of it. They would just give it to you with their hands and you didn't know where those hands had been. But after awhile I stopped thinking about it and just ate the food anyway. If we really wanted to, we could have driven back to the Marine camp any time and gotten a hot meal. But it was like, 'Do I really want a meal that badly that I would risk taking a convoy out through the city?' Maybe not.[19]

Christian gave another perspective:

We ate Iraqi food about every day. . . . Could you live on it if you had to? Yes. Did you lose weight? Absolutely. When I was there I lost 42 pounds. You survive. I don't want to paint this grave picture, but you just did what you had to do to get by. In terms of food, there were tons of care packages from home. We lived on soup and we cooked in our rooms a lot. We were lucky—one of our guys was a chef. He was very creative with some of the stuff he came up with. We started to run the unit like an SF unit. We had team rooms and food and we just made do with what we had.[20]

Water was rarely an issue, and the ASTs could get all the bottled water they needed from both US and Iraqi sources. Tennyson, with a 3d Division battalion that later deployed to Tall Afar, stated, "There was lots of bottled water . . ." but then added, "Water to wash with was a problem, though. . . . When we were in Tall Afar at our outpost, we didn't have any running water until we managed to get a pump down to the spring next to the [outpost] and pumped in wash water."[21]

Ammunition was another commodity in great supply, but most of the advisors did not take it for granted. Charnock was one of them. He remembered that in Kuwait, he and the members of his team were concerned there would not be enough of a resupply in Iraq so they decided not to shoot up their ammunition while on the live-fire ranges. "We'd just stand up there, go through the motions, and then keep all our rounds," he explained. He later came to believe it had been a good decision. When one of the teams that had been identified to depart early from Taji to join its unit was getting ready to leave, it had only a small basic load to take along. Charnock was able to provide those advisors with more from his own stash. He probably need not have worried though, because ammunition was one class of supply of which there was plenty in Iraq. Charnock added that when he got to Kirkush, ". . . the Marines actually were very helpful. They had [an ammo] bunker set up with everything imaginable and they let me go in there and take what I needed."[22]

Equipment, on the other hand, was a major concern. Instead of the HMMWVs and crew-served weapons they expected to receive, some ASTs received little or nothing in the way of proper equipment, at least initially. Some teams had Toyota pickup trucks for team vehicles. Few had the up-armored HMMWVs, crew-served weapons, SINCGARS, and BFTs they had anticipated. Charnock was on a team that was one of the exceptions. "When I got there I signed for everything we were supposed to get and that's what we got. We got two Humvees, a .50 cal and a M249 squad automatic weapon (SAW). That was it." On the other hand, some of the equipment brought over from the states was cause for concern:

> It was bad equipment. . . . We brought over PVS-5s [night vision goggles], which are crap. . . . They're very hard to work with. The active duty guys were walking around with PVS-14s. I would have been happy with a pair of PVS-7s, but the 5s were what we took over there and carried with us the whole time in their big green boxes. We ended up getting 14s, though, from the Marines, but I can't say everyone got that kind of stuff. I feel lucky that we fell under the Marines because they had everything they needed and they took good care of us.[23]

Maintenance was another issue. It is one thing to have the equipment on hand, it is still another to keep that equipment operational. In the case of Dan Christian's ASTs at Namuniyah, they relied on Iraqi soldiers to perform some basic repairs on their HMMWVs. They also established an informal relationship with a support unit from the 56th Brigade, Texas National Guard, located 30 kilometers away at Camp Scania, for acquisition of parts, oil changes, and other minor work on their vehicles. "We did everything we could to beg, borrow, steal, leverage American ingenuity, and establish relationships to get done what we needed to get done," he recalled.[24]

BG Schwitters was acutely aware of the conditions under which the advisors were living. Jim DiRisio recollected that the general was out often checking on the teams:

> General Schwitters did a lot of traveling. At any given week, we were probably out of the office 4 or 5 days. We were visiting the ASTs, giving them support, letting them know we were there, trying to find out what they needed. That was always difficult, though, because some of them lived in pretty Spartan conditions and there was a lot of frustration on their parts about what they didn't have. They didn't have access to the American PXs and sometimes they didn't even have access to decent food or water because they were embedded with Iraqi units. It was hard to go out and sit down and ask them how they were doing and what they needed because we would just get bombarded with complaints about mail, food, water, being able to take showers, and needing translators. There

was no shortage of problems to be solved. We tried to solve them as best we could.[25]

Schwitters agreed with that assessment:

> Every day we wrestled with the question of how to improve what we were doing. In hindsight, if we'd been able to predict the future better, we certainly would have set up a much more robust and resourced effort for both logistics and life support. Life support was the one area that was a continual struggle—providing our ASTs a safe and secure source of life support, whether that's food, water, or what I'll call 'quality of life' issues. We didn't want them bathing in pond water or worse, for instance. We wanted them to have the means to keep themselves sustained.[26]

While he was aware of the problems facing his advisors, as a career Special Operations officer, Schwitters also knew there was a point of diminishing returns. He explained that living a lifestyle that approximates what one could expect in America,

> . . . runs exactly contrary to the principle of embedding yourself and living like they do. T.E. Lawrence certainly talks eloquently about the need to become one of them. So we had a cultural clash between what you or I as a leader would want for our soldiers and the compromises someone in that position would find makes them most effective. If you want to live over in your own little walled compound with good food, showers, TVs, weight rooms, a morale, welfare and recreation (MWR) sustainment package once a week or month and Internet access, well, that runs square against developing the relationships upon which effectiveness hinged.[27]

Many of the Iroquois Warrior advisors either understood this principle when they arrived or came to learn it while they were there, but predictably there were also some who never understood it. Unfortunately, those were the few individuals who complained the most and likely understood the mission the least. The effectiveness of those advisors to their Iraqi units was questionable at best.

The experiences of the 98th Division advisor teams in Iraq during 2004 and 2005 were as varied as the locations at which they served. Each team encountered a unique set of circumstances, events, units, and personnel with which they had to contend and interact with as they worked to improve the Iraqi Army. On arrival at their respective duty stations, each team found their Iraqi unit at a different level of organization and readiness than those of their brother ASTs. Each Iraqi division, brigade, and battalion had been organized at different times. Indeed, some battalions had not yet been organized. Compounding the differences between units was the quality and dedication of their previous ASTs. Thus, the Iraqi units and their leaders were all at differing levels of knowledge, experience, and training, all of which presented a unique set of advantages and disadvantages for their new advisors. To provide a clearer, and hopefully more cohesive, explanation of what the 98th Division ASTs accomplished during their year's tour, it is necessary to provide a description of the collective ASTs experiences by division.

The Advisor Experience—The 5th Iraqi Division

The Iraqi 5th Division, also known as the "Hadeed Division," was organized in April 2004 at KMTB. It was commanded by MAJ General Ahmad Hlaybos. On the arrival of the 98th Division ASTs, the 5th Division consisted of the 3d, 7th, and 9th Brigades. The 3d Brigade had completed its basic training some time before and had already been engaged in a few minor operations. The 7th Brigade was just completing basic training and preparing to go "operational." The 9th Brigade, with the exception of its officers, was nonexistent. It would begin basic training in early December.[28]

In April 2005, the division would undergo a major reorganization as part of an overall plan developed by the MOD that did away with distinctly designated units and gave all divisional subordinate units a uniform set of designations. In this reorganization, 3d and 9th Brigades were redesignated as the 1st Brigade, 5th Division, and 3d Brigade, 5th Division, respectively. The brigades' subordinate battalions were redesignated the 1st, 2d, and 3d Battalions. Concurrently, the 7th Brigade was transferred to the 1st Division as that division's 4th Brigade, and replaced by the 32d Brigade, Iraqi National Guard which was redesignated as the 5th Division's new 2d Brigade.[29] (See appendix C for a more detailed explanation of this reorganization.)

The senior advisor for the 5th Division was COL Parsons. Parsons had originally been assigned to the C2 Cell in Taji; however, while he was at Fort Bliss in early September 2004, Parsons learned in a phone call from MG Robinson that the 5th Division's senior advisor slot had come open. Robinson asked him if he wanted the position, to which he responded that he did. Parsons soon was on his way to go through the training at Camp

Atterbury and ended up in the first Atterbury mobilization group to arrive in country.[30]

When he arrived at Taji in late October, Parsons learned that the 5th Division already had units preparing to go to Fallujah (the entire 1st Division was already there). The 3d Brigade had been ordered to move two battalions there to support the 1st Marine Division's assault on the city, and an additional brigade, the 7th, soon was to follow. The 3d Brigade had to have its units in place to support the Marines before the 7 November start date. The division headquarters was to move to Fallujah on 10 November, and the 7th Brigade would follow after that. Therefore, the 5th Division ASTs were ordered to link up with their units at KMTB as soon as possible.[31]

The teams for the 3d Brigade and its subordinate battalions flew out on 1st Cavalry Division Blackhawks. They were accompanied by part of Parsons' division team. Because Mob-1 was made up of the volunteers who had waived their right to a 30-day delay, Parsons' divisional AST only had 5 of its authorized 10 men present at Taji. The remainder would follow in Mob-2, about 3 weeks later. Even with only five of his troops present, there was difficulty in getting them all to the KMTB in a timely fashion due to the space available on the choppers. Parsons and one other member made it out to the KMTB on time. The other three, including Scott McConnell the G3 advisor for the division, were delayed for 2 days by severe weather.[32]

Parsons' team backfilled an AST from the 95th Division (IT). That team had been there about 6 months and had taken the division staff through the basic training period.[33] All was not well with that team, however. McConnell's counterpart, who had only been thinking about "getting out of Dodge," was not only the G3 advisor but also the OIC of the team. Apparently the lieutenant colonel who had been the OIC had, some time earlier, "fallen out of favor with the [rest of his AST] and scooted back to Baghdad" and the major was required to take charge.[34]

Of course, the 5th Division AST was not perfectly prepared to assume the mission either. In addition to missing half of its members, there had been no decision on who would assume each of the specific duties on the team, except that Parsons would be the advisor to the division CG. McConnell recalled the team had to hold "huddles" away from the Iraqis to find out "who was good at what and who wanted to do what as far as the staff positions" after they arrived in Kirkush.[35]

The integration with the Iraqi staff, on the other hand, went well despite the organizational difficulties of the AST. Parsons gave his impressions of their reception and the division commander:

They welcomed us. They were excited to have the American presence and support and so we had a very good working relationship. The guy I was working with was not an individual who had been vetted through General Petraeus and MNSTC-I, but he turned out to be a pretty solid guy. He probably wasn't the best military commander you could have had as a commanding general of an Iraqi division; but while we didn't need to make them as capable as the United States Army, we had to make them mission capable to fight the insurgency. To me, his prior military experience and his caring for soldiers made it easy for us to link up and gain synergy early on. His staff was welcoming of our efforts and we aligned very quickly with them.[36]

In theory, the 5th Division was fortunate to have Major General Ahmad and his key subordinates. Ahmad, the deputy division commander, and the chief of staff had all been members of the old Iraqi Army. They were also veterans of the Iran—Iraq War and so possessed knowledge of and experience in combat operations. In reality, that experience did not seem to translate into ability, at least not immediately. "They were not capable of planning, developing a plan from intelligence, nor could they perform a mission on their own," Parsons recollected. ". . . I don't believe any one of them—even with their wealth of experience in actual combat operations—could develop a mission plan and move forward."[37]

This lack of ability was compounded by the mindset of the division's staff officers. McConnell described them as "a bit disjointed and fairly disengaged." He went on to explain that after the team took over from the previous AST, ". . . the whole flavor of where the division staff was seemed to be primarily focused on garrison training and garrison operations. The emphasis [should have been] on how you keep in touch with units that are in combat. There was one whole brigade deployed forward and they had no mechanisms to get in touch with them, other than by courier, which to us seemed absolutely ludicrous and very ineffective."[38]

This situation was apparently due in part to the fact that most of the officers and NCOs on the staff had been recruited at their hometown of Numaniyah and desired (and schemed) to get the headquarters transferred back there. "That's where most of these officers and NCOs were recruited from and that was where they all lived around," McConnell recalled. "They all wanted to be based within 45 minutes of their homes so they could go home at night or on the weekends. They were preoccupied with that whole thing and basically in denial that they had a brigade that was actually fighting the fight."[39]

To complicate matters, the AST had to rely on only two interpreters. The five members of the team had to share them and so the time each member could spend with his Iraqi counterpart was limited. "It was really slow going at the start," McConnell recalled. The lack of interpreters left time for the advisors to work on their responsibilities to the US side of operations, such as the various reports that had to be rendered to CMATT. But even that had a downside, as McConnell explained:

> My experience (and a lot of other people's experience) was that it was easier to stay involved with the American side of the piece. Doing the American reports, doing the American coordination, working with the Coalition force that was there at Kirkush and trying to get in touch with the people in Baghdad. It was almost like, 'I can do this. Let me take care of this stuff.' Getting in with and building relationships with the Iraqis took second fiddle.[40]

Fortunately, Parsons and Ahmad hit it off well in their relationship. Soon after the transition, both men departed Kirkush and spent the next month in Fallujah and Tikrit observing what the 3d Brigade units were doing to help the Marines. The excursion did a get deal to cement the bond of trust between the two soldiers, but the absence of the two leaders was a strain on both the division staff and the AST. Neither man was there to provide the guidance and set policy and direction for their respective units. Therefore, little progress was made in developing the division staff and the division as a whole. This situation was remedied shortly after their return in early December. McConnell described what happened:

> . . . Colonel Parsons and General Ahmad came up with a plan that they would send a slice of the 5th Division AST and the 5th Division headquarters forward to Fallujah to work with the Marine regiment there, to be in charge of the two Iraqi Army brigades and the battalions that were working in Fallujah. That did a couple positive things. It got us embedded, living and breathing 24/7 with the Iraqi Army staff. It also showed them what actually went on forward in combat and how the Coalition works—how we get in, move around and communicate. I'd say it was very tenuous and uncomfortable the whole time we did it and maybe it wasn't as effective as a division staff leading the fight; but as far as a training tool and us showing

them firsthand what the 5th Division should be doing, it was effective. Talk about indoctrination by fire—that was definitely it. It was either stupid and lucky or absolute brilliance, depending on how you wanted to look at it.[41]

At the brigade and battalion level, Iroquois Warrior advisors encountered many of the same and many different experiences as those at division level. In the case of MAJ John C. Curwen, OIC of the AST for the 6th Battalion, 3d Brigade, it was decidedly different. On one of the two initial ASTs that were rushed out of Taji to link up with their units, Curwen and his men arrived at the KMTB about the end of October. There, they discovered the 6th Battalion, less one of its companies, had already deployed to Fallujah. One member of the outgoing AST, SFC Michael Kingsbury, was there with the company, but was not deploying forward. Curwen and the others peppered Kingsbury with questions about the unit, the mission, and the area. The team also met their interpreter, Muhammed, and was able to get a sense for the unit and the KMTB before they left, not knowing whether the battalion would ever return there.[42]

Riding in a 5-ton truck with jury-rigged armor, the team accompanied the last company of the 6th Battalion on its journey to Fallujah. The convoy passed uneventfully through Baquba and Baghdad. West of Baghdad, the convoy was hit by an IED that went off about 75 meters behind the 5-ton that Curwen was riding in. The IED, which was apparently hidden under the body of a dead dog, caused only superficial damage to one of the 12 Hyundai trucks that served as personnel carriers for the Iraqi soldiers. No troops were injured in the blast. The convoy continued to move and approaching Abu Ghraib, it was struck by a second IED. The second one went off about 300 meters behind Curwen, this time very close to one of the Hyundai trucks. The line of trucks continued to move out of the blast area, then stopped to allow leaders to check on their troops. Two Iraqi soldiers had been injured and were evacuated to a field hospital.[43] After a rather harrowing introduction to convoy operations in Iraq for the 6th Battalion AST, the convoy finally pulled into East Fallujah Camp that evening.

Curwen and his AST were met at Camp Fallujah by MAJ Peter Fedak, the outgoing AST OIC. Fedak's team was known as the "Timberwolves" and was actually an O/C team from the CMTC at Hohenfels. From Fedak, Curwen learned the 6th Battalion was down to about 230 soldiers. Like a number of other Iraqi battalions, there had many desertions in the 6th after a recent incident where 49 soldiers from the 7th Brigade had been captured and executed while going home on leave. Even more 6th Battalion troops deserted after being told they would be sent to Fallujah to conduct operations.[44] Fortunately, the battalion's leadership was essentially intact and had suffered no desertions.

Despite the weakened state of the 6th Battalion, Curwen noticed that Fedak and his men had done a credible job working with the unit. He was impressed with the way Fedak and his team worked with the staff and saw that the Iraqi soldiers conducted their operations at least like moderately trained soldiers. Curwen remembered ". . . watching the soldiers, watching how they moved, and how they reacted to different situations, it was clear that they had a lot of the basic soldier skills like moving spread out—although there were times when they would bunch up. There were times when you had to remind them of certain things, but generally their tactical movements and planning were good."[45]

When Curwen's AST arrived, the 6th Battalion and Fedak's team were preparing to participate in Operation AL FAJR, the reduction of the insurgent stronghold of Fallujah, which was to start on 7 November 2004. The battalion formed part of the security perimeter holding the insurgents in while other units attacked south through the city to destroy or capture as many of them as possible. Though the RIPTOA began when Curwen's team arrived, Fedak held the reins of control through the assault. Curwen recalled that the transition was not very smooth or complete:

> It was a little bit more chaotic than I think either they or we would have liked given the nature of the fact that we were literally hours—a day to 2 days—prior to the start of the offensive. And so a lot of pieces had to be put together quickly and they were probably concentrating as much on the tactical mission that they were advising the 6th Battalion on as they were transitioning with us.[46]

Curwen's team completed the transition about 11 November while operations were still ongoing. That day, Curwen escorted Fedak to a local landing zone, put him on a chopper, and assumed responsibility for the 6th Battalion.

For the next month, the 6th Battalion conducted foot patrols and coordinated searches or manned traffic control points in the suburbs of Fallujah and virtually all of the towns surrounding it. About the beginning of December, the battalion received notice it would deploy back to the KMTB in two segments. The first started back on 3 December and was followed by the remainder on 6 December. At Kirkush, Curwen began the long process of retraining the battalion as it began to receive new recruits to replace those lost before the deployment.[47]

Figure 18. Elements of the 2d and 4th Companies, 6th Iraqi Battalion, clear a route north of Fallujah headed toward Al Karmah in December 2004.

In contrast to Curwen's experience, Matt Jones, the OIC for the 18th Battalion, 7th Brigade, found a different set of circumstances when his team arrived at Kirkush in early November. "The team we were replacing didn't even know we were coming and there was already a major on the ground who thought he was staying for another 4 months. They only had five guys," he recalled. The members of the outgoing AST were from a USAR training division, probably the 95th Division, and were in Iraq on 120-day or 180-day orders. The team had never left the compound because the 18th Battalion had been in basic training and was not yet operational. In fact, when Matt Jones and his team arrived, the battalion was on its post-basic training leave so no soldiers were present.[48]

An incident occurred just prior to Matt Jones' arrival that reinforced to all the Iroquois Warrior ASTs just how dangerous the advisor mission was going to be. On 24 October, three battalions of the 7th Brigade completed their basic training. Immediately following the graduation parade, the troops were loaded on trucks, buses, and minivans to transport them back to their hometowns for several weeks of leave. A group of 3 minivans, carrying 49 soldiers of the 17th Battalion, was ambushed at a fake police checkpoint near the Iranian border about 95 miles northeast of Baghdad. The soldiers were forced out of the vans, ordered to lie face down in the sand, and each summarily executed with a bullet to the back of the head.[49] This incident, and the brigade's pending orders to go to Fallujah, had a significantly detrimental impact on the morale of the brigade and on many units of the Iraqi Army.

For the first 20 days that Jones and his team were at the KMTB, there were no soldiers, just some of the battalion cadre. Jones used that time to have his team work with the Iraqi officers and concurrently attempt to secure the necessary equipment they would need to operate in the upcoming mission to Fallujah.

Like Curwen, Matt Jones' AST inherited two up-armored HMMWVs. Unfortunately, these vehicles did not possess any turret armor for the crew-served weapons. The vehicles also did not have radio mounts. Additionally, the team's radios, brought with them from the United States, were older SINCGARS models. "They were just crap," Jones explained. "We had radio problems all the time." Jones, therefore, decided to fix the problem. The team first went over to the local US unit, the 30th Infantry Brigade from the North Carolina National Guard, to try and get newer radios and other equipment. Failing there, they traveled down to Numaniyah and met with limited success in getting some support there, but still no new radios. The team would have to do with what it had.[50]

The Iraqi leave period passed quickly and soon it was time for the soldiers to return. Jones and his team were detailed to go out to the various pick-up points and escort the soldiers back to the KMTB. This had two purposes: first, to provide the soldiers some security on their return trip to prevent a repeat of what had happened to the soldiers of the 17th Battalion; and second, to facilitate the actual return of the soldiers. Jones explained, "If we didn't go and pick them up, nobody would return." As it was, only about 400 of the battalion's 750 soldiers actually returned from leave.[51]

On returning from this escort mission, Matt Jones learned of the Ahmad–Parsons plan to move the 7th Brigade to Fallujah to reinforce the 3d Brigade. The orders went out to the brigade on 1 December that directed it to move on 7 December (although the brigade did not actually depart until the 14th for sundry reasons). The very day they received the movement order to Fallujah, an additional 200 soldiers, all of whom refused to serve outside of what they considered their home area, walked out the front gate. Incredibly, one of the deserters was the battalion commander. "He stole his pistol, his staff car—a Chevy Lumina—and an AK-47. We never saw him again. That wasn't exactly a good day for morale," Jones remembered.[52]

The good news was that the battalion XO, Major Karasul Amir Karasul, was a dedicated and professional soldier. Karasul happened to be a Kurd whom the soldiers respected and trusted. He had served in the Peshmerga before the war and possessed a great deal of combat experience and knowledge of how to lead men. This officer was to provide his unit a quality of leadership in the ensuing months that was apparently uncommon for most Iraqi battalions.

Despite the mass departures (it was not technically desertion because the Iraqi soldiers were there voluntarily and not yet bound by law to remain), Jones knew that his team and the battalion's leaders had to get ready for what they would face in Fallujah and there was no time to spare. But cultural differences were going to be a part of the challenge:

> We'd set up these training schedules that went from 0500 physical training all the way until 2200 at night, and it just didn't happen. It's hard to get the Iraqis to train for more than 4 hours a day. If we could get 6 hours of training in a day, that was a good day. We would do round robin training where we'd do reflexive firing, some very basic close-quarters marksmanship, to include a live-fire battle drill with some shoot houses we put up. We did convoy operations and we did patrolling. We had from 1 December until the 15th, and if we got 8 training days in all of that I would be surprised. They had holidays and other things going on. What we had to do was focus everything on getting them there alive.[53]

At about the same time that Matt Jones was getting his troops ready to move to Fallujah, the division's 9th Brigade was beginning its basic training. SFC Dennis Ewing, a drill sergeant from the 1st Battalion, 390th Regiment in Buffalo, New York, had been assigned to the AST for the 9th Brigade's 26th Battalion. Like most of the other ASTs for the 5th Division, Ewing's team linked up with its battalion at the KMTB, although in Ewing's case the battalion at this point consisted only of an officer and NCO cadre. Thus, the team spent the first several weeks working with the battalion's leaders, at least those that were present. Ramadan was in full swing, so many were on leave for the holiday.

Ewing recalled that much of his effort during this period was focused on NCO team building. The battalion's NCOs were a mixture of prior-service soldiers and a number who had gone through a short NCO training course. Collectively, Ewing felt that these men had about as much leadership and training experience as a US soldier might have when he completed basic training. "We concentrated on the NCOs becoming leaders," he remembered. "We went to the range, did individual fighting movements. We figured if we could train them up to a semi-standard, they would be better off when they were actually showing their privates how to go through things." Having this time to work with the unit's NCOs was a bonus. According to Ewing, ". . . a lot of [ASTs] didn't have that luxury. They already had teams that were up and running and had missions. Then they had to more or less train their NCOs and officers at the same time they were training the privates."[54]

Once all the officers and NCOs returned, the team departed with the cadre and traveled to Numaniyah where the 9th Brigade's soldiers would go through basic training beginning the first week of December. Once at the NMTB, the team helped their unit leaders get the thousands of Iraqi recruits in-processed, through the medical exams, and assigned to their new platoons, companies, and battalions. They then started the troops through 8 weeks of basic training. When asked about the AST's and brigade's most significant accomplishment during this period, Ewing blandly stated, "There were no casualties. . . . I don't think there was anything really bad. I think uniformly the standards were just not there. There was no desire to learn."[55]

In January, about half way through the brigade's basic training, Christian arrived at the NMTB to take over from the mentally questionable brigade AST OIC. As he engaged in the transition process with his US counterpart, he quickly came to realize that he faced two major problems. The first was the garrison commander, and the second was his own team.[56]

From his counterpart, Christian learned that the garrison commander, a US Army colonel, was for some reason hostile to the ASTs and was resistant to providing them any support. "So right off the bat I have this built-in contentiousness going on just between the Americans, which is really something you just don't want to have to deal with. There's enough fighting going on outside the gate."[57] The second issue was the more serious of the two.

The 9th Brigade AST was one of three in the 5th Division that was not exclusively manned by 98th Division soldiers (although all three had division personnel assigned and were led by Iroquois Warrior OICs). This team had USAR personnel from Oklahoma, Kentucky, and the East Coast. Christian explained, "Some of the soldiers who were there, quite frankly, were really not cut out to be on [an AST]. They didn't want it. They were only doing it because they were ordered to do it, not because they elected to do it or thought they could do it." This posed problems in a number of ways, not the least of which was that the Iraqi leaders could sense it. Christian had to act quickly and make changes to remedy the situation:

> I met with various key leaders throughout the organization whom I felt I could trust and whom I thought had the ability to assess soldiers' capabilities as to what the mission requirements were. That's what it was really all about. Then I just moved people around and put them where I felt appropriate to get the job done, where I had confidence they could do a good job and no one was going to get hurt. Those who couldn't do the job, I found different jobs for. Although these other jobs were equally as important, they weren't necessarily on the front lines. It was really a chess game to make sure everyone was in the right place; and at the end of the day, it seemed to work out pretty well.[58]

While the 9th Brigade started basic training, the 7th Brigade, in accordance with the Ahmad–Parsons plan, moved to reinforce the 3d Brigade at Fallujah. Matt Jones remembered that in his AST's efforts to "get them there alive," the team spent the last 3 days at the NMTB on convoy operations and then departed on 15 December. "We convoyed down on the 15th with 52 vehicles," he explained. "They were driving Nissan pickup trucks and Hyundai cargo trucks. We got steel to reinforce the doors of the cargo trucks and the beds and welded PKM machine gun mounts on the personnel trucks. They had three or four machine guns mounted on them apiece. There were no plates underneath, though, still a wood floor."[59]

The convoy departed at about 0900 with what the Iraqi leadership counted as 251 soldiers and drove west to Taji escorted by a security team from the 30th Brigade. En route, one soldier decided it was time to leave. "He just jumped off a truck north of Baghdad and took off. He didn't take his rifle; he just ran away," Jones recalled. At Taji, the convoy picked up a team from the 1st Cavalry Division and started southwest to Fallujah on what was described as "a bad road." Just out of Taji, the convoy was struck by an ambush. The AST was quickly involved in the fight:

> It was a complex attack with multiple improvised explosive devices (IEDs) and small arms fire. The Iraqis stopped in the kill zone and one Iraqi was hit in the throat. Two of my guys on the AST had to get out of the vehicle they were driving. They were traveling with RPKs. They engaged the enemy and then kicked the Iraqis back onto their vehicles, threw the body in the back so we could treat

him. The 1st CAV escort team was doing their best to suppress the enemy, and it was a pretty raging firefight back and forth for awhile. So we got out of the kill zone and treated the kid. We were fortunate to have an outstanding Navy corpsman attached to us as well. We medically evacuated the kid via helicopter but he died anyway.[60]

As the convoy approached Fallujah, a Marine escort team took over and led it into the East Fallujah Camp. The Iraqi leaders immediately began sorting out the unit. "The Iraqis did a pretty good job reorganizing and getting their guys straight and settled," Jones remembered, but there was one glitch:

> We [asked] the Iraqis how many soldiers they have and they say 256. 'How is that possible? We lost two!' But they were adamant about it. Numbers in Iraq are always iffy. The Marines asked how many soldiers we had and we said, 'About 200-ish.' They were angry. 'What does that mean? You don't know how many soldiers you have?' 'Nope. We don't. We can't speak Arabic and we can't count them all, and if they can't do it, oh well.'[61]

At this point, with all the departures, the companies in the 18th Battalion were down to about 45 men each.

Over the next 2 days, the 18th Battalion went through a training exercise with its assigned counterpart unit, the 3d Battalion, 1st Marines. After the training, the 18th Battalion conducted a relief in place with one of the 3d Brigade battalions that had been sent to Fallujah before the assault. Matt Jones' battalion took over a number of outposts on 18 December. He remembered that the city was still live with insurgents who had not been killed or wounded in the battle or who had not fled to other cities such as Samarra:

> [Our outposts were] all pure Iraqi positions, no joint positions, and none of the positions were fortified. They were just houses that had been taken in the fight. The city was still very active. The Marines were still losing people. Current operations were ongoing. One of the Marine battalions had cleared some buildings in the center of the city that they thought were suspicious, and apparently they'd missed a lot of people. The city was a free-fire zone at the time. It was a lot of fun. You could shoot anything that moved at night. They were chasing down a lot of insurgents, catching them on thermals, and then the Marines

and the Iraqis would chase them through the city and try to get them.[62]

On 19 December, the battalion began active patrols with the Marines in the city. Initially the patrols consisted of four Iraqi soldiers with each Marine squad. Each patrol would go out three or four times each day. Those troops not on patrol would remain at their outposts pulling local security and fortifying their positions. The work with the Marines was invaluable to the new Iraqi soldiers. Jones recalled that the Marines treated the Iraqis as soldiers and their leaders as leaders—they did not denigrate them. Thus, through mutual trust, the Marines were able to significantly increase the capabilities of the Iraqis, at least at the soldier level. "The individual soldiers really jumped ahead that first month. The Marines taught them proper urban patrolling and room clearing techniques. They taught them the things they do best and so the soldiers were getting a lot better."[63] They needed to be better because there was an important mission on the horizon—the Iraqi national elections.

The immediate objective for the Marines and the Iraqis was to produce a secure environment by January to allow the elections to go forward. As with other Iraqi units, the 18th Battalion provided security at polling sites to provide a clear Iraqi presence while the Marines secured other key locations such as intersections and main thoroughfares to provide ease of access for voters. According to Jones, the elections went "flawlessly," although there were actually few voters left in the city. The only incident of note was that the insurgents attempted to rocket a polling place just after the polls closed at 1630. ". . . it landed like 50 meters past the tent," Jones said. "We were all just standing there watching the rockets come in and laughing. We were like, 'Come on, man. Can't you do any better than that?'"[64]

Parsons agreed that the elections in Fallujah went well, given the recent events there. The Coalition units surrounding the city were vigilant about who was let back in after the fighting. That, combined with the overall security effort in the city and at the polls, produced a positive outcome. Parsons remembered:

> All our Iraqi soldiers who were there in the city were able to rotate through and vote as well. I thought it was a great accomplishment. It gave them a feeling of success, where they could build toward the objective of the election and ultimately get people in to vote. Even though people were afraid, they were coming out of their homes and voting. It was really a confidence builder.[65]

The 5th Division Headquarters (Forward) had arrived at Fallujah at about the same time as the 7th Brigade. The intent of bringing the headquarters slice and two of the 5th Division's brigade headquarters to Fallujah was to allow the 1st Marine Division to gradually start letting those headquarters take over operations in the area. The forward headquarters was attached to the 1st Marine Regiment, commanded by Col. Michael Shupp. Like Jones, McConnell remembered that working with the Marines was largely a positive experience. "The regiment was great as far as supporting the whole concept," he said. "They gave us logistics support, equipment, beans and bullets, the whole nine yards. They bent over backwards to support the Iraqis, helping them set up a base of operations and learning logistics and whatnot." However, the relationship was not perfect. "The piece that kind of fell apart was the Marine regimental command using the 5th Division headquarters staff to run the Iraqis. They actually had communications and links from the Marine regiment all the way down to the Iraqi battalions, which cut off the Iraqi division and brigade leadership of any responsibility for running battles."[66]

One could argue that the Marine effort to consistently control the subordinate unit operations was self-defeating in terms of allowing the Iraqis to take over control of operations in Fallujah. In reality, the 5th Division's forward headquarters was not really a functional organization. The level of training of the headquarters staff did not enable it to assume control as originally envisioned by the Marines, and the division's subordinate units were likewise not ready to take responsibility for patrol sectors. As a result, in January the I Marine Expeditionary Force headquarters made an assessment of the situation. " . . . they realized that the 5th Division wasn't doing anything but occupying terrain and buildings that needed to be given to somebody else," McConnell recollected. "So, if they weren't going to bring anything to the fight, then they were going to go back to base." The problem was that CMATT resisted sending the division back to the KMTB. "We knew we needed to go but we couldn't. We were caught between a rock and a hard place," McConnell explained. Finally in February, CMATT relented and the division forward headquarters returned to Kirkush later that month.[67]

As for the rest of the 5th Division units in Fallujah, the 7th Brigade remained there to continue operations with the Marines. The 3d Brigade headquarters and the 6th Battalion were returned to the KMTB, which was now filled to the brim with the recruits of the 9th Brigade as well. The 5th Battalion was sent to Taji because there was not enough billeting for that battalion at Kirkush. There the battalion performed perimeter security duties for the next several months.

The 5th Division scheduled both of these battalions for rebuilding and retraining, since they had lost so many troops to desertion before the fighting in Fallujah. The battalions were to be refilled with so many recruits that they would essentially be untrained units and would require retraining.

The 3d Brigade's other battalion, the 7th, had been sent to Samarra when the others departed for Fallujah. The team XO for the 7th Battalion's AST was MAJ Lawrence "Larry" Bradley. Bradley had been commissioned in the Regular Army in the early 1990s and had served with John Curwen in the 1st Battalion, 30th Infantry at Schweinfurt, Germany. Bradley had left active duty about 10 years before, but retained his commission in the IRR. Though he had been promoted through the ranks to major over the ensuing years, he had not participated in drills with a Reserve unit. "I hadn't worn a uniform regularly for 10 years," he explained. Therefore, it came as a surprise for him to receive orders for active duty and service in Iraq in August 2004. Dutifully answering his orders, he completed the weeklong refresher training at the Fort Benning CRC and was sent to Camp Atterbury as a filler for the 98th Division. By coincidence, the first person Bradley met when reporting into the division's command post building at Atterbury was Curwen. As an outsider to the division, Bradley was happy to see a familiar face. He had not been told anything about the mission and was not informed as to what role he would be assigned. Curwen, however, "tried to poop me up on what was going on as best he could," Bradley recalled.[68]

After completing the training at Atterbury and in Kuwait, Bradley arrived in Taji around 23 November. Even though he had been with the 98th Division mobilization group for 2 months at this point, he still did not know what his job was going to be. That soon changed. About his third day there, he was finally notified that he was going to be an advisor for the 7th Battalion, 3d Brigade. He was to replace an officer who either refused or failed to perform his duties with that unit. By the beginning of December, Bradley was on a chopper headed for Samarra.[69]

The chopper landed at FOB 7, a small compound located about 2½ miles from the city. As the chopper approached the compound to land, Bradley remembered that seeing the voluminous amounts of paper and garbage blowing through the post and all the trash caught in the concertina wire surrounding the camp caused him to believe that the 7th Battalion must be a very ill-disciplined unit.[70]

At FOB 7, Bradley linked up with the OIC of the AST, MAJ Peter Mucciarone, an Infantry officer assigned to the 98th Division's 7th Brigade.

The team had been with the 7th Battalion only about 2 weeks before Bradley arrived and was now at full strength with his arrival. Though it was among the first ASTs to deploy into a combat zone, Mucciarone's team possessed only one up-armored HMMWV. The other HMMWV was a standard "rag top."[71]

As the XO, Bradley was responsible for developing supply and logistics support for the team. In this he was lucky that the local US unit was the 1st Battalion, 26th Infantry from the 1st Infantry Division. Though the battalion was not liable to provide any support if it chose not to, Bradley discovered that the various supply and maintenance NCOs and officers from the unit were amenable to help the AST when they could.[72]

The 7th Battalion, including the battalion's leaders, was a mixture of Sunni, Shi'a, and Kurds. "We never had any problems between soldiers in our battalion due to tribal differences, though," he explained. The main problem was that the battalion would lose 50 to 60 troops a month to desertion. These were replaced about once a month with 50 to 60 more. "They'd just show up at the gate on trucks," Bradley remembered.[73]

The constant turnover of personnel required a continual process of training the new soldiers, both at the individual level and at the more practical collective level. Compounding the problem was that the troops were required to have 1 week's leave per month (which was standard for all units of the Iraqi Army). They would depart on a Friday morning and return the next Friday evening—if they returned at all. Additionally, the battalion had the mission of securing its own compound and conducting various missions, such as cordon and search missions and manning tactical control points (TCP) in and near the city.

The solution to this problem was that Mucciarone and the battalion commander developed a schedule where each of the battalion's four companies was assigned to a specific task for a period of 1 week:

    1 Company—Patrolling, TCPs, cordon and search
    1 Company—FOB defense
    1 Company—On leave
    1 Company—In training

Over a month-long period, each company was able to rotate through all the tasks and ensure the battalion met its basic obligations.

As Bradley got to know the leaders and soldiers of the 7th Battalion, he came to realize the battalion was not as undisciplined as he initially believed. "Their ways are not our ways," he explained. "Once I lived with the Iraqi soldiers for a while, and came to understand what they were about, I realized that they were committed and dedicated to the mission. They would do the job."[74]

In January 2005, MNSTC-I began to implement a series of fundamental changes to the advisor effort in Iraq. The first change, which took place that month, was the redesignation of AST to MiTT. The intent of this change was to provide psychological reinforcement to the Iraqis, and Coalition soldiers too perhaps, that the teams' mission was to transition the responsibility of the fighting to the Iraqi Army. Another change was the decision to integrate the ING into the Iraqi Army. This change had little immediate impact, but it would lay the groundwork for providing those units a formal MiTT later. Though these steps were predominantly psychological, there were more substantive changes in the works, but they would not take place until later that spring.

The 5th Division MiTTs began to settle into a routine that allowed them to work on coaching, mentoring, and advising their units. After the January elections, the location and activities of the division's units would remain relatively constant. This was particularly true of the division headquarters.

Back at the KMTB, Brad Parsons and Scott McConnell began working on making their division staff capable of planning and conducting at least minor operations at the brigade and division level. It was a great challenge given the language and cultural barriers and the limited number of interpreters. Much of the effort to move the division headquarters toward competence began with Parsons and the division commander:

> I spent a lot of time speaking to General Ahmad about what it meant to be the commander of an Iraqi division of over 5,000 soldiers. We talked about what his responsibilities and roles were, how important it was for him to get clear guidance from higher headquarters (that being the Minister of Defense and the Iraqi ground forces command later on). He had to be in sync with them operationally. That was a very challenging effort because, culturally, they are always swayed to do personal agreements with their senior leadership. For example, we would go to Baghdad to meet with the Minister of Defense and the ground forces commander and get agreement (in their terms) to support efforts that the [division commander] felt were important. That kind of obviated what we were trying to do and I explained at length how we operated in the US Army, how we take our guidance from higher as

far as missions are concerned, and that [guidance] would come down from corps to division, from division to us at the 5th Division Iraqi Army. It was all synched and coordinated from the highest headquarters down to the lowest. Although they understood what we were trying to tell them, they just weren't going to follow that plan.[75]

Though cultural differences impeded some progress, Parsons recalled that the team was successful in other areas:

We did a lot of battle staff exercises with them in order to teach them to work as a staff. We presented challenges to them and watched them react to changes in the environment as if it was a real combat operation. We put them through scenarios that had [the division] losing troops and equipment and had them perform resupply efforts. We presented medical evacuation issues. There were logistics, fuel and water supply rationing, ammunition [problems], you name it. We challenged them on different scenarios in order to get them to react and battle track and work as a staff to provide information up to their higher headquarters, as well as provide guidance down to the subordinate unit commanders so they could take appropriate actions.[76]

As the G3 advisor, McConnell remembered the staff presented significant challenges in spite of the fact that many had prior military experience:

We had to teach them simple things like just how to use grid coordinates. Their army wasn't used to using grid coordinates. They would just estimate where things were. For example, they would say, 'Here it is, just southwest of that town on this road outside this village.' They really had no idea where exactly they were headed. They couldn't track engagements with any kind of accuracy or consistency. It just didn't exist prior to us working with them.[77]

As the division AST worked toward creating a functioning staff, the 9th Brigade ran its units through basic training and prepared them for active combat operations. The brigade completed its basic training at the end of January 2005 and the troops departed on 2 weeks of block leave around the beginning of February. Meanwhile, once he was able to get his inherited brigade AST in order, Christian began preparing for the next step in the brigade's evolution into an operational unit.

Christian went to work talking with the headquarters that owned his AO, the Multi-National Division Central-South (MND-CS). The Polish Army manned the MND-CS headquarters, but the division also included Ukrainian, Romanian, Salvadoran, and Bulgarian soldiers. Christian's brigade had no defined mission, so in negotiating with the Poles he attempted to acquire one. However, the Poles had no territory or even small, finite missions they were willing to give to the 9th Brigade. Christian then went to talk to the nearest US unit and came up with the same answer. Therefore, just as at Taji (where he found useful work in repairing and improving the concertina wire), Christian again took the initiative and created his own mission.[78]

Working with the brigade staff and coordinating with the local ING unit (actually a former ING unit by this time), he divided the Wasit province into operational sectors. Once the 9th Brigade's troops returned from leave and the subordinate units were run through a series of validation training events, the brigade was ready to take a few baby steps on actual missions. Ewing recalled that his battalion's first operation was a "split mission" that included multiple tasks:

> We started doing patrols with our battalion and we had set up checkpoints in the vicinity of Numaniyah. We also did a direct recruiting mission which was a supplement to the basic training. Units would send new potential soldiers down (we had ASTs training them) and then they were being shipped out throughout the whole country to fill shortages within the units. We had some of our ASTs on that while the others were with the battalion doing missions. . . . [the operations were] just basic, touchy-feely missions—setting up checkpoints, walking through local villages, weapons caches, and stuff like that.[79]

Through March and April 2005, the 9th Brigade, now nicknamed the "Al Karrar," or Warrior Brigade, and its subordinate battalions ran missions like those described by Ewing. The brigade's significant events log for April provides an idea of the kinds of operations that 9th Brigade units were performing and the results of those efforts:

Date:	Location:	Event:
3 Apr 05	AO Sword	1st Bn found dead body floating in the canal. HN [host nation] victim had throat slashed. No further info.

9 Apr 05	MB 771503 TCP #2	While conducting convoy security from NMTB to MND-CS border, 3d Bn and US escort observed a firefight ongoing between US forces and insurgents. Unknown US forces advised the convoy to turn around.
16 Apr 05	ANMTB	3d Bn soldier died of self-inflicted gunshot wound in his barracks.
21 Apr 05	AO Sword NB105103	IP [Iraqi Police] advised IA of ordnance cache. Located, secured, and transported to the NMTB range for disposal. Cordon and searches conducted on local homes. Nothing else found, no arrests (2d Bn).
23 Apr 05	AO Sword Shumali Bridge	2d Bn stopped HN vehicle containing 5 AK-47 rifles at the TCP.
23 Apr 05	AO Sword NA 133997	2d Bn on patrol located ammo cache. Destroyed 49 57mm AA rounds, 6 rockets, 117 mortar rounds, and 4 artillery rounds.
24 Apr 05	AO Sword Shumali Bridge	2d Bn found dead body floating in the canal. Appeared to be HN civilian with gunshot wound to the head.
26 Apr 05	AO Sword Shumali Bridge	2d Bn detained 10 Afghan civilians who were traveling through Iraq from Iran. They had only photocopies of their passports. They were handed over to the IP.[80]

In May, the 9th Brigade began to conduct larger operations. The first of these was a brigade-level mission called Operation COBWEB conducted 6 through 10 May 2005 in the area north of Suwayrah, Azizyah, and Zubaydiyah. The brigade's mission was to "locate, eliminate, and prevent the establishment of insurgent sanctuaries in northern areas of Iraq's Wasit province." It was a mission designed to be relatively low-key and simple to teach these units basic techniques in tactical movement, communications, and cooperation with higher headquarters and adjacent units. The mission was conducted in coordination with the 1st Polish Brigade Combat Team and elements of the Iraqi 8th Division.

The 4-day sweep was quite successful with Ewing's 2d Battalion (formerly the 26th Battalion) producing the greatest results. During the

Figure 19. LTC Dan Christian (center), advisor to the 3d Brigade, 5th Division, provides recommendations to the brigade commander, Colonel Rhaman (right), on the deployment of troops during Operation COBWEB.

mission, the 2d Battalion uncovered a number of caches that included AK-47s, RPG-7s, IEDs, electrical wire, and a number of the distinctive black uniforms of Saddam's former Fedayeen forces. The unit also captured a number of DVDs that contained anti-Iraq government propaganda and video clips of the execution of several MOI officials. The most significant haul, however, was 29 suspected insurgent fighters that were captured and taken off the streets.[81]

In talking with a reporter from *The Advisor*, MNSTC-I's newsletter for advisors, Christian told him, "Cordon and search missions such as these not only allow the Al Karrar brigade to have a substantial impact on the insurgency's ability to operate, but also enable the brigade to improve on its tactics and techniques for future operations." The brigade commander, Colonel Rahman Jerry Chalib, explained through an interpreter, "We hope to use the extensive intelligence information that we gathered from this discovery to assist the planning of additional missions in the future."[82] That future mission was not long in coming.

Ten days after the conclusion of COBWEB, the brigade conducted a larger cordon and search mission appropriately dubbed Operation PENINSULA. This operation, which had the same objectives as the earlier mission, was conducted by sealing off the base of what was a peninsula formed by the Tigris River. It was roughly a 5-kilometer square area that had been considered by intelligence personnel to be rather tame in terms of insurgent activity. Thus, it was also considered to be another good training mission for a relatively new brigade.

The operation began in the morning with one battalion conducting the seal, and the other two moving through their assigned sectors conducting the search. Much to everyone's surprise, the haul on this mission was greater than on COBWEB. After several small firefights, the brigade ended up detaining 187 suspected insurgents, of which 67 were made official prisoners after military intelligence personnel questioned them. The amount of captured materiel was much larger too. Christian explained, "We filled five or six dump trucks worth of weapons, anything from AK-47s to rocket-propelled grenades (RPGs), dynamite, C4—all kinds of stuff." As it turned out, the brigade conducted three more raids of that area before the 98th Division left in the fall of 2005 and turned up quite a few more caches. Christian later recalled rather dryly that the results were "really interesting for an area that was considered dormant, and not really critical, to be such an active area for insurgents."[83]

Though these missions were quite successful, Christian and the other MiTT members felt that their greatest success came with Operation FISH NET II held on 8 July. Since the MiTT mission was to prepare their Iraqi units to be ready to operate on their own, they developed a concept for a cordon and search mission north of Numaniyah that would be entirely Iraqi planned and run. Christian recalled the results:

> It was very successful and brought in more insurgents and more caches. They received the mission, they planned the mission, they conducted the mission, and they did retrograde operations back to the Numaniyah Training Base with no US support. We sat back and just watched. We pointed out opportunities for improvement, pointed out things they needed to consider in terms of mission planning or mission execution, but they did the whole thing— and at the end of the day, that was what we were there to do.[84]

Though Christian and his advisors had brought their brigade to a higher level of capability, that did not mean their job was done nor was it any less dangerous. Operation FISH NET II concluded just after noon that day and the Iraqi troops loaded their vehicles to convoy back to the NMTB. Christian's two brigade HMMWVs, accompanied by two 5th Division MiTT HMMWVs and two Polish "Scorpion" vehicles from the MND-CS, were along to provide escort support. The convoy departed a little after 1300 and moved south-southeast on Route BISMARCK headed for Numaniyah. About 30 minutes later, the last vehicle in the convoy, an M1114 (up-armored HMMWV) manned by members of the brigade MiTT, was hit by an IED.

In the HMMWV were five advisors: LTC David P. Wait, the brigade XO advisor, was the vehicle commander; CPT Paul Bollenbacher was the driver; SSG Jose Rodriguez was the gunner; CPT Peter Mollineaux and Chief Petty Officer Hyde, a Navy corpsman, rode in the rear seats. The blast threw shrapnel into the right side of the vehicle and smashed the ballistic glass at the right rear seat where Mollineaux was sitting. Fragments of the IED, or perhaps spall from the inside of the truck, lashed at Mollineaux, Hyde, and Rodriguez. Wait and Bollenbacher escaped injury, other than being rattled by the blast and perhaps sustaining some hearing loss.

Christian, located in his M1114 two vehicles to the front, heard and felt the blast. The gunner, First Sergeant (1SG) Joseph B. Joie, turned to see the smoke and debris from the explosion. Christian ordered his driver, MAJ Micheal L. Eller, to turn around and go to the assistance of the other vehicle. By the time they got there, Bollenbacher had managed to drive his HMMWV about 100 meters farther down the road and stopped. There Joie and Bollenbacher provided first aid to the wounded soldiers while Wait and Christian pulled security.

The two vehicles began receiving small arms fire from the vicinity of a water treatment plant to the northeast of their position. Within the next 20 minutes, Eller called for a medical evacuation (MEDEVAC) and four additional M1114s arrived (two division MiTT HMMWVs and two Marine HMMWVs) to help with security. With the arrival of those vehicles, some equipped with .50-caliber M2 machine guns, the fire from the treatment plant became sporadic. That, in turn, allowed the landing of the MEDEVAC helicopter directly on the road at about 1425. The three wounded men were loaded on the chopper and were taken to Camp Echo for treatment.

As testimony to the rugged durability of the M1114 issued to the advisor teams, in addition to saving the lives of those three soldiers, the vehicle required only three new tires (which were changed on the spot) to be driven away. Christian and the six HMMWVs arrived at the NMTB at about 1730 that afternoon.[85]

At about the time the 9th Brigade was starting its post-basic training operations, the 3d Brigade was coming out of its rebuilding efforts and was ready to start active operations again. John Curwen's 6th Battalion had been manning eight guard towers on the perimeter fence at the KMTB since its return in December. Between December and April, the battalion

Figure 20. Medical evacuation operation for the four 3d Brigade advisors
wounded by an IED just after the conclusion of Operation FISHNET,
8 July 2005.

went through the process of rebuilding and retraining. It was a difficult
experience, Curwen recalled. "It was painful because we didn't get all the
soldiers at once. We got them like 100 here, 150 there. And as each new
group of brand new green recruits came in, it was back to basic training or
taking the seasoned soldiers and helping to train them on how to do some
of the basic soldier tasks."[86] The team also worked with getting the unit's
sergeants to understand the duties and responsibilities of NCOs, but that
too was problematic.

Adding to the difficulties was that the 30th Infantry Brigade had been
replaced at the KMTB by the Tennessee National Guard's 1st Squadron,
278th Armored Cavalry Regiment (ACR). Unlike the 30th Brigade, the 1st
Squadron had no desire to help Curwen and his team, nor was it enamored
of the Iraqi soldiers of the 6th Battalion. Curwen remembered that the
Guardsmen's view was essentially, "We're large and in charge, and we
really don't care what you do with your Iraqi soldiers. Just keep them out
of our way."[87]

The attitude of the Tennessee Guardsmen was not lost on the Iraqi
soldiers. Curwen explained:

> You know, they tolerated us, but parts of the regiment
> were always convinced that certain elements within the
> Iraqi units were going to attack them late one night, to
> the point where they put up an interior guard—Camp
> Caldwell [where the 278th was billeted] occupied a corner

of the Kirkush Military Training Base. There were towers around the entire perimeter of KMTB. When 278th came in, they put in jersey barriers and guard towers on the *interior lines*. . . . When [the Iraqis saw], you know, posts on the inside of the base and it wasn't always manned, but when it was manned and you'd see the American soldier whose weapon is pointing not outwards but is pointing inwards, the language doesn't matter.[88]

Fortunately, the prevalent attitudes of the 278th ACR did not last long due to a transformation in its relationship with the 6th Battalion. Another fundamental change to advisor operations occurred in the first couple of weeks in May. Over that period, the command and control of the MiTTs was transitioned from the CMATT to a new headquarters designated the Iraq Advisor Group (IAG), which was commanded by BG Sherlock.[89] In keeping with the new policy of transitioning the burden of the conflict to the Iraqi Army, this command worked directly for the CG, MNC-I, LTG Thomas F. Metz, rather than for Petraeus. The MiTTs were now required to report to the IAG and were MNC-I assets rather than MNSTC-I's responsibility. Concurrently, MNC-I assigned each Iraqi division to one of the corps' MSCs and provided each battalion and brigade a Coalition counterpart unit that was responsible for assisting the training of its Iraqi unit and the administrative and logistical support of its MiTTs. Some Coalition units had to create more MiTTs "out-of-hide" to advise the many former ING units that were integrated into the Iraqi Army as the 2d, 4th, and 6th Divisions, as well as for the new 8th Division and 9th Mechanized Brigade. The Coalition units also had responsibility for employment of the Iraqi unit on missions in the Coalition unit's area of responsibility (AOR).

In theory, this arrangement provided better command and control of the MiTTs and the Iraqi units for actual operations, better logistics support to and security for the MiTTs, and more resources (air support, artillery, intelligence, etc.) to support the higher collective training requirements of the Iraqi brigades and divisions. In practice, it often fell short of meeting the goals.

Under this new program, the initial counterpart units for the 5th Division were as follows:

Division headquarters	Headquarters, 42d ID
1st Brigade	1st Squadron, 278th ACR
2d Brigade	3d Brigade, 3d ID
3d Brigade	None

Though Parsons provided his reports to the IAG on administrative and logistical matters, his boss for day-to-day operations was now MG Joseph J. Taluto, CG of the 42d Division. As part of the transition to MNC-I, Parsons had to develop an assessment of where the 5th Division and its subordinate units were in terms of readiness and capabilities, and that assessment went to Taluto for review. The report was part of a process to develop standards in terms of readiness for Iraqi units and a timeline to meet certain levels of operational capability.[90] Apparently, at least some of the burden was placed on the US counterpart units to ensure their Iraqi units met the timeline. McConnell stated that the 42d Division developed a plan, without any input from the 5th Division MiTTs, on how they were going to meet the readiness and time requirements:

> When we got their briefing, they looked at us and said,
> 'Oh, you're a division-level team. We're not going to be
> at division-level operations until 2006. You just stay here.
> Do CPXs [command post exercise], do garrison training
> and somebody will pick you up when the time comes. In
> the meantime, we're going to go back down to company
> level and revalidate all their training from company level,
> to battalion, then to brigade.'[91]

In other words, the 42d Division was going to start retraining the 5th Division units at the company level without any consideration of whether the units needed it or not. It was a "one-size fits all" approach to working with the Iraqi units. No one had apparently bothered to read Parsons' assessment, nor had the 42d Division attempted to find out from the people who had fought, ate, and slept with the very units they were assigned to train, where those soldiers thought the unit was in terms of capability. McConnell explained with some frustration: "They basically invalidated everything that had been done and disregarded all that experience, not only of the [MiTTs] but of the Iraqi staffs as well. They were taking them back down to ground zero, reassessing them, and then retraining them according to their standards."[92]

Parsons' 5th Division MiTT spent the rest of their time in Iraq basically working with the division staff on planning and training skills, routine staff work, and occasionally a CPX, but there was to be no practical experience in planning and controlling actual unit operations. As a result, Parsons recalled: "We never took them into an operation, nor did we ever take them to where we could sign off on territory completely where they were in control."[93]

In theory, logistics support to the MiTTs by the US counterpart should have improved when they switched over to MNC-I, and in some instances it did. The difference, however, was entirely dependent on the attitude of the US counterpart unit commander and his view of MiTTs and the mission to transition the fight to the Iraqi Army. Some unit commanders understood the big picture and went to great lengths to support the advisory effort. Others gave it as little attention as possible. Most were somewhere in between. Parsons described his perception of the problem:

> When we were under MNSTC-I and CMATT, their effort was to make the Iraqi forces the top priority. When we got transitioned from MNSTC-I and CMATT and fell under the MSCs, they were already in the AO as the warfighters—and so they saw it as a threat to drawing down on resources they had, because the mission was changing on them. Now, they not only had to play the combatant role but they also had to be the support arm for the advisor teams. I believe that transition stuck in the craw of a lot of MSCs. I don't think it was well received by a lot of the MSC commanders, quite frankly.[94]

Surprisingly, Curwen found that once the 278th ACR became the official counterpart unit of his brigade, its attitude toward the MiTT mission reversed course 180 degrees:

> Again, to their credit, the 1st Squadron completely reorganized their troops to support the training mission, and although they, by mission, didn't have to give me many soldiers to plus up my AST team—I think it went from . . . I had 10 and I think they had to bring me up to 15 or 16 on their own through task analysis and working with me—they determined or decided that it was better to give me more soldiers so that not only the battalion had an advisory team, but each of the companies had . . . either a six- or seven-man team. The battalion had enough people where you could actually work with the staff. We could work with the S1, the S4, each of those sections, and give them the attention that they really needed. We could work with the companies to help them finish rebuilding and training the soldiers up to the standards where they needed to be.[95]

Two days after the 278th provided men to function as advisors with Curwen's team in early April, they were out on their first mission with the 6th Battalion. Two days later, the battalion was ordered to send two

Figure 21. SSG Christopher Dill and Emad, a unit interpreter, at a checkpoint north of Fallujah in December 2004. Dill was killed in action 4 months later near Balad Ruz.

companies to an area south of Balad Ruz, near a town that American soldiers nicknamed "Turkey Village." The area was predominantly Sunni and a known trouble spot. There was a wide open field there about 2 kilometers square that, during Saddam's day, was rumored to have been a place for local farmers to hide crops to prevent their confiscation by the state. Intelligence gained from an informant by a Special Forces A-Team, or Operational Detachment-Alpha (ODA), indicated insurgents might now be using the area to hide weapons and ammunition. The 6th Battalion was ordered to go there and conduct a search.

For the search, the battalion commander selected the 1st and 4th Companies. SSG Christopher Dill, a drill sergeant from the 2d Battalion, 390th Regiment in Webster, New York, was assigned as an advisor to the 3d Company. Dill, who had served with a combat engineer battalion with the 24th Infantry Division in the first Gulf War, had already seen combat in this conflict. The previous November, when the 6th Battalion was in Fallujah, Dill had dismounted from the safety of his armored HMMWV to help his Iraqi soldiers clear a building defended by insurgents. He was awarded the Bronze Star for Valor for his actions that day.[96] Now he volunteered to go along on the mission to Balad Ruz, even though his company was not going to be involved. Since it was the battalion's first

154

two-company operation and the first mission conducted with an ODA, he wanted to see how such operations would be conducted.[97]

The detachment of the 6th Battalion arrived in the search area about 0900 on 4 April 2005 and began the search. The effort continued in the designated zone uneventfully until about 1330. At that point, the search had covered about 70 percent of the required area, so the ODA team decided to take their informant farther south to another location. It was an area determined to be suspicious based on aerial photographs. The ODA, mounted in two M1114s and escorted by Dill in another HMMWV and two Iraqi gun trucks, drove down to take a look. About 45 minutes later, Curwen got a call from one of the vehicles saying the element had come under fire. Curwen immediately decided to send most of his MiTT (which now included the 278th advisors) to the rescue, because they were at hand and he could quickly get them there to reinforce. He felt it would take the Iraqi soldiers too long to assemble, load their trucks, and get there in time. Curwen did order the Iraqi commanders to start the vehicle loading process and follow later.

Curwen and most of his advisors took off to the south. En route he was trying to make radio contact with the advisors who had gone forward because the situation was unclear:

> They knew they were taking fire from the south or from the southeast. But it was sporadic. They're in contact, then they're not, then they are. We ended up following them down the same road that they took to that area. I had, when I went down there, my 1114 plus, I want to say, two others that traveled down there, and ended up setting up on either side of the ODA trucks and my other M1114 that was down there with them. The situation that developed was a combination of rifle fire and machine gun fire, RPG-4s, and sporadic mortar fire.[98]

Curwen recalled, ". . . the people who were down there had significant stocks of RPGs and other munitions. It wasn't just stuff that they happened to be carrying." Whether the insurgents happened to be training in the area and were surprised, or they knew the 6th Battalion was coming and were preparing an ambush, is not clear. Whatever it was the ODA had run into, it was at least an organized body of insurgents who were clearly well equipped and willing to fight.[99]

Once Curwen's vehicles arrived, the weight of the fire from the crew-served weapons on the M1114s caused the insurgents to change tactics. They now began to break contact and retreat south, only to resume the fighting once the advisor vehicles were on the move. Eventually, the MiTT and ODA came to an area criss-crossed with irrigation canals and berms that forced the vehicles to stay on the road. The insurgents continued to fire at them, but because of the terrain it was difficult for the advisors to pinpoint where the fire was coming from. Finally, the ODA was able to coordinate for air support and soon two AH-64 Apache helicopters arrived in the area. Although the choppers were unable to do much damage to the dismounted insurgents who were using the ditches for cover and conceal-ment, they did detect several vehicles behind a tree line to the south of the enemy positions and called in two jets. Within minutes, the jets were on station and released a 500-pound bomb at the trucks behind the trees. Curwen remembered that the strike "took care of the trucks and vehicles. The battle damage assessment wasn't tough. We saw pieces of what they had go flying into the air."[100]

Just after the air strike, the 1st and 4th Companies finally arrived, dismounted, and began to sweep toward the last known enemy positions. Dill and three advisors from the 278th pushed out with the Iraqis to clear the ditches to their front. The line had advanced only a short distance when suddenly the enemy opened up with heavy automatic weapons fire from a trench line about 150 yards away. It was accurate and heavy. "It was hitting right around the soldiers and they [weren't] making any headway," Curwen recalled. Several Iraqi soldiers were wounded or killed in quick order. The troops seemed to be caught in a planned kill zone and became pinned down. Dill, 2LT Christopher Rule, SSG Stephen Kennedy, SGT Robert W. Betterton, and two members of the ODA dismounted from their vehicles to move down and render assistance. These men, too, were quickly pinned down. Within minutes, all four advisors had been hit. Rule's and Betterton's wounds were not too serious, but Dill's and Kennedy's were. Kennedy was hit in the side where the round just missed striking the Small Arms Protective Insert (SAPI) plate in his Kevlar vest that would have probably stopped it and let him off with a severe bruise. Dill was struck in the neck, just above the vest. Soon after Dill and Kennedy were hit, other advisors quickly dragged them out of the kill zone and moved them to the 1114s for protection. In the meantime, someone had called for MEDEVAC choppers.[101]

When the MEDEVAC arrived at about 1600, the fighting was at a lull. "We had a sense when they were MEDEVAC'd—Sergeant Kennedy and Sergeant Dill—neither of them were doing too well," Curwen explained. In fact, both soldiers died later that day. In addition to Kennedy, Dill, Rule, and Betterton, the MEDEVAC choppers evacuated at least two dead and eight wounded Iraqi soldiers, but the fighting was not yet over.[102]

The two Iraqi companies now pushed forward again. Curwen was with the 4th Company on the right; the 1st Company was on the left. About two-thirds of the way across a field that was bordered by a bushy tree line to the south, the 6th Battalion came under fire again, this time from the tree line now only 80 yards away. The insurgents threw grenades at the 1st Company, which began to pull back. Curwen, however, led the 4th Company all the way to the tree line. The bad guys were now to his left and the 1st Company had retreated back to the jump-off line across the field. Moreover, the M1114s were now parked at the far end of the tree line.[103]

Curwen was clearly in a dilemma. He could not fire down the tree line at the insurgents for fear of hitting his vehicles; the vehicles could not fire at the insurgents for fear of hitting the troops of the 4th Company; and the 4th Company could not advance along the tree line for fear of being mistaken for insurgents by the 1st Company, now in positions back across the field. Curwen motioned over his interpreter and asked him if he thought the company would be embarrassed if it was pulled back before finishing the insurgents off. They had gotten this far and Curwen did not want to crush their morale, especially after the casualties the battalion had sustained. "I'll be honest, I was in no big hurry to run down the bush line to find these insurgents," he remembered. "We pulled back."[104]

It turned out to be a good call. Just as the unit was moving back away from the tree line, the remaining insurgents attempted to sprint across the road south toward safety. But the gunners on the M1114s were ready. The insurgents were cut down in a hail of fire from the vehicles. Soon after, a muffled blast came from the tree line. ". . . I saw something fly up in the air and it wasn't parts of bushes," Curwen said. Apparently, one of the insurgents had committed suicide with an explosive. That event ended the fighting; it was now dusk.[105]

The 6th Battalion completed the search and collected the enemy dead, weapons, and ammunition. The battalion had killed 13 insurgents and probably more. There were a number of enemy wounded too, as evidenced by the various blood trails found. But the cost to the battalion was also high. The unit sustained 2 Iraqi soldiers killed in action and 13 wounded, in addition to the 2 dead and 2 wounded Americans. The battalion reconstituted and reorganized that night, protected by a C-130 gunship and mounted elements of the 278th ACR that had been sent down as reinforcements.[106]

It appears the fighting south of Balad Ruz must have broken the insurgent threat in that area, at least for a time. For the rest of his time in Iraq, Curwen and the 6th Battalion conducted patrolling operations in the area west of that city, while the 7th Battalion, back from Samarra, patrolled the areas to the east. No tactically significant actions occurred in those areas during the remainder of the tour.

When reviewing the efforts of the various 98th Division ASTs/MiTTs that worked with the 5th Division, the advisors that served on those teams draw a picture that reflected mixed results. On the one hand, the advisors were not able to bring the units as far as they might have wished. Parsons lamented that his team never got the division headquarters far enough along to plan and conduct actual operations. Scott McConnell estimated that "on a scale of 1 to 10, we took them from a 1 up to a 5 or 6 level. There was certainly still a lot of room for improvement."[107]

On average, however, the 5th Division advisors were very proud of what they accomplished with their Iraqi units. At the division level, while the headquarters did not ever conduct a real operation, Parsons believed the staff was at least "capable of developing and preparing to execute a mission."[108] McConnell agreed: "By the time we handed it off to the 80th, though, they were a moderately competent division staff that could work together through serious issues. They could actually do battle tracking, communications, and they could come up with some kind of plan and guidance for their subordinate units."[109]

At the brigade level, Dan Christian was very satisfied with what his team was able to achieve. He believed that when he handed the old 9th Brigade off to the succeeding MiTT, the brigade could plan a mission, conduct it, and return to the FOB, "and they could do it all on their own."[110] Dennis Ewing was satisfied with his team's results as well. He recalled that the old 26th Battalion was "pretty close to being a working asset by themselves, without American support, so we were pretty happy with the turnaround."[111]

By the fall of 2005, it was clear the Iroquois Warriors had not brought the 5th Division to the point that it could plan and conduct even the simplest of division operations. That would be a difficult goal to achieve even for an active duty MiTT drawn from a US Army division staff. Parsons and his advisors were able to bring the staff to the point were it was ready to at least begin attempting such a task. At least one of its brigades, the 9th, was conducting brigade-level operations on a recurring basis, and one other, the old 3d Brigade, was probably capable of such an effort. The battalions of those brigades were planning and conducting basic missions at the battalion level as well. At the very least, it can be said that the 5th Division advisors built a good foundation for the 80th Division MiTTs to build on and take the 5th Division to the next level.

The Advisor Experience—The 3d Iraqi Division

Figure 22. CPT Ari Moskowitz, staff advisor to Headquarters, 3d Division, Iraqi Army, provides 9mm pistol familiarization training to members of the 3d Division staff at Al Kasik Military Training Base, Iraq, in December 2004.

The headquarters of the Iraqi 3d Division began organizing about June 2004 at the Al Kasik Military Training Base. Major General Khursheed Saleem Hassan Al Dosekey, a highly respected Kurd soldier with a lot of combat experience, commanded the division. Khursheed was also apparently serving part-time as the deputy commander of a large Peshmerga force. Verbally, the general supported the Iraqi government and its policies, but it was never clear where his true loyalties lay though, as one officer intimated, one may surmise they were with the Peshmerga if push ever came to shove. Shipman recalled:

> He told us many times that he really felt we needed a new Iraqi Army and he supported an integrated army with Arabs and Kurds serving together. His frustration was that the southern soldiers, who were mostly Arab, would go away and not come back again because they didn't want to be in Kurdistan or close to Kurdistan, which is where our base was. Even though he wanted to have a diverse unit, it was difficult to maintain that. Consequently, the

people they recruited to come in on this direct recruit program were mostly Kurdish soldiers. The balance tipped much more heavily on the Kurd side.[112]

Unlike the 1st and 5th Divisions, the 3d Division's organization remained constant, with the exception of one battalion, during the 98th Division's tour in Iraq. It consisted of the 4th, 5th, and 8th Brigades, which would later be redesignated as part of the Iraqi Army reorganization in April—May 2005 as the 1st, 2d, and 3d Brigades, respectively. When the ASTs began to conduct their link-ups in November and December 2004, most of the division was at Al Kasik. The 4th Brigade had completed its basic training in October, and was ready to begin operations. The 8th Brigade was still in basic training and would finish in mid-January. The last brigade, the 5th, did not exist except for the cadre, which was located at Fort Tall Afar.[113]

The senior advisor for the 3d Division was COL Sanford Holman, later the commander of the 80th Division's 1st Brigade at Fort Meade, Maryland. Holman had just been reassigned from the 80th Division to the headquarters of the 98th Division as the G4 in the summer of 2004 and soon after accepted a position on the battle roster to serve as a division senior advisor for the deployment.

Holman's deputy was LTC Shipman. Shipman was one of the advisors who kept the same assignment from the time his name was placed on the battle roster in June until he arrived at the 3d Division in November. That would change about April 2005 when he was promoted to colonel and reassigned as the senior advisor to the Iraqi 2d Division.[114]

The 3d Division's ASTs were made up entirely of personnel who had deployed with the 98th Division, although a number were fillers from other USAR divisions. The teams were deployed from Taji to the AKMTB over several weeks due to the existing AST's rotation dates and the various levels of training of each of the brigades. Thus, the ASTs for the division headquarters and the 4th Brigade were the first to travel to Al Kasik during the beginning of November. The majority of the advisors were flown into the AKMTB, but Shipman was placed in charge of the ground convoy to transport the teams' brand new up-armored HMMWVs to the base.[115]

The convoy departed Taji about 7 November and took Highway 1 north toward Turkey. Shipman guided his serial of vehicles to tag along with other convoys so that there was strength in numbers in the event of an attack. En route, the convoy stopped a number of times at FOBs to remain overnight, refuel, and link up with another convoy that happened to be going its way. What should have been a long 1-day trip, or perhaps a trip consisting of 2 short days, turned into a 5-day trip. "We didn't really know where we were going and many of the units we were tagging along with were new to the theater too," Shipman reflected. Luckily, the group latched on to a 25th Division Stryker company headed to Mosul. Shipman recalled that the unit, as new to Iraq as his own, "was outstanding. The company commander even had his people call ahead and make reservations for us at lodging so we could stay at the FOB in their area when we got there, because it was going to be about 2200 at night when we pulled in. They took great care of us."[116]

On 9 December, Shipman's cluster of vehicles, still guided by the Stryker unit, reached FOB Marez, just south of Mosul near the airport. Shipman and his convoy remained there for 2 days waiting on another convoy that was heading west to Al Kasik. It happened that a Stryker company was heading there on the morning of the 11th.

Departing FOB Marez in the morning, the convoy reached city center about 0900. As they passed through the city Shipman recalled, "Our pucker factor was very high because we sensed something was wrong."[117] He further explained, "There were places where people were running away from the roads or moving away from us as we were coming through, but we didn't have any enemy contact." The convoy kept moving and turned left onto the road that would take it to Al Kasik, 30 miles to the west. Shipman's detachment arrived at the AKMTB to find out from the evening's television news that almost the entire 1,800-man Iraqi brigade stationed there and the city's police had walked off the job. The city had been left to the insurgents before the convoy passed through.[118]

At the AKMTB Shipman learned the 3d Division was headquartered in a temporary location while the permanent headquarters building was being renovated. The renovation was necessary because that building and one of the mess halls on the base had been heavily damaged by truck bombs the previous August. "By the time we got there, they had really beefed up security and cracked down so things like that wouldn't happen again," he remembered.[119] That may have been true at the AKMTB, but the 3d Division ASTs would soon find out it was not true everywhere.

By the time Shipman had arrived with the HMMWVs, Holman's division team had completed its RIPTOA with the previous AST. The outgoing advisors spent only 2 days with Holman and his people. Shipman recollected, "I don't think our team really felt that the outgoing team had a lot to contribute."[120] The transition for the battalion and brigade teams apparently took a little longer and was at least more satisfying in terms of information the outgoing teams had to offer.

In the case of the 8th Brigade, its ASTs were particularly lucky as those battalions were still in basic training. Shipman recalled,

> ... our advisors overlapped with the Australian training unit that was there doing the training with them. That was a pretty successful handover. It took longer. The Aussies didn't just dump it on our guys. They probably took 5 to 7 days—and the Aussies were there for quite some time after that before they pulled out. They were there to assist as needed.[121]

For Tennyson, assigned to the 12th Battalion, 4th Brigade AST, the RIPTOA experience was enlightening, to say the least. He was finally about to find out what was in that black box he had been pondering over since his arrival at Camp Atterbury. The team that Tennyson's AST was replacing consisted of only four individuals—a major, a captain, and two sergeants. These soldiers had been part of another AST, but had been pulled away to take the 12th Battalion through its basic training. As the battle handover proceeded, Tennyson discovered the black box held something different than he had imagined. "The whole time leading up to us getting [to the AKMTB], we had been thinking we were going to be doing some training with these guys," Tennyson explained. "Instead, [we learned the 12th Battalion was] the only operational Iraqi battalion in Al Kasik—in that whole northern territory."[122]

This state of affairs caused Tennyson concern. First, his assessment was that the battalion was not really trained and, therefore, not ready for active operations. "They only knew the basics," he explained. His second concern was the battalion's leaders. He remembered that some were "total slugs. We ... had other officers who were pretty lazy and not well respected. They didn't treat their soldiers well." On the other hand, there were also those who were good leaders and some with combat experience. Tennyson described one particularly good officer: "We had one company commander who was former Peshmerga and a very strong leader. The soldiers respected him and he really cared about his soldiers. They would follow him anywhere. He was always in the lead."[123]

Another division-wide problem was desertion. When the ASTs began to arrive at Al Kasik, many of the division's soldiers were at home for the Ramadan holiday. As with the 5th Division, the soldiers were being targeted by the insurgents as they were going home and when they returned from leave. Shipman recalled:

> Some were beheaded and their bodies were strewn along the roads in Mosul and west toward Al Kasik. It was a very

difficult time for the division. . . . The Kurdish soldiers had an easier time coming back because we were way up north and it was a shorter distance they had to travel. The soldiers from the south, though, really had trouble coming back because of the distance and the insurgent threat. There was a certain amount of attrition. It's hard for me to put a percentage on it but it could go as high as 40 to 50 percent.[124]

Another source of attrition was payday. Tennyson explained that the battalion "would get new soldiers in, they'd get a paycheck, go on leave, and then they would not come back. Every month there were new soldiers or else the soldiers we had just trained weren't there anymore."[125]

After the transition of authority with the outgoing teams, the incoming ASTs settled in to begin work with their units. Shipman described his AST's relations and its work with the 3d Division leadership and staff:

General Khursheed was always very receptive. He was extremely cordial and his staff was cordial and appreciative in the normal style. There was all the usual drinking of chai (tea). We met with him every day for 1 to 2 hours in the morning and the rest of the day we didn't interfere with his internal operations. We did the same with the staff. Because of our senior advisors' approach to how we would do this, we did not colocate with them in their building or living quarters. We had a Coalition block over on one side of the base, and a mile and a half away was the Iraqi compound where their division headquarters was. We'd go over, work with them, and then go back to our side of the base.[126]

For Tennyson, the process of settling in was a little more exciting than for those advisors at the division headquarters. His team was immediately going into active operations with the 12th Battalion. The first mission was a relatively simple one and it took place only 2 days after Tennyson's team took over.

Like the rest of the 4th Brigade, the vast majority of the soldiers of the 12th Battalion were on leave for the Ramadan holiday when the team arrived. Many of the soldiers were Kurdish and so were not very far from home. The routine for the 3d Division was to drive its Kurdish soldiers to a secure drop off point in Kurdistan about 45 minutes north of Al Kasik and let them off there to start their leave. At the appointed time about a week later, trucks would return to that point and pick up the soldiers to bring them back to base. The AST's first mission was to escort the convoy up to Kurdistan and return. At this point, however, Shipman had not arrived with the teams' HMMWVs, so the advisors rode in the civilian vehicles the previous team had been using.

Just north of Al Kasik, the convoy was hit by IEDs. Tennyson described the incident:

> We were going through a narrow area through some mountains and there was a daisy-chain of five mortar rounds. They were pretty small, though, and nobody was seriously injured. The fins on them were 6 inches. They were 120s, I guess. Luckily they were right on the edge of the road and our guys were driving in the center of the road. The way they were emplaced, each of them made a crater that was about 3 feet in diameter and a couple feet deep.

Fortunately, because of the amateurish emplacement of the mortar rounds, the blast effect went straight up instead of into the vehicles. Tennyson continued: "They just didn't have them directed correctly. We had one soldier who received some shrapnel in his head but it was nothing serious. The van he was in was fine. . . . When this happened, we were rolling out in our team Yaz Jeeps and the outgoing AST team brought their Durango out afterwards. It all happened about 10 minutes outside of Al Kasik."[127] In short, it was another startling introduction to the realities of advising in Iraq.

The hazards of serving in Iraq were driven home more deeply the following month. In late November, the first operational brigade in the division, the 4th Brigade, received the mission to send two battalions to begin expanding the cleared areas around Al Kasik. The 10th Battalion was sent to Tall Afar to begin operations there, and the 11th Battalion was sent to FOB Marez in Mosul to operate in that locality.

In Mosul, the 11th Battalion was responsible for manning an outpost across the city from the main FOB. Each company spent about a week at a time there manning the post and conducting visibility patrols in that part of the city. SFC Paul D. Karpowich, a drill sergeant in the 1st Battalion, 417th Regiment at Pennsauken, New Jersey, and now on the AST for the 11th Battalion, was at the outpost from about the 7th through the 21st of December. Previously a paratrooper with the 82d Airborne Division, Karpowich had left the Regular Army but remained in the Army Reserve.

On 21 December, Karpowich's unit returned to FOB Marez in Mosul, and he was looking forward to his first prepared meal in 2 weeks. He and the team medic, Petty Officer Second Class Isidoro Dacquel, went over to the mess hall and enjoyed a hot dinner. Near the end of the meal, Dacquel told Karpowich to relax and he would go gather up the Iraqi soldiers as they came out to form up and return to their billets. Dacquel was outside and had just ordered one of the soldiers to put out a cigarette when an explosion ripped through the mess hall. As soon as the debris stopped falling, Dacquel charged back into the facility to begin treating the wounded, but it was too late for Karpowich. A suicide bomber, disguised as an Iraqi National Guardsman, had set off an explosive device that killed Karpowich and 22 other soldiers and wounded another 60. Karpowich, the 30-year old Freeland, Pennsylvania, native, was the first of five Iroquois Warriors to give their lives for their country during the deployment.[128]

Figure 23. CSM Robert Riti, senior enlisted advisor to the 3d Iraqi Division, and his Iraqi counterpart inspect election banners and election equipment prior to distribution by Iraqi Army forces before the 30 January 2005 Iraqi National Elections.

Part of the purpose in deploying units to Mosul and Tall Afar was to prepare for the January elections. As in the 5th Division area, the 3d Division units were employed to increase security in various areas to facilitate the conduct of the elections. The 12th Battalion was sent to a small town of about 4,000 people north of Al Kasik. Tennyson recalled that the battalion set up a cordon around the town and sealed it off and then began gathering intelligence from the local populace:

You would always have somebody come up to you and say something like, 'Hey, that guy has weapons and he also has some pictures of Saddam. He's talked about shooting helicopters.' So they'd go in and maybe find one little picture of Saddam and an AK [-47]. Well, what are we supposed to do with him now? There wasn't a whole lot there to arrest him on, but they would hold people like that and release them later on. We had a lot of that.[129]

Through the intelligence gathering effort, the battalion was able to round up about 30 suspects and, perhaps as a result, the elections went off without a hitch. After the elections, the Iraqi battalion commander decided to take the suspects back to Al Kasik for further questioning. "The . . . commander had reason to believe these guys knew things so he detained them for the weekend and wouldn't accept any risk with the suspects. In the end, most of them were released, though." It turned out the reason why so many were released, apparently, was that the informants and most of the arrested men were from families that were feuding with one another.[130]

Following the elections, the division went into a recruiting drive to replace the men who had deserted. The battalions were each down to about 400 men and needed to be brought back up to something closer to full strength. The effort was apparently focused on prior service soldiers who could be directly recruited into battalions and trained there to shorten the lag time from enlistment to employment in actual operations. But there were problems with the process as Shipman explained:

We were allowed to do this direct recruit program. It was a bit complicated and I'm not sure we ever did it exactly right, but basically commanders could direct a recruit— former military soldiers—into their unit and train them through a structured training program. What ended up happening was probably less structured than that. A lot of them came up from Numaniyah where they were in-processed. Some of them got a little training down there but most got none. They were brought up on buses to Al Kasik over the next several months and then brought into our unit, integrated into the units. They were supposed to be kept separate in a training platoon/company/battalion to go through the basic training again, a refresher, and then put into the units. What actually happened, though, was that a lot of them got integrated right into the units because they were former soldiers. People just assumed they knew what they were doing.[131]

After the elections, the 12th Battalion began stepping up its operations in and around Al Kasik. It conducted raids, cordon and search missions, and "cordon and knock" missions, in addition to the routine security and TCP missions it was already performing. Tennyson recollected, "Those were the first real infantry type missions they were doing, other than just driving down the road and securing it so they could move back and forth to go on leave, or setting up a checkpoint. They started gaining proficiency in those kinds of skills."[132]

But apparently each company was not improving at the same rate. The battalion commander kept using the company of the former Peshmerga commander to do the hard missions, and the captain would, in turn, rely on about 20 or so reliable soldiers who were themselves former Peshmerga fighters or members of his family. Tennyson explained, "We relied a lot on the Iraqi leadership to handpick their guys for the main efforts on missions, which had the effect of hiding the lack of training for the rest of the battalion."[133]

Figure 24. Advisors and soldiers of the 3d Iraqi Division detain suspected insurgents following roadside ambush near Rabiah in January 2005.

Despite the disparity in unit selection for missions, the 12th Battalion ASTs, by now redesignated as MiTTs, attempted to equally train and advise every unit in the battalion. The advisors helped the companies put together "shoot houses" for training on entering and securing buildings. They assisted the battalion staff with convoy training and other operations. The advisors tried to explain the correct methods and techniques for conducting a wide range of collective tasks, but the efforts did not always bear fruit. "It was always frustrating because I'd sit down with the Iraqi S3 and go through some planning factors on a battalion movement and it seemed like he got it," Tennyson remembered. "When they went to execute, though, if I wasn't right there he would just go back to the old way of doing things."[134]

In April the 12th Battalion was transferred to Tall Afar to replace the 10th Battalion. Tall Afar is located about 30 miles west of Mosul. Pre-war, the city boasted a population of about 250,000 people, mainly of Turkish descent. However, because of the insurgency the population may have been as low as 150,000 by the time the 12th Battalion arrived.

In the center of the city on a slight rise sat an old Ottoman-era fortress or castle that had been used by the British during their stay in the area after World War I. Both the ING and the local government, including the police headquarters, were using it when the 12th Battalion arrived in April to garrison the position. The battalion also manned another combat outpost large enough to accommodate one company at a location on the northeast outskirts of the city.

The local US unit, the 2d Squadron, 14th Cavalry, was part of the Stryker brigade from the 25th Infantry Division. The 12th Battalion began conducting operations with that unit soon after its arrival. "We were actually working closely with one of the infantry companies, going on missions and doing cordon and searches and raids," Tennyson recalled. The missions were sent out from the two outposts into various areas of the city. Tennyson described the procedure:

> From there [the outposts], we were doing presence patrols out into the neighborhoods, just short ones where we'd go out for 45 minutes or an hour and then come back in. They were doing pretty good. We would take them into the friendly areas just for practice. On a few occasions, they ended up in firefights. They were still making mistakes but it didn't cost them any lives on those operations. They were still having problems maintaining accountability of their people while on foot patrol. The company commander would get up front and he'd just go, while our [MiTT] would be splayed out throughout the battalion trying to keep track of everything.[135]

Though the patrols eventually began going into worse areas of the city, the battalion suffered few casualties from these forays. Most deaths and injuries came from IEDs. Another source of casualties came from what might be described as sightseeing from the fortress walls. ". . . you could see the whole city from this thing," Tennyson remembered. "It had the old parapets with the arrow slits and everything. There was lots of cover. Guys would stand up on the wall and look out, and we had a few guys get shot doing that."[136]

Around April and May 2005, the 3d Division began to experience a number of changes that affected how it and its subordinate units operated. The most important of these was the command changeover from CMATT to the IAG. Another was the arrival of the 3d ACR commanded by COL H.R. McMaster. The assumption of responsibility for the Mosul—Al Kasik—Tall Afar AOR by the 3d ACR instantly changed how the 3d Division operated. McMaster dictated everything that was going to happen with the Iraqi units in his AOR. He went so far as to coordinate SF ODAs to work with the Iraqi units on operations rather than their own MiTTs. "The challenge became that, just when the 3d Division felt like they were beginning to gain some autonomy, in came the 3d ACR and the ODA teams," Shipman explained. He further described the shift:

> The ODAs took over a lot of the tactical operations [with the Iraqi units] and 3d ACR took over the battlespace management and major combat operations, including clearing out Tall Afar of insurgents. The MiTTs thus took a secondary role and [they were] largely [relegated to] working with the battalion, brigade, and division staffs and doing mostly logistics and personnel advising, not the operational advising—which was being done by the ODAs.[137]

Under the 3d ACR's management, MiTTs became extraneous because between the ODAs and the cavalry regiment's advisors, the actual MiTTs were considered strap hangers on actual missions. "The ODAs or the 3d ACR advisors would tell the unit MiTTs 'we got it' and tell them to stay back on the post during the missions," Shipman recalled. "The MiTTs were not welcome to go along."[138]

The 3d Division also began to deploy more units farther out and away from Al Kasik in June, mostly near the Syrian border to help interdict illegal border crossings along that line. The 8th Brigade sent one of its battalions to Rabiah, another to Sinjar, and a third to Al Biaj, to support the border security effort. However, as these battalions deployed, the division lost control over them. Shipman explained:

So [these battalions] were being pushed out and asked to be more operational, but they were also losing their autonomy because they were getting way more oversight from the 3d ACR and others than they had been getting before. From supporting a counterinsurgency operation and working with a national army [standpoint], it was a difficult situation. The Iraqi division commander was really no longer the division commander. He was now taking very direct orders from an Army colonel in the American Army.[139]

Soon after the 3d ACR settled in to Al Kasik, the 3d Division MiTT was trying to hurry the process of getting Major General Khursheed and his staff to move into the newly renovated headquarters. There were a number of reasons why Shipman (the acting senior advisor since Holman had returned to the United States on mid-tour leave) was pushing for the move. First, the division MiTT was working out of offices on the US side of the base. Shipman knew that to have the best impact on the division staff, he and the MiTT needed to be working in the same building on a daily basis. Second, he had plans to set up a model TOC in a room he had picked out for the Iraqi staff to see and use so they could learn how to operate a tactical headquarters. Third, Shipman had picked out a room in the headquarters that was considered secure enough for setting up a SIPRNET site so the team could operate its terminal and do routine business there rather than at its old offices on the US side. Most of these plans went to naught however, because the 3d ACR had demanded space in the headquarters so it could maintain a presence there for liaison and coordination purposes. The regiment took over the SIPRNET room leaving only the model TOC room for the MiTT. No wonder Shipman later described the relationship between the 3d ACR and the MiTTs as "tense."[140]

The impact of the 3d ACR's mode of operations was clearly felt at the battalion level as well. Tennyson described his impressions:

> . . . it was like the reigns got pulled way back and the Iraqis were told to stay in the outpost. I think they [the 3d ACR] were afraid of a bloodbath, but I don't really know. I never had an opportunity to talk to the squadron commander. When they came in, they wanted to try the diplomatic route again so all the operations that were ongoing—the cordon and searches, the presence patrols, the occasional firefight—that all stopped. The 3d ACR wanted to meet with the mayor and the police chief. There were a whole lot of meetings with the elders and such.[141]

There was another downside to these changes from the advisor point of view: "I think the Iraqis lost some proficiency, though. They had just started to get decent with the presence patrols on a small level," Tennyson recalled.[142] The implication was that the longer the Iraqi troops remained in garrison, the more their operational skills eroded.

Though the initial methods of operation by McMaster and the 3d ACR seemed a little heavy-handed (at least toward the MiTTs and their Iraqi units), the relationships did improve with time. The longer the commanders of the ACR worked with the MiTTs of the 3d Division, the more they came to rely on them. Tennyson explained, "I think once they realized what kind of asset we were, any time they wanted to get Iraqi soldiers they knew they just had to call us."[143]

In May 2005, as part of the major Iraqi Army reorganization, the MOD decided to transfer the 11th Battalion at FOB Marez to the new 2d Division, because the battalion had been there so long and was in that division's AO. To replace the 11th Battalion, the 109th ING Battalion, located in Tall Afar, was assigned to the 3d Division. The 109th was assigned to the 4th Brigade and soon after was redesignated as the 2d Battalion, 1st Brigade, 3d Division (the old 4th Brigade was redesignated as the 3d Division's 1st Brigade).

Since it had been an ING unit, the 2d Battalion had never had an AST or MiTT. At the time of the transfer, Holman was still on leave so Shipman, as the acting senior advisor, approached LTC Joel Armstrong, XO for the 3d ACR, and requested the ACR provide a MiTT for the battalion. Armstrong agreed the regiment should provide the team, but the personnel for it never materialized. In May, Shipman decided to create a MiTT out of hide and selected newly promoted LTC Terrence K. Crowe, formerly of the old 21st Battalion in the 8th Brigade, to head the new team. Because the team was ad hoc, Shipman could only provide an additional captain and three NCOs to help man it.[144]

While serving in his former battalion, Crowe had gained a reputation for leading from the front. MAJ Michael T. Ansay, a MiTT OIC from a sister battalion, said:

> LTC Crowe is largely responsible for the success that our brigade had in the north of Iraq. LTC Crowe's team led the way with captured insurgents, recovered weapons and explosives, and the collection of intelligence information. In fact, my team and my Iraqi battalion are heading into an area where LTC Crowe previously worked. I was amazed at all the intelligence his team handed off to me

and all the great work they completed there. I have been blessed to move into an area that LTC Crowe has largely cleaned out.[145]

Encounter with History

Figure 25. LTC Terrence Crowe.

In early June, Crowe's battalion received a routine mission to conduct patrols in and around Tall Afar. The battalion had been performing these operations for some time, but had only recently been operating with units of the 3d ACR. The mission was to sweep part of the city in coordination with the tanks and Bradley Fighting Vehicles (BFV) from the regiment. On 7 June, parts of the 2d Battalion, with Crowe and his team going along, moved into the city on trucks, escorted by the 3d ACR. At the designated point, the Iraqi soldiers jumped off their trucks and began dismounted patrols in the targeted area. Ansay described Crowe's actions on such missions:

> Foot patrols inside the cities are by far the most dangerous missions. Your only level of protection is your body armor. Not surprisingly, soldiers are very reluctant to lead

off on such patrols. Being the great leader he was, LTC Crowe would not ask his Iraqis or his team members to do anything he would not do himself. Therefore, he repeatedly led off on such patrols. He would continue to do so until the Iraqis and his team members gained their own confidence.[146]

Leading his battalion through the dangerous, dirty streets of Tall Afar, Crowe skillfully advised the commander on maneuvering his units to maintain the advantage over any insurgents that might decide to oppose the movement. In fact, the enemy had decided to do just that. The 2d Battalion soon ran into a pocket of enemy fighters who opened fire with automatic weapons and rocket propelled grenades. From the top of a two-story building, an insurgent found Crowe in his sights and pulled the trigger. Within a second or two, Crowe was hit twice—once in the leg and once in the groin. Though wounded, Crowe was able to crawl to cover. Part of the 2d Battalion was now pinned down and the call went out to bring up the vehicles of the 3d ACR. The intent was to secure the area and get Crowe out as quickly as possible for medical treatment.

While they waited for the cavalry to come to the rescue, the men of the 2d Battalion hunkered down and fought back. Amazingly, Crowe continued to fire, but he was seriously wounded. Hit in the femoral artery, he was quickly bleeding to death. In fact, before the mounted element arrived, Crowe had died.[147]

Soon after this incident, Shipman was reassigned from the 3d Division to be the senior advisor to an Iraqi division that was formerly an ING unit. Unlike the units of the 1st, 3d, and 5th Divisions, the battalions of the ING had been stood up by various Coalition units using men largely from a given tribe from a specific geographical area. Also unlike the original three Iraqi Army (IA) divisions, the ING units were not intended to be used outside their home area. The only advisors made available to these units initially were those soldiers that Coalition units could spare. Thus, in terms of useful training and advising by a professional team of soldiers, the coverage for ING units was very uneven and dependent on whether the commander of the counterpart Coalition unit saw the mission as important or useful. When the ING was integrated into the Iraqi Army in early 2005, MNC-I and MNSTC-I began to put greater emphasis on advising those organizations. That is, in part, how Shipman and Crowe ended up advising these former ING units.

Shipman, along with an ad hoc six-man MiTT, was reassigned as the senior advisor for the 2d Division which was headquartered at Al Kindi, a suburb of Mosul. The counterpart unit helping to advise and train the 2d Division was the 1st Brigade, 25th Infantry Division, a Stryker outfit. In contrast to the 3d ACR, Shipman recalled, "The Stryker Brigade treated us fabulously and gave us a great deal of support."[148] The units of the 2d Division had been doing actual missions almost from the day they were organized. They had not gone through any kind of basic training, but had learned their skills on the job. When Shipman and his MiTT arrived, the division had been pulled back into garrison and was starting the process of going through a more formal training program that would, in theory, bring its units up to the proficiency levels of the first three regular army divisions.

Shipman began working with the Stryker brigade to provide organized MiTTs to the division's subordinate units. Despite the lack of an initial formal training program, and although there had been no MiTTs at brigade or battalion level to advise the units, Shipman explained that "the 2d Division was much more integrated with the 1/25 Stryker Brigade [than had been the case with the counterpart units with the 3d Division]. [The 2d Division was doing] operations jointly and had been since the fall. A lot of those battalions had already married up with companies and battalions from the Stryker Brigade and were doing operations."[149]

Shipman's time with the 2d Division was short-lived. In June 2005, a formal MiTT under COL Michael Cloy arrived in country to take over from Shipman's team. Shipman was then reassigned to advise the Iraqi police chief for the Nineveh province, a job he held for the rest of his tour.[150]

Back in the 3d Division, Tennyson's battalion was also in the process of trying to refit and retrain, but his team, and the ODA now assigned to help train the unit, was running into a familiar problem. The revised training plan was to run a schedule similar to that described by Mucciarone's battalion in the 5th Division: two companies on missions in Tall Afar, one company in training, and one company on leave. The problem was that instead of the troops of the company on leave taking only 1 week, many soldiers would come back 5 or even 10 days late. As a result, the company designated to be in training rarely achieved any significant training results before it had to rotate into the actual mission cycle. Having a truly volunteer army clearly had its disadvantages, but there were also extenuating circumstances as Tennyson described:

> It was bad. It doesn't take 2 weeks to take your money home and hand it to mama. They wanted to go home and relax for a couple weeks. Granted, some of these guys had

real problems at home. We often had guys come back who had lost two or three of their family members while they had been gone, because someone came and shot them. They had major issues at home and if I was in the same situation I don't know if I'd stay with the army. I might be at home defending my house as well.

As a caveat, Tennyson went on to say, "There were also guys, though, who took advantage of it and would take as much leave as you'd let them."[151]

In August the 3d Division lost its third advisor. SFC Robert V. Derenda, a drill sergeant from Ledbetter, Kentucky, was assigned to the 3d Battalion, 398th Regiment of the 100th Division. He was a filler, but in fact, he had formerly been a member of the 98th Division when he lived in New York. Assigned to a MiTT in the 8th Brigade, Derenda and SFC Brett E. Walden of the 1st Battalion, 5th Special Forces Group, were traveling together in a HMMWV escorting a convoy near Rabiah on 5 August. The Iraqi driver of a civilian fuel vehicle apparently lost control as he was passing the convoy. The truck swerved into the oncoming lane and into Derenda's HMMWV. Both soldiers were killed in the accident.[152]

Within the next month, many of the 3d Division advisors were rotating home. In reflecting on their experiences, the Iroquois Warriors that served with the 3d Division provided a varied assessment of how well their mission was executed in Iraq. Shipman provided a rather balanced appraisal:

> This was not a mission for which we were trained or are habitually established to do. We have great drill sergeants and great instructors whose jobs are to do individual training in an administrative classroom environment or in a very controlled basic training environment. Very few of them, though, had any tactical or operational experience going into this mission, so it was quite a steep learning curve. Many of us have come back and said, 'We really learned a lot.' We learned a lot working with tactical forces like the Stryker Brigade, 3d ACR and doing operations. Some of the things we learned, though, were by mistakes that we made. We weren't necessarily the right unit for the job, but I think we acquitted ourselves as well as we could have.[153]

Tennyson was perhaps more pointed in his evaluation. "I think there was a lot of bad stuff and we were lucky things didn't go a lot worse than they did for a lot of our teams," he said. He then added,

The 98th Division has a lot of capable leaders. If you give them a mission, they can train for it. But the black box mission we got—of just being told we were going to advise and support a foreign army—is not good enough. I think knowing exactly what we were going to do would have alleviated a lot of issues and given us a chance up front to correct a lot of things we had to struggle through once we were in country.[154]

The Iroquois Warrior advisors in the 3d Division were, perhaps, not as far along as those of the 5th Division in bringing their division and brigades to a level where those headquarters were capable of planning, conducting, and controlling tactical operations. Part of the reason is that, as a whole, the 3d Division was behind the 5th in terms of dates of organization, dates of basic training completion, and arguably, in the level of experience with actual combat operations. One wonders also about the impact of the 3d ACR's efforts when it arrived in the area to sideline the MiTTs and assert direct control over the 3d Division units. Of course from the Iraqi perspective, one would have to ask that question of the unit leaders. At the very least, it must have been a bit confusing, and perhaps even alarming, for the Iraqis to have the teams with which they had been working on missions now be told by another American unit to stay away from operational missions. Still, all considered, it seems that the Iroquois Warrior advisors of the 3d Division also laid a good foundation for follow-on MiTTs to build on.

The Advisor Experience—The 1st Iraqi Division

The advisor experience for the Iroquois Warriors in the Iraqi 1st Division was largely different than that of the 3d and 5th Divisions. The differences were primarily centered on two things. First, the majority of the ASTs/MiTTs in the 1st Division were manned by Marines. The ASTs for the division headquarters, two brigade headquarters, and five of the nine battalions were exclusively Marines. The 98th Division provided only four battalion teams to the 1st Division and a few soldiers to the 1st Brigade AST.

The other difference was that by the time the 98th Division ASTs fell in on their respective battalions in November, those units had already been organized and in combat. Some battalions had already worked with several groups of advisors prior to the 98th Division's arrival. The Iroquois Warriors coming into the 1st Division would find no green units to advise—they were already veterans.

The 1st Division had been organized in May 2004 at Taji from battalions and brigades that were formed as part of the IIF. The IIF was a division-size, elite force that was intended to be trained specifically in counterinsurgency (COIN) operations and employed wherever it was needed in Iraq. Once the decision was made later that year to train all Iraqi units in COIN, the unit's distinction as the IIF was lost, but its pride in being designated as the 1st Division and in being the first division to be formed in the new Iraqi Army carried on.

Initially composed of just two brigades, the 1st and 6th, the division received its third brigade about December 2004 when the 2d Brigade was reassigned from the 5th Division. It gained a fourth brigade in April 2004 when the 7th Brigade was transferred in, again from the 5th Division. As part of its mission, the 1st Division was responsible for operations in Anbar province and thus became involved with Operation AL FAJR in Fallujah in November 2004 where five of its battalions were involved.

Fallujah is where MAJ Swartwood's battalion was located when a Marine officer showed up at the Green Hotel at Taji looking for him the day after Thanksgiving. The officer, Col. Ronald Baczkowski, was the senior advisor to the Iraqi 1st Division. Baczkowski told Swartwood that his AST would fly out of Taji that night to Fallujah where they would link up with their Iraqi unit, the 1st Battalion, 1st Brigade. Accordingly, Swartwood assembled his team, moved to the airfield, and flew out about 2300. The choppers landed on the US side of Camp Fallujah in the wee hours of the next morning.

There, Swartwood and his men met LTC Marcus DeOliveira, the senior advisor for the 1st Brigade AST. DeOliveira recalled that the team landed at Camp Fallujah and, ". . . because their aircraft got there late, I did not have as much time as I wanted with them. I think I had a bit less than an hour and then they were passed off to the teams they would transition with to go into Fallujah to start the transition process. It was not the best case scenario—a relief in place in Fallujah while operations were on-going."[155]

In the meeting, DeOliveira laid out his expectations of the team and just what it was they were going to be doing. DeOliveira remembered telling them "they had to execute operations alongside those they advised so as to . . . understand what the unit they advised was capable of doing." He also stressed that "being an advisor was not about teaching but building relationships and trust. . . ."[156] Swartwood later recalled that DeOliveira's pitch was the first information on what exactly he was going to be doing as an advisor in Iraq, other than what he had gleaned from the Internet.[157]

For his part, DeOliveira was somewhat taken aback by some of the advisors he received on the three teams that came to his brigade. "I am not sure what they were told before they got to me or how much they heard what was told them," he explained. "There was much talking about being told they were only going to be teachers and not have to go out. That was not my idea of being an advisor. I fully expected they go out and fight alongside their units."[158]

The unrealistic impressions of the advisors' mission, formed before mobilization and fostered through Camp Atterbury, Camp Virginia, and Taji, were now cleared away, and the stark reality of what their actual duties entailed was driven home. The expectations for advisors to participate in combat operations and live in the same Spartan conditions as their Iraqi counterparts immediately caused a few of them to balk and protest. "I was a bit disappointed with some complaining," DeOliveira recalled. "This was the kind of complaining I would expect of much more junior personnel than those on the teams." He was also concerned by the quality of some of the soldiers he was provided:

> I think of the three teams that came to me (one brigade and two battalions) there were 28 or 29 individuals. Of these, one I sent away his first day in Fallujah. He was extremely overweight and not able to operate in a combat zone. Two officers were moved to better positions than initially suited them. One NCO deliberately shot himself. One NCO was caught trying to send a pistol back to the US. Two other NCOs were sent away for medical reasons.[159]

DeOliveira was also concerned about the soldiers' level of ability given the previous combat experience of the battalions in his brigade. "I needed real infantrymen, artillerymen, and logisticians," he said. "The skill sets I needed were not all there and I had to move some people around and have some do things other than originally intended in order to get at people's strengths. Overall we got things done but there was more friction than needed."[160]

After meeting with DeOliveira, Swartwood's team next met with the outgoing AST. MAJ Hunter Floyd led the team. Floyd's team was composed of reservists from the Fort Lewis brigade of the 91st TSD. They had all volunteered for the mission and had been there for about 6 months. Significantly, they were all O/Cs from the same lanes training battalion at Fort Lewis, Washington, and as such, had made a cohesive team. Though they may have been particularly suited for the mission, just like their CMTC counterparts, the Powder River boys were ready to go home. Swartwood described the transition:

> MAJ Floyd did a pretty good job. He gave me a lot of information and my team said they received a lot of information from the people they replaced as well. The problem was that it was only 2 days and we could have gotten a lot more information if we had had more time. It would have been nice to have gotten more information from them. . . . They'd been there for six months and said, 'Six months is too long to be with these Iraqis. We want to leave.' My team was pretty gung-ho and we could tell the other guys wanted to leave so we simply said, 'We're ready to take over.'[161]

In retrospect, of course, Swartwood realized that his team was not ready to take over and the combat veterans of the elite 1st Battalion knew an opportunity when they saw one. Swartwood's men were the fourth ASTs to work with them and the Iraqis knew their new advisors were green. He explained,

> . . . for a period of time, they took advantage of the fact that we were the new guys and did some stuff that circumvented the rules that were in place. For example, at that point we were working with the 1st Marine Division and they were giving us supplies. They would come out to the field once a week and give us supplies, in addition to stuff we'd get through the Iraqi chain. However, the Iraqi supply chain didn't work very well so we would get most of our supplies from the 1st Marine Division. At first, my AST didn't have a good grasp on that procedure so the Iraqis would take stuff that we were supposed to get.

Swartwood chalked that up to the short transition. He later allowed that Floyd "may have given me that information but I just may not have grasped it all in that short period of time."[162]

The 1st Battalion was considered the best unit in the Iraqi Army. It was not only first in name, but also first in fact. The 1st Battalion was the original infantry battalion to be formed and was organized at Kirkuk in August 2003. Relatively well trained, it was the only Iraqi unit to be given its own sector of operations during the battle of Fallujah in November 2004. When Swartwood's AST arrived, the battalion was still securing that area of the city. "There was a lot of pride among the Iraqis at being the 1st Battalion,

1st Brigade, 1st Division, as being the first unit stood up. They saw themselves (and other Iraqis saw them) as the Americanized Iraqi battalion," Swartwood recalled.[163]

The lack of experience of their new advisors was also a concern in the initial integration. Swartwood stated, "They had been through combat already and we were coming out there as pretty green. None of my team had seen combat. As a result, we thought the Iraqi soldiers would initially look at us as being perhaps not quite worthy or at least not quite as good as the advisors we'd replaced." Swartwood later determined that he should not have been concerned. "It ultimately didn't end up that way because the Iraqis view the Americans as superior forces," he said.[164]

Though the 1st Battalion possessed a lot of pride, it did not mean that everything was well within the unit as Swartwood soon discovered. One of the things that Floyd failed to mention was that the 1st Battalion Commander, Lieutenant Colonel Ali Jabbar, had been accused of embezzling. Since there was no banking system to speak of in Iraq, there was no such thing as automatic deposits either. Each month, the Iraqi soldiers were paid in cash. Ali had received an entire month's payroll while the battalion was in Fallujah and it soon disappeared. Ali then had the temerity to ask his soldiers to help him make it up by donating money left over from their previous payroll that they had not been able to take home because they had been in Fallujah for so long. Swartwood, now aware of the situation, understood from DeOliveira that Ali would be relieved before leaving Fallujah to return to its base at Rustamiyah.[165]

About 3 weeks after it arrived in Fallujah, the 1st Battalion was relieved of its mission by a battalion of the 8th Brigade. Swartwood's AST accompanied the 1st Battalion back to Rustamiyah. The problem was that Ali had not been relieved. As a result, the battalion XO, the S3, and two company commanders left in disgust when they arrived at Rustamiyah. Swartwood explained, "They thought [Ali] was dishonest and not a good officer. They transferred out of 1st Battalion because they felt Colonel Ali should have been relieved and he wasn't. They couldn't work for him. They were very good officers too; it really was a shame."[166]

The plan at Rustamiyah was for the battalion to go on about 2 weeks' leave, and then begin a retraining cycle. When the troops returned, the battalion went to the ranges and the advisors took their units through various training exercises for the next month, then it deployed to Mosul to prepare for the elections.

At Mosul, the 1st Battalion entered the AO of the 1st Brigade, 25th Division. The battalion was given a sector covering the southeast portion of the city. There they set up in a number of abandoned buildings and began visibility patrols. As in most of the other areas where the Iraqi Army was on patrol during the elections, everything went relatively smoothly. The battalion returned to Rustamiyah and from there conducted operations with units of the 10th Mountain Division and the 3d Infantry Division in the spring. Later in the summer it deployed out to Ramadi and conducted missions there with the 2d Marine Division.[167]

At about the time the 1st Battalion was performing its missions with the 3d Infantry Division, the 7th Brigade was reassigned from the 5th Division and became the 4th Brigade of the 1st Division. Along with that brigade came Matt Jones and Brian Charnock. Both had been serving with their battalions in Fallujah until that time.

Figure 26. A typical haul of ammunition confiscated during one of the Iroquois Warriors' many search missions conducted in conjunction with their Iraqi Army units.

After the January elections, Jones recalled that Fallujah became relatively quiet. There was time for the advisors to work with their units on squad-level training and conducting presence patrols. Then in April, at about the same time the brigade was transferred to the 1st Division, the enemy began to stir once again. "We started to have more activity on the peninsula," Jones explained. "Fallujah sits on the river and the peninsula region is in between Fallujah and Ramadi. . . . There was more activity out there and we lost a kid to an IED attack. From that point on, the city started

181

to turn [ugly] and the IEDs in our area became rampant. There was one IED a day, and that was just in our battlespace."[168]

Matt Jones' battalion (officially redesignated as the 3d Battalion, 4th Brigade, but unofficially continued using the 18th Battalion designation) rapidly shifted focus from presence patrols to anti-IED operations. The task became almost impossible. Jones remembered, "we were very unsuccessful in keeping them out of the city. There were so many armaments lying around. You could dig in almost every yard and find buried 155-millimeter artillery shells. We found a cache with 220 120-millimeter rounds all buried in this guy's yard. It took four trucks to haul them all away."[169]

In April the 18th Battalion was also assigned a new counterpart unit, the 3d Battalion, 4th Marines. Jones worked with that unit to integrate his Iraqi troops into the battalion's operations. In doing so, he also wanted the Iraqi battalion to move to the next higher level of operations. He explained how he accomplished it:

> . . . we developed a plan with them [the 3d Battalion, 4th Marines] to do an operation every 10 days. It would be a company operation but we'd call it a battalion operation so the battalion staff could do the planning. That way, the Iraqi staff could do the planning and issue the order. The Marines did a great job of integrating the battalion and company staffs of the Iraqis into the planning and execution. The Iraqi battalion commander, the S3, the translator, and I would go to the Marine base and we'd sit through the op order brief. They'd always issue it verbally. We'd sit through the rock walk and any other briefs that needed to be done.[170]

Once through the information gathering with the Marines, the advisors guided the staff through the development of the operations order and then had them issue the order to the company or companies going on the mission. The company would then conduct the mission with the Marines.

By late spring, the units of the 18th Battalion were conducting some fairly sophisticated operations. Jones explained:

> We started doing company operations where companies would have their own search lanes. They'd do a cordon and search with the Marines, doing joint operations. Then we developed battalion battle drills. We had a battalion IED battle drill and, within that, we had a MEDEVAC drill. We had one company who had a Republican Guard

officer and he started doing his own activities. By May, they were doing about one joint patrol a day. If a company sent out three or four patrols, two of them might be with MiTTs and the other two were all Iraqis.[171]

Though his Iraqis were making progress, there were still problems. One of the issues concerned the conduct of the Quick Reaction Force (QRF) missions:

> We had a lot of fights over the QRF. Every company was supposed to have a QRF, plus they were supposed to have a standing battalion QRF—and that QRF went out two or three times a day. They were lackadaisical on it and one time we really lost it. We were very upset because they weren't using it properly. They were endangering lives because they weren't doing what they were supposed to and weren't moving like they were supposed to move.[172]

By late summer, the 18th Battalion was conducting true battalion-level operations. Jones recalled that it conducted at least two battalion cordon and search missions before his MiTT left Iraq. For one mission, the 3/4th Marines even attached an engineer squad and a psychological operations team to the battalion. The willingness of the commander of the 3d Battalion, 4th Marines to work with and respect the 18th Battalion is much of the reason why the Iraqi battalion advanced so far while he was there. According to Jones:

> I give the Marines a lot of credit because they treated the Iraqi battalion commander like a battalion commander. The biggest problem we had over there was the attitude of, 'Oh, it's only a f------ Iraqi.' Well, if that Iraqi is a battalion or brigade commander and you want him to operate at a certain level, you have to treat him at that level. If you're going to treat him like a private, he's going to act like a private. If you treat him like a battalion commander and his battalion fails to follow through on a mission, you need to call him on the carpet and ask him, 'Battalion commander, where were your soldiers?' Then he'll answer to you. But if you just go grab his soldiers, he won't answer to you.[173]

Though it was in the same brigade as the 18th Battalion, Charnock's 16th Battalion did not seem to have progressed as far, but it too continued to make progress after being reassigned to the 1st Division in April. At that time the battalion was still in Fallujah, but soon after was moved to Al Kharma, a town about 7 miles away.

At Al Kharma, the Marines had set up four platoon-size observation posts (OP) from which to watch the city and conduct presence patrols. Intelligence indicated some of the insurgents that had escaped Fallujah had gone there. The commander of the 16th Battalion's Marine counterpart unit felt the Iraqi unit was trained well enough to take over the positions in Al Kharma and clear the town. In turn, that would release a Marine company for operations elsewhere. Charnock described the operation:

> [The 16th Battalion] took over the city and did a whole clearing of the city when they first got there. It was an Iraqi-led mission. We were just there for support. . . . They did that and then set up at the OPs the Marines had. The Marines cut their men in half and kept about a squad or two at each OP. We put one member from the AST at each OP as well. We were responsible for patrols for so many hours during the day and were to respond to anything.

Once the city was cleared, the 16th Battalion settled in to routine patrolling. "We were mostly a reactive force at that point," Charnock recalled.[174] After securing Al Kharma, the 16th Battalion continued minor operations until it moved to Taji later that summer. There it would conduct its RIPTOA with the incoming 80th Division MiTT in September.

On balance, the Iroquois Warrior advisors and their Iraqi brigades and battalions assigned to the 1st Division seem to have benefited from their association with their counterpart Marine units. It appears that Marine commanders were somewhat more positively disposed to both their Iraqi units and the advisors that were assigned to them. They were more willing to integrate the Iraqis into combat operations and support them with resources, both logistical and operational, when they needed it.

The fact that the 1st Division units were already combat veterans did not seem to have a long-term impact on their relationship with the 98th Division's "green" advisors. From the evidence, it seems the MiTTs, along with help from both Army and Marine counterpart units were able to significantly increase the operational capabilities of the Iraqi units to which they were assigned.

Of course, as in the case of the teams with other divisions, the overall progress was good in some areas, minimal in some areas, and at best, flat in others. Success was not achieved in all areas with all units. Some of the failure to progress can be laid at the feet of the Iraqi leaders and soldiers and some of it can be attributed to the advisors. For example, Charnock initially developed a slightly negative perspective toward the Iraqi soldiers and their leaders based on his own military experience: "When we got them I was skeptical of what they could and couldn't do. . . . These guys [didn't] have a lot of upper leadership. Their NCOs were pretty much just their best privates." Matt Jones reinforced this view by stating, "The Iraqis will never operate at the level the Americans operate at. We're head and shoulders above them."[175]

On the other hand, the advisors, or at least the process used to select them, were not entirely blameless. Jones made the argument:

> An advisor in combat is not someone who sits back with a clipboard and goes through the Army Training and Evaluation Program (ARTEP) and says, 'Yes, you did this right. Yes, you did that right.' Instead, you are actively engaged in combat operations. You're side-by-side with your Iraqi counterpart. There are times when you're more directive than other times and times when you, as the advisor, have to tell them exactly what to do because of the urgency of the situation. There are other times, though, when you're going to be accepting a greater amount of risk than with regular Coalition forces because you need to sit back and let them learn. You need to go into the mission with an open mind and with a good understanding of how to operate in a combat zone. The problem we had was that we had way too many officers and NCOs who went over there who had never been operational in their life and didn't have a clue how a battalion operates in combat. If you don't know how a battalion operates in combat, you certainly can't know how a brigade is supposed to operate in combat—not at Combined Arms and Services Staff School (CAS3), not on a staff somewhere, not teaching a class, but how a battalion *really operates*.[176]

Obviously, many of the personnel from the 98th Division selected to be advisors did not have the skills and experiences, at least initially, that Jones describes. Many of them did learn the skills on the job and, if they were one of those who were positively disposed toward the mission and their Iraqi soldiers, were likely to be very effective in helping to bring their assigned unit to a higher level of capability.

If the advisory efforts in the 1st Division were not entirely successful, it seems many advisors who served with the division feel they were, at least, largely successful. Though skeptical initially, Charnock proudly related that the 16th Battalion made good progress:

> These guys came a long way. By the end, we would send them out on patrols by themselves. They would go out and they would be responsible for patrols all on their own. They would find stuff and bring people back, get intel. They did a lot of things. Of course, they still made a lot of mistakes and we had to help them, but I would expect that from an American unit as well. . . . I definitely trusted them a lot more toward the end and I didn't have any trouble going out with them by myself if need be. Many times, it would be me and maybe one other American. We'd go out into the city, do a patrol, and I felt almost as safe as I would with an American force.[177]

Matt Jones believed the 18th Battalion was likewise a better unit, with some caveats, than the one that existed before his team arrived:

> By the end, they were doing some battalion operations within their lanes and they were getting fairly successful with some counterinsurgency missions. They were very good at raids and at exploiting intel that they gathered through their own sources. They were somewhat constrained in the detention process, though, which was kind of crappy. The system for detention wasn't working very well. They have a different view of the Constitution than we do and they operate in their own ways certain times, but they were very successful at exploiting human intelligence. For example, say we grab the triggerman of an IED. That same night, we'd probably hit two or three houses.[178]

In short, many of the Iroquois Warriors who served on the ASTs/MiTTs would concur with the way Swartwood summed up the advisor experience: "I'm very proud of what I did and what my team accomplished over there." DeOliveira would also agree. Despite, the rough start with a few of his Iroquois Warrior advisors, he later commented, "Overall I am very proud of every one of them for putting their lives on the line and working at improving the units they advised."[179]

The Iraqi Advisor Group and the Phoenix Academy

It is important to note two additional significant aspects of the advisory effort in Iraq developed by soldiers of the 98th Division—the Iraq

Advisor Group (IAG) and the Phoenix Academy. Though the academy would eventually become part of the IAG, the two had distinctly different geneses.

In December 2004, General George W. Casey, CG of the MNF-I, decided he wanted to formalize the AST concept for all Iraqi Army divisions, including those of the ING (soon be integrated into the Iraqi Army). Up to that point, the advisor effort for ING units had been left up to the discretion of the Coalition counterpart unit commander. Some units provided their ING battalion with a lot of advisor support, and others provided nothing. Casey directed that beginning in January the Coalition counterpart units would provide enough personnel and equipment for a standard MiTT for ING battalions, brigades, and divisions, and for some of the new Iraqi Army units that were scheduled to be organized.[180]

As various changes to the advisory effort began in January 2005 (ASTs changed to MiTT, ING integration into the IA, designation of Coalition counterpart units to work with the units of the regular IA, etc.), the MNC-I staff realized a need for a headquarters between MNC-I and the MiTTs to supervise those teams and ensure some level of standardization of the counterpart-provided MiTTs. Petraeus had two brigadier generals assigned to the CMATT headquarters where only one was needed (a situation which apparently possessed all the friction one might expect). The MNSTC-I CG thus volunteered Sherlock to MNC-I to start up and command the IAG. The offer was accepted and Sherlock began the effort to establish the IAG in January 2005, largely with personnel from the 98th Division.[181]

The charter of the IAG was not to command the MiTTs. Effective about 1 April, the MiTTs were to become answerable to the MNC-I Major Subordinate Commands to which they were attached for tactical control (TACON). Sherlock and his new headquarters were to be responsible for receiving and compiling the reports of the MiTTs, ensuring their administrative and logistical support (which was to be provided predominantly by the counterpart unit), ensuring standardization of MiTT organization and functions across all the teams, and developing a standardized training program for incoming advisors. The IAG was additionally responsible for the RSOI of new advisors coming into country that were generated as a result of RFFs for MiTTs to be assigned to the new IA divisions (the 7th through 10th Divisions) being organized that year.

On 1 April 2005, the IAG officially took over responsibility for operational MiTTs (those of the 1st through 6th Divisions). Newly arrived MiTTs remained under CMATT control until such time that their IA unit was declared operational and assigned a counterpart unit. At that point, the MiTT was transferred to the TACON of its counterpart unit and the administrative control of the IAG. Eventually, the IAG would be responsible for about 80 MiTTs based throughout Iraq.[182]

The genesis of the Phoenix Academy was the idea of BG Schwitters and COL Kienle, the CMATT Chief of Staff. Schwitters later described the rationale for the school:

> We recognized around the November/December 2004 timeframe that the training of the [advisors] coming in— regardless of what service or unit they were from—needed to be finished off, and it could only be done by guys who had been doing the advisory support mission and doing it successfully. So we made that part of the force flow. The idea was to continue to use the training at Camp Atterbury as the initial platform, and then they would come into Kuwait and get collective training in the environment. . . . From an operational and mission perspective, we needed to finish that training off in the [actual] environment, led by successful AST leaders as well as cultural experts, and also give them the opportunity to go out and do [represen- tative missions] in the local area. We wanted them to go out and actually be able to train on entry control points and take some low-risk convoys out. We wanted them to have a chance to go out and do these things before they were out on their own and training the Iraqis to do them. That was the reason for Phoenix Academy.[183]

As part of his responsibilities as the CG, IAG, Sherlock was directed to develop a comprehensive training program for MiTTs that began with the training at Camp Atterbury. The IAG developed a three-tiered effort (Atterbury, Kuwait, and Taji) based on an improved version of what the 98th Division experienced for its deployment. The third tier evolved from the 2 days of Iraqi history and culture classes into a 10-day program that became the curriculum of the Phoenix Academy.

The ideas for what was needed for this curriculum came from an advi- sor conference held by Schwitters at Taji in January. At the conference, the advisors were canvassed for what they thought was needed by incoming advisors to adequately prepare them for the MiTT mission. The informa- tion gathered from this conference was provided to Sherlock who then turned to the 98th Division C2 Cell to function as a curriculum develop- ment team. LTC Robert Lawless (who became the cell OIC when Cipolla left), Joe Friedman, and five others sat down in March to develop the schedule and write the lesson plans. Friedman recalled that the team tried to put realism into the training:

> Some classes were an hour; some were half a day. Most of it was classroom but there were a few hands-on practical exercise types of blocks [such as] 'How do you work with Iraqis through an interpreter?' So the [class object] was to set up a traffic point. We had the new ASTs in country get with interpreters and some MPs (who were Iraqi soldiers already stationed there). They would instruct the MPs on how to set up a traffic point through the interpreter. That was a block called 'Working with Interpreters.'[184]

The planning team's concept also brought in serving advisors to function as instructors and to talk to the students about the realities of advising in Iraq. Additionally, the team wanted to bring in Iraqi soldiers and leaders to talk to the students and answer questions about serving with Iraqi units, Iraqi culture, customs of specific locations, etc. The planning effort was a lot of work, but it eventually paid off and was conducted more or less as planned. "I was personally very proud of what we did there because, in 6 weeks, this went from concept to having the first large group of students walk in the door," Friedman remembered.[185]

The first class of advisors to attend the Phoenix Academy was actually advisors for SPTTs, which included some Polish and El Salvadoran advisors. By the time the C2 Cell turned permanent ownership of the academy over to the IAG in June, 700 students had completed the course.[186]

The IAG and the Phoenix Academy were successful 98th Division projects that brought greater capabilities, order, and professionalism to the advisory effort in Iraq and helped MNSTC-I get beyond the ad hoc operations it inherited in June 2004. Both the IAG and the Phoenix Academy were just beyond their formative stages when they were handed over to the 80th Division, which began arriving in country in June 2005.

Relief in Place/Transfer of Authority with the 80th Division

The RIPTOA with 80th Division elements that were deploying to replace the 98th Division began in July 2005, starting with the handoff of the IAG between Sherlock and Brigadier General John P. McLaren, Jr., the ADC of the 80th Division (Institutional Training). To prevent what had happened to their soldiers when they arrived, Sherlock and the IAG developed a formal, in-depth, 2-week RIPTOA process that was conducted between the MiTTs of the 98th Division and those of the 80th Division. The intent was for the 98th Division MiTTs to take their replacements through a specific series of events (such as an introduction meeting with their interpreters and the Iraqi unit, a guided tour of the base, inventory of team equipment, instruction on operations peculiar to the AO, introductions to the Coalition counterpart unit, etc.). The handoff also consisted of a more formalized "left-seat, right-seat ride." The concept of this process was that for the first week or so, the outgoing team would be in charge of advisor operations on missions. The outgoing team would drive the vehicles, operate the radios, and provide actual advice to the Iraqi units. The incoming team members would simply observe and ask questions. For the second week, the roles would be reversed and the outgoing team would provide a critique. Once the RIPTOA was complete, the new team was in charge and the outgoing team would travel to the Green Hotel at Taji to await transportation to Kuwait.

The quality of the battle-handoff between the 98th and 80th Division advisor teams perhaps lay in the eyes of the beholder. McLaren felt that the 98th Division teams were not always committed to the plan:

> There was a specific checklist that was developed to make sure you covered all these topics and there was a reporting requirement that came back as to what had to be done to have an effective turnover or transition between the teams. It was very dependent upon the personality of the actors involved. We tried to make the most efficient transition happen possible but, again, when you have that diverse of an area, I would say some went well and some didn't. Some of the problems were guys who just wanted to get out of Dodge as fast as they could. It was specifically me and Brigadier General Richard Sherlock calling folks and saying, 'If you're not happy with the transition, the guy doesn't leave.' We took that attitude with every single team. If the arriving team was not satisfied that everything had been covered sufficiently for them to feel like they could take over, then we weren't going to let the other team go.[187]

On the other hand, the 98th Division advisors were not always impressed with their replacements either, as Charnock related in his experience:

> The 80th Division guys came in to replace us with a 10-man team. They weren't happy. I think they believed the same things we did initially about simply being trainers when they got there. We had to tell them that the Iraqis

didn't need any more training; they were doing the real stuff every day. I think they were told that they weren't going to be leaving the wire too much. Then they found out where they were going to be living, there was no wire. They pretty much lived in a house in the city with neighbors who were Iraqis. They didn't really want to go out on many missions. We had some trouble right in the beginning where Marine generals had to step in and tell them to do things because they were saying they wouldn't do certain things. The handoff didn't go well. They didn't like us because we were telling them they had to do these things, like going on missions with the Iraqis. They kept saying no, that that's not what they were told they were going to be doing. They had a bad taste in their mouths for us.[188]

Tennyson's team had some trouble with its replacements as well, but some things turn out for the best:

We did spend a lot of time with them, though, a lot of time with our Iraqis, and we tried to build up the relationship between them and the 80th guys. Before we left, they were on one of their first missions with the Iraqis, into Tall Afar, and they got hit with an IED. Nobody got hurt, but it was a good wake up call for them because we were having some trouble conveying to them certain details about things. We were getting down to the nitty-gritty details about where they should put each Humvee. I think that incident got their attention. When they got back in, they wanted to know everything. It was the one good IED.[189]

In the case of the 5th Division team, Parsons and McConnell may have gone too far, but as they had learned, better too much than too little:

They showed up in the middle of the night on these Chinooks. We piled them into trucks and bed them down for the night. The next day, we had a big welcome for them. The Iraqi Army, Colonel Ahmad and his whole staff, put on a big meal to welcome them in. They got indoctrinated to Iraqi food and culture. We did a couple briefings with them. From then on, it was just a daily update brief with a deliberate list of tasks that had to be completed. We had a huge binder with a wealth of information concerning the whole story, from when we first picked the unit up to pictures of things that were done in Samarra, Kirkush, and Numaniyah. We gave them CDs, binders, operations orders, and schools plans. I think we overwhelmed them, having them drink from the fire hose, but I honestly believe that when we left they had a good handle on where they needed to go next, what to do and how to do it.[190]

While it is likely that not every 98th team did their handoff as well as they might have, the Iroquois Warriors that were replaced by LTC Paul Ciesinski's 80th Division MiTT certainly did, as Ciesinski himself attests to both their transition efforts and the job they did with their Iraqi unit:

That was . . . LTC [Stephen T.] Udovich's team. It took about 10 to 14 days and they took it seriously. They were well under TOE strength; they were about 60 to 70 percent strength. . . . They took us all throughout the area of operations (AO) and they did their honest best to get us to learn our AO and the challenges we would face . . . the 3d Brigade was becoming more and more confident due to Udovich's team, to the 3d ACR working with them, and due to an SF officer who was working with them. . . . When [Udovich] took over, they couldn't even get out the gate in a convoy. They couldn't feed themselves. They couldn't fuel. They couldn't arm. They couldn't pay their soldiers, and that was having major repercussions on retention. But, Udovich's team and 3d ACR worked hard on these things while the ODA worked strong on squad and platoon level combat skills: raids, cordon and searches, and those types of things.[191]

One thing seems to be evident about the 98th Division's RIPTOA efforts with the 80th Division—the transition experience for the 80th Division personnel coming into Iraq was clearly more organized and thorough than that received by the Iroquois Warriors. It is possible that some of the 80th Division's advisors possessed the same "we know it all" attitude that plagued the MiTT that Tennyson's team had to deal with, and therefore, missed some of the details their outgoing teams were attempting to convey. As Swartwood admitted, there may have also been details that were passed on to them that they did not absorb due to a short transition as in Swartwood's case in the transition with MAJ Floyd. The detailed checklist and reporting procedures dictated by the 98th Division's

RIPTOA process, if followed correctly, should have given the incoming teams ample opportunity to listen, observe, and learn before the Iroquois Warriors departed. By all reckoning, after their transition the 80th Division MiTTs should have been the beneficiaries of a solid foundation of advisory experience and of Iraqi units that were ready to proceed to the next level.

Although it is arguable whether the advisor mission was more important to the overall MNSTC-I operation than the other tasks performed by the Iroquois Warriors, it was clearly the mission that garnered the most controversy concerning the decision to employ a DIVIT to meet MNSTC-I's needs. The question of whether or not these institutional training soldiers had the skill sets to do the mission was answered. Moreover, the answer was, predictably, yes and no, which would have been true of almost any group of soldiers that could have been sent over. The Iroquois Warriors did possess the basic training and small unit collective training skills needed for most battalions of the 1st, 3d, and 5th Divisions. With the exception of two battalions of the 1st Division, the other battalions that the 98th Division advisors worked with were just out of or still in basic training and others were still not yet formed. The tactical and technical skills that these DIVIT soldiers brought to the mix were probably about right. The purely advisory skills they needed were, just like those soldiers before them, learned on the job, and for the most part they learned them well.

As the various ASTs completed their left-seat, right-seat rides with their 80th Division counterparts, and as those Iroquois Warriors on the staffs and training teams transitioned with their replacements, they all prepared to move to Taji for outprocessing and the trip home. Compared to their movement to the theater and their subsequent experiences in Iraq, the movements to Taji and Kuwait were anticlimactic. It was difficult at times to get the soldiers back to Taji due to transportation problems, but all 98th Division soldiers got back to the Green Hotel in time to catch their flights to Kuwait. At that point, to most Iroquois Warriors the delays and holdovers they would experience did not matter. They were going home.

Notes

1. Headquarters, Coalition Military Assistance Transition Team, PowerPoint Brief, "Coalition Military Training Assistance Team Command and Control (C2) Cell, Headquarters CMATT, undated, *passim.*

2. LTC Joseph Friedman, interview by author, Combat Studies Institute, Fort Leavenworth, KS, 5 November 2006, 5.

3. Ibid., 4.

4. Headquarters, Multi-National Security Transition Command-Iraq, Support Unit, "Requirements Assessment," Enclosure 4, "Army Support to MNSTC-I Requirement," 3 August 2004, 7–8.

5. Headquarters, Multi-National Security Transition Command-Iraq, Support Unit, PowerPoint Brief, "Assessment," 3 August 2004, 2.

6. LTC James DiRisio, e-mail to author, Subject: Number of ASTs, 1 February 2007.

7. Both BG Schwitters and LTC DiRisio commented on the excellent performance of these soldiers.

8. COL Sean Ryan, interview by author, Joint Center for International Security Force Assistance, Fort Leavenworth, KS, 21 December 2006, 4.

9. Friedman interview, 5 November 2006, 5.

10. BG Frank Cipolla, telephone interview by author, Combat Studies Institute, Fort Leavenworth, KS, 20 November 2006, 3.

11. BG Richard Sherlock, interview by author, Office, Chief of the Army Reserve, Pentagon, Washington, DC, 16 November 2006, 11.

12. COL Douglas Shipman, interview by author, Headquarters, 98th Division (IT), Rochester, NY, 3 November 2006, 5.

13. MAJ Scott McConnell, telephone interview by author, Combat Studies Institute, Fort Leavenworth, KS, 12 December 2006, 7.

14. MAJ Matthew Jones, interview by author, Headquarters, 98th Division (IT), Rochester, NY, 4 November 2006, 7.

15. SSG Brian D. Charnock, interview by author, Headquarters, 98th Division (IT), Rochester, NY, 4 November 2006, 3–4.

16. LTC Daniel Christian, interview by author, 98th Division Headquarters, Rochester, NY, 3 November 2006, 4.

17. BG James Schwitters, telephone interview by author, Combat Studies Institute, Fort Leavenworth, KS, 13 December 2006, 4.

18. COL Bradford Parsons, telephone interview by author, Headquarters, 98th Division (IT), Rochester, NY, 3 November 2006, 7.

19. Charnock interview, 4 November 2006, 9.

20. Christian interview, 3 November 2006, 11.

21. MAJ Jeffrey E. Tennyson, interview by author, Headquarters, 98th Division (IT), Rochester, NY, 3 November 2006, 10.

22. Charnock interview, 4 November 2006, 8.

23. Ibid.

24. Christian interview, 3 November 2006, 11.

25. LTC James DiRisio, interview by author, Headquarters, 98th Division (IT), Rochester, NY, 3 November 2006, 7.

26. Schwitters telephone interview, 13 December 2006, 4.

27. Ibid.

28. McConnell telephone interview, 12 December 2006, 7.

29. Headquarters, Coalition Military Transition Team, PowerPoint Brief, "10 Division Proposed MOD Forces Organization Chart, Version 3," 8 March 2005.

30. Parsons telephone interview, 3 November 2006, 4.

31. Ibid.

32. McConnell telephone interview, 12 December 2006, 6.

33. Parsons telephone interview, 3 November 2006, 5.

34. McConnell telephone interview, 12 December 2006, 7.

35. Ibid., 6.

36. Parsons telephone interview, 3 November 2006, 4–5.

37. Ibid., 5.

38. McConnell telephone interview, 12 December 2006, 7.

39. Ibid., 8.

40. Ibid., 9.

41. Ibid.

42. LTC John C. Curwen, telephone interview by author, Combat Studies Institute, Fort Leavenworth, KS, 8 February 2007, 2–3.

43. Ibid., 4–5.

44. Ibid., 3–4.

45. Ibid., 6.

46. Ibid., 7.

47. Ibid., 9–10.

48. Jones interview, 4 November 2006, 6–7.

49. *The Middle Ground* web log, available at http://themiddleground. blogspot.com/2004/10/patriots-and-soldiers-iraq-fallen-49.html, accessed 3 November 2006; Edward Wong, "Ambush Kills 50 Iraq Soldiers Execution Style," *The New York Times*, 25 October 2004.

50. Jones interview, 4 November 2006, 7.

51. Ibid.

52. Ibid.

53. Ibid., 7–8.

54. SFC Dennis Ewing, interview by author, Headquarters, 98th Division (IT), Rochester, NY, 4 November 2006, 3.

55. Ibid., 4.

56. Christian interview, 3 November 2006, 4–5.

57. Ibid., 5.

58. Ibid.

59. Jones interview, 4 November 2006, 8.

60. Ibid.

61. Ibid.

62. Ibid., 9.

63. Ibid., 10.

64. Ibid.

65. Parsons telephone interview, 3 November 2006, 5.

66. McConnell telephone interview, 12 December 2006, 10.

67. Ibid., 11.

68. MAJ Lawrence Bradley, telephone interview by author, Combat Studies Institute, Fort Leavenworth, KS, 7 February 2007.

69. Ibid.

70. Ibid.

71. Ibid.

72. Ibid.

73. Ibid.

74. Ibid.

75. Parsons telephone interview, 3 November 2006, 6.

76. Ibid.

77. McConnell telephone interview, 12 December 2006, 9.

78. Christian interview, 3 November 2006, 6.

79. Ewing interview, 4 November 2006, 4.

80. 3d Brigade, 5th Division, "Significant Events Log, 1 Dec 04–25 Aug 05."

81. CPT Paul Molineaux, Multi-National Security Transition Command-Iraq, "Iraqi Soldiers Wrap Up 'Operation COBWEB,'" *The Advisor*, 14 May 2005, 7.

82. Ibid.

83. "Significant Events Log"; Christian interview, 3 November 2006, 7.

84. Christian interview, 3 November 2006, 7.

85. MAJ Michael L. Eller, "Consolidated Report: IED Ambush Attack of 3d Brigade, 5th Division (Iraqi Army)," 8 July 2005.

86. Curwen interview, 8 February 2007, 10.

87. Ibid., 11.

88. Ibid.

89. Sherlock functioned as the deputy CG of CMATT until he took over as the CG of the IAG.

90. Parsons telephone interview, 3 November 2006, 6.

91. McConnell telephone interview, 12 December 2006, 11.

92. Ibid., 12.

93. Parsons telephone interview, 3 November 2006, 6.

94. Ibid., 8.

95. Curwen interview, 8 February 2007, 11–12.

96. Timothy J. Hansen and Jocene D. Preston, ed. *An Encounter with History: The 98th Division and the Global War on Terrorism: 2001–2005* (Washington, DC: Government Printing Office, 2006), 258–59.

97. Curwen interview, 8 February 2007, 12.

98. Ibid., 14.

99. Ibid.

100. Ibid., 15

101. Ibid., 15–16.

102. Ibid., 16.

103. Ibid., 17.

104. Ibid.

105. Ibid., 17–18.

106. Ibid., 18.

107. Parsons telephone interview, 3 November 2006; McConnell telephone interview, 12 December 2006, 9.

108. Parsons telephone interview, 3 November 2006, 5.

109. McConnell telephone interview, 12 December 2006, 9.

110. Christian interview, 3 November 2006, 7.

111. Ewing interview, 4 November 2006, 6.

112. Shipman interview, 3 November 2006, 6.

113. Ibid., 6.

114. Ibid., 1–2.

115. Ibid., 4.

116. Ibid.

117. COL Douglas Shipman, telephone interview by author, Combat Studies Institute, Fort Leavenworth, KS, 14 February 2007.

118. Shipman interview, 3 November 2006, 5.

119. Ibid., 2.

120. Ibid., 5.

121. Ibid., 6.

122. Tennyson interview, 3 November 2006, 4.

123. Ibid., 6.

124. Shipman interview, 3 November 2006, 6.

125. Tennyson interview, 3 November 2006, 6.

126. Shipman interview, 3 November 2006, 7.

127. Tennyson interview, 3 November 2006, 5.

128. *Stars and Stripes*, "Coming to Grips with a Close Call at Mosul," available at http://www.estripes.com/article.asp?section=104&article=33002&archive=true, accessed 11 October 2006; *Fallen Heroes Memorial*, "Fallen Heroes of Operation Iraqi Freedom: Lt. Col. Terrence K. Crowe," available at http://www.fallenheroesmemorial.com/oif/profiles/croweterrencek.html, accessed 3 November 2006.

129. Tennyson interview, 3 November 2006, 7.

130. Ibid, 7.

131. Shipman interview, 3 November 2006, 6.

132. Tennyson interview, 3 November 2006, 7.

133. Ibid.

134. Ibid.

135. Ibid.

136. Ibid.

137. Shipman interview, 3 November 2006, 8.

138. Shipman, telephone interview, 14 February 2007.

139. Shipman interview, 3 November 2006, 8.

140. Ibid., 7–8; Shipman, telephone interview, 14 February 2007.

141. Tennyson interview, 3 November 2006, 8.

142. Ibid., 8.

143. Ibid., 11.

144. Shipman, telephone interview, 14 February 2007.

145. "Fallen Heroes of Operation Iraqi Freedom: Lt. Col. Terrence K. Crowe.

146. Ibid.

147. Ibid.

148. Shipman interview, 3 November 2006, 10.

149. Ibid., 9.

150. Ibid., 9; COL Douglas Shipman, e-mail to author, Subject: RE: Your Interview Transcript, 24 January 2007.

151. Tennyson interview, 3 November 2006, 8.

152. Hansen and Preston, *Encounter with History*, 262–63.

153. Shipman interview, 3 November 2006, 10.

154. Tennyson interview, 3 November 2006, 11.

155. COL Marcus DeOliveira, e-mail to author, Subject: Iraqi 1st Brigade, 4 March 2007.

156. Ibid.

157. MAJ Roger Swartwood, interview by author, Headquarters, 98th Division (IT), Rochester, NY, 3 November 2006, 7.

158. DeOliveira e-mail, 4 March 2007.

159. Ibid.

160. Ibid.

161. Swartwood interview, 3 November 2006, 7–8.

162. Ibid., 8.

163. Ibid., 9.

164. Ibid., 8.

165. Ibid.

166. Ibid., 9.

167. Ibid.

168. Jones interview, 4 November 2006, 11.

169. Ibid.

170. Ibid.

171. Ibid., 11–12.

172. Ibid., 11.

173. Ibid., 12.

174. Charnock interview, 4 November 2006, 5.

175. Ibid., 6; Jones interview, 4 November 2006, 13.

176. Jones interview, 4 November 2006, 12–13.

177. Charnock interview, 4 November 2006, 6.

178. Jones interview, 4 November 2006, 12.

179. Swartwood interview, 3 November 2006, 10; DeOliveira e-mail, 4 March 2007.

180. Sherlock interview, 16 November 2006, 8. The ING was established 3 September 2003 as the Iraqi Civil Defense Corps (ICDC). The ICDC was designed to be raised and advised by Coalition units and used to complement Coalition operations. It was redesignated as the ING in July 2004 and integrated in the Iraqi Army about April 2005.

181. LTG David H. Petraeus, interview by author, Headquarters, Combined Arms Center, Fort Leavenworth, KS, 11 December 2006, 8.

182. MG John P. McLaren, Jr., telephone interview by author, Combat Studies Institute, Fort Leavenworth, KS, 14 November 2006, 3. Actual control of some MiTTs was delayed by as much as 2 weeks due to operational activities.

183. Schwitters telephone interview, 13 December 2006, 6–7.

184. Friedman interview, 5 November 2005, 8.

185. Ibid.; The C2 Cell was integrated fully into the IAG in May 2005, but continued to perform the RSOI function for incoming MiTTs until its RIPTOA with the 80th Division.

186. Sherlock interview, 16 November 2006, 11; Friedman interview, 5 November 2006, 12.

187. McLaren interview, 14 November 2006, 5.

188. Charnock interview, 4 November 2006, 6.

189. Tennyson interview, 3 November 2006, 9.

190. McConnell telephone interview, 12 December 2006, 12.

191. LTC Paul Ciesinski, interview by Dr. Christopher Ives, Combat Studies Institute, Fort Leavenworth, KS, 13 October 2006, 9–10.

Chapter 7

Redeployment and Summary

If they are to succeed, they must do so on their own.

SGT With

As the RIPTOA process between the 98th and 80th Divisions progressed through the summer and fall, Lawless, in charge of what had become the IAG C2 Cell, managed the movement of staff personnel at MNSTC-I, CMATT, CPATT, the advisors teams, and other Iroquois Warrior individuals and elements from their respective duty stations back to the Green Hotel at Taji. From there, the cell would arrange for transportation to the BIAP and for space on flights to Kuwait.

The procedure seemed simple, but as with many military operations, there were variables that could not be controlled. The biggest problem was the date and time for departure flights from the BIAP to Kuwait were not known until at best 48 hours beforehand, and to ensure a given mobilization group was boarded on its assigned flight was a zero-defects operation. All levels applied pressure to ensure nobody missed their scheduled flight. If a MiTT was at Tall Afar, it had to complete its RIPTOA before it could go to Taji for outprocessing. If the incoming team was late, that immediately posed a problem. Once the handoff was complete, transportation had to be arranged to get the team to Taji and choppers were not always available. Once at Taji, the outprocessing checklist had to be completed, which included all officer efficiency reports, noncommissioned officer efficiency reports, and awards.[1]

Friedman explained that to ensure people did not miss their flights, Lawless would "move these ASTs to Taji and they'd be there for a couple days, not knowing when they were going to leave because we didn't know when the flights were. We didn't want to send them anywhere because we might not get them to all the steps in time. Colonel Lawless had to 'swag' in getting people to Taji, and sometimes they sat for a while. Some people understood and some didn't."[2] Once at Taji, however, everything else seemed to go relatively smoothly for the remainder of the journey home, at least in terms of transportation arrangements. Additionally, the C2 Cell at Taji was in frequent contact with the rear CP at Rochester letting Rick Monczynski and the rear CP know when personnel were flown out to Kuwait.

After Friedman's stint as a curriculum developer with the Phoenix Academy, Lawless sent him to Camp Arifjan in Kuwait to manage the

C2 Cell's efforts to receive Iroquois Warriors coming in from the BIAP, organize them into their original mobilization groups, and coordinate their movement from Kuwait to their CONUS mobilization training post. Friedman also let Monczynski know when flights left Kuwait.[3]

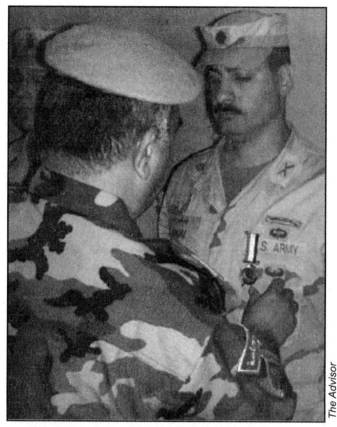

Figure 27. Just prior to his departure from Iraq, MAJ John Bovina receives the Iraqi General Service Medal from Brigadier General Abdullah for his services as an advisor to the Iraqi 4th Division.

Back in the states, the rear CP was able to track each group of soldiers as to their arrival dates and times at Indianapolis and El Paso. MG Robinson had directed a colonel or above from the division be on hand to welcome each flight home, and he personally attended a number of these arrivals (as well as the "Welcome Home Warrior Citizen" ceremonies conducted at various home station locations after demobilization). Once the mobilization groups went through the process of turning in weapons and equipment, filling out appropriate demobilization paperwork, and going through a medical exam (all of which took several days), the troops were flown home to start a well-deserved 30-day demobilization leave. By December, almost all of the division's soldiers were home.

Though the 98th Division did not deploy as a division to Iraq, the deployment, mission, and redeployment was clearly a division effort. Although approximately 600 soldiers from the 98th deployed overseas, the remainder of the Iroquois Warriors still had to perform all the basic training, MOS, OES, and NCOES missions the division had been assigned for FY 2005, just as MG Wilson had directed. The division successfully accomplished those missions and still supported the MNSTC-I mission.

As far as the Army was concerned, when the 98th's soldiers went to Iraq they went as individual fillers. As such, their parent unit could have washed their hands of them; however, Robinson established the rear CP cell for the duration of the mission. The rear CP kept track of what was going on with his soldiers in Iraq, provided those soldiers with what support he could from this side of the Atlantic, and tried to anticipate the return of those troops who came back early (some wounded or worse) so their families could be notified. He also insisted on leadership presence on the troops' return and sent administrative teams to Fort Bliss and Camp Atterbury to help those installations put the Iroquois Warriors through the demobilization process quickly and efficiently.

In Iraq, there was no division headquarters yet the C2 Cell, and officers such as Jody Daniels and Ann Pellien, expended a great deal of effort to track where the division's soldiers were, what they were doing, and what their status was, particularly those wounded. Their efforts were not always successful, but logically, there need not have been any effort at all other than that provided by MNSTC-I—that is unless there was some sense of unity, an esprit, which existed to bring these individuals together as a team before the deployment. And indeed there was.

Although the Iroquois Warriors went to Iraq as individuals, they maintained their unit identity, if only psychologically, and often called on each other in ways that other members of the MNSTC-I would not. When Sherlock needed to organize the IAG, for example, he turned to the division C2 Cell to help form the new command. When he needed the Phoenix Academy created, he turned to the same group. When Shipman needed to create the MiTT that the 3d ACR failed to provide, he turned to other Iroquois Warriors to meet the need. When Parsons needed someone to help train the 5th Division staff on various staff skills, he turned to a 98th Division MTT. There was clearly a unit spirit maintained among the

Iroquois Warriors in Iraq that transcended the patch they wore on their left sleeve.

The part of the division that went to Iraq performed a wide array of missions for MNSTC-I and performed them, by all accounts, successfully. Almost overnight, the division was able to rapidly increase the staff capabilities of the MNSTC-I, CMATT, and CPATT. What was originally billed as a training mission, morphed into an advisory mission by the time the survey team developed its requirements assessment for LTG Petraeus. By March 2005, the division was manning over 30 MiTTs and had personnel serving on a number of others. In various other assignments, the 98th Division had soldiers serving in every province of Iraq, Kuwait, and Jordan.

Most Iroquois Warriors who served in Iraq agreed they were glad to get home, but also, they were proud of what they, and the "division," accomplished. Most also agreed the mission was a worthwhile experience. Many said they would be willing to do it again. They also believed what they accomplished contributed to the long-term success of a long-suffering country. Perhaps SGT Julian With from Schenectady, New York, packing to leave to go home in July 2005, said it best:

> This place is a learning experience to say the least. I have made several new friends and I have changed my opinion of the Iraqi culture. The people I have worked with have told me that because of me and the other Americans they come in contact with on a daily basis, that they have seen a different side to the Americans than what Saddam had taught them. They have been there to see us laugh and to see us cry when we lost some dear friends. It is weird—I can't wait to get home but at the same time I feel bad for leaving because I have made some very good Iraqi friends, but I understand that if they are to succeed they must do so on their own. It is kind of like raising a child and watching them take their first steps and hoping they don't fall flat on their face.[4]

In June 2006, the mission of training advisors for the Iraqi Army was transferred to the 1st Brigade, 1st Infantry Division at Fort Riley, Kansas. At about the same time, the 108th Division (IT) began taking over the MNSTC-I mission from the 80th Division. By 2007, a fourth USAR training division was identified to assume the mission that summer. From June 2004 on, the MNSTC-I evolved from an ad hoc group of individuals to an efficient command capable of training, advising, and supporting the

Iraqi Army. The advisory effort also evolved from a collection of soldiers who learned their new duties on the job to trained advisor teams with an understanding of their mission and who possessed effective advising methodologies.

The trends have been in the right direction, but the future still holds the answer to whether the Iroquois Warriors, along with the string of other Army Reservists who followed them, fully succeeded in helping MNSTC-I and the Iraqi Army keep from falling on their face. The answer will be revealed when, and if, the Iraqi Army finally assumes the lead in active combat operations in their own country and consistently wins.

Notes

1. LTC Joseph Friedman, interview by author, Combat Studies Institute, Fort Leavenworth, KS, 5 November 2006, 10. By several accounts from 98th Division personnel, the administrative procedures to outprocess the division's soldiers at Taji were broken. At the time of this writing, several officers and NCOs have not received their efficiency reports or end-of-tour awards.

2. Ibid.

3. Ibid., 11.

4. SGT Julian With, *Times Union Blog*, "Returning Home, 25 July 2005, available at http://blogs.timesunion.com/wartime/?p=42, accessed November 2006.

Chapter 8

Analysis and Conclusions

They should be justly proud of what they did.

LTG Petraeus

The activities of RC units in recent years have provided numerous revelations about the state of the Regular Army and the Reserves in the early 21st century. Most revelations, it is safe to say, have been in the positive column of the ledger. For the first time since the Korean War, the Army conducted a large-scale activation and deployment of RC units into war zones and did so in a relatively quick, smooth, and efficient manner. Moreover, the Army Reserve and National Guard units sent to Iraq and Afghanistan have been given meaningful and challenging missions that have enabled them to positively contribute to the war effort. This is especially true for the National Guard combat arms brigades sent to those theaters.

Unlike World Wars I and II, there has been no wholesale relief of RC general officers from their commands (and subsequent replacement by Regular Army officers) before their units deployed. Every RC command has deployed into theater under its assigned general officer commander, and the vast majority have remained in those commands throughout their combat tours. This is both a testament to the increase in executive ability and professionalism of the RC general officer ranks and to the trust and confidence placed in those abilities by the Regular Army.

Additionally, the US Army has seen an ever-increasing willingness to deploy National Guard division headquarters to places like Bosnia and Kosovo, as well as to Iraq, to command both active and RC brigades and battalions to conduct myriad and complex missions.

However, on the "improve" side of the ledger there are a few issues concerning the employment of RC units that this monograph has attempted to illustrate and that bear further analysis. Some of those are the use of Reserve units to perform non-METL missions, the use of Reserve units to provide individual fillers versus unit solutions to mission requirements, and the complications of AC/RC integration under the historical biases held by members of both components. There are also issues of a more general nature that are worth reviewing. These include the selection, training, and support of advisors and the issues associated with establishing ad hoc organizations. A further discussion of these issues is provided to educate Army leaders from all components, and all levels, for future consideration.

General Issues

Ad Hoc Organizations

MNSTC-I, an ad hoc organization, was assigned a crucial mission that needed to be performed even as it was being created. To be efficient and effective, it had to transition beyond ad hoc methods and procedures. To succeed, it had to function like a permanent organization with standardized routines and methods of operations. That capability, in large part, is what the 98th Division was able to contribute to the success of MNSTC-I's early efforts.

British military historian Sir Michael Howard once remarked, "I am tempted indeed to declare dogmatically that whatever doctrine the armed forces are working on now, they have got it wrong. I am also tempted to declare that it does not matter that they have got it wrong. What does matter is their capacity to get it right quickly when the moment arrives."[1] His quote is, at least, partially applicable for the US Army's situation immediately following the end of major combat operations in Iraq in 2003. The US Armed Forces were not prepared to rebuild the Iraqi Security Forces after the collapse of the Saddam regime. The US Army did not even have doctrine regarding rebuilding the armed forces of a defeated nation to get wrong.

What is applicable is that once the deed was done, the United States needed to begin rebuilding Iraqi military forces quickly and get it right. Whether it was done quickly is not within the purview of this work as the mission is still ongoing as this is written. More relevant is the question of whether we got it right. The definitive answer to that question will have to wait for history to unfold, but perhaps a preliminary attempt is appropriate.

MG Eaton received his mission to build three new Iraqi divisions in June 2003. Typically, SF units would be brought in to perform such a mission and some were; however, SF units, including the two National Guard groups, were already stretched thin with other missions in the GWOT. Thus, Eaton had to build an ad hoc training and advisory organization from the ground up. He did so by submitting various RFFs to fill the 330 plus trainer/advisor positions envisioned to support the initial three divisions. The personnel to fill these positions were acquired through the process of having Human Resources Command assign the requirements to commands throughout the Army. What Eaton ended up with was an array of soldiers who ran the gamut from Regular Army combat arms O/C teams from the Combat Training Centers and Marines (many of whom possessed actual combat experience) to noncombat arms soldiers from the RC and a sprinkling of Navy corpsmen. All were on orders for varying lengths of time, which caused a replacement nightmare.

The quality of advisor personnel that CMATT was receiving from its beginning in 2003 to September 2004 appears to have been as varied as their sources. Of course, quality is a relative term. Doubtless, nearly all were good soldiers, but some were not suited to the role of being a unit advisor by temperament and training. Most of the ASTs were collections of individuals who did not jell into functional teams until sometime into their deployment, if ever. As related earlier, BG Schwitters estimated that only about a third of those teams were effective in performing their duties with their Iraqi units.

When the 98th Division mobilization groups arrived in Iraq, what the CMATT received with the new ASTs was not far removed in terms of quality from the original teams. While none of the 98th teams were made up entirely of O/Cs or combat veterans, most (though not all) had been working together for at least 2 months and many of the individuals were familiar with each other because they often came from the same hometown units. Some were temperamentally suited to be advisors; some were not. The major difference was that the package CMATT received from the 98th at least possessed a uniform standard of training and all were in Iraq for a minimum of 9 to 10 months. The same was true for the personnel going to work on the various staffs and base support operations within MNSTC-I. What the 98th provided MNSTC-I, in addition to the work its soldiers performed, was some breathing space for transitioning from what was clearly an ad hoc seat-of-the-pants effort by CMATT under the CPA to what became a relatively well-structured organization (MNSTC-I) that had established an orderly process for integrating and rotating the follow-on units (i.e., the 80th and 108th Divisions). While the whole operation was not perfect, by the time the Iroquois Warriors left the record shows that at the very least they helped MNSTC-I to be well on its way to getting it right.

Adoption of LTG Helmly's concept for a permanent FA-TRAC would preclude many of the problems faced by Eaton and Petraeus when standing up an ad hoc effort like MNSTC-I. The command could focus on preparing for this mission during peacetime. When the next conflict materializes where rebuilding or retraining a foreign army becomes necessary, the

FA-TRAC could be reinforced with the needed parts of a training division and deployed to perform the mission for which they had been trained.

The FA-TRAC concept may require training divisions to assume another mission—that of advising foreign army units in addition to training an army. This, of course, would complement the mission provided by SF units, but would also require coordination with that community. The addition of that mission, in turn, requires the Army to create a doctrine for advising foreign forces so training divisions can develop viable and standardized training programs to meet requirements of an advisor mission.

Militating against such a plan is that in a period of limited budgets will the Army see value in maintaining such a specialized organization in the force structure? One senses that the answer, for now, might be yes given our experience in Iraq.

Non-METL Missions

Much of the argument over the decision to send a DIVIT to reinforce MNSTC-I centered on the skill sets needed for advisor duties versus the skill sets of the 98th Division soldiers. This facet of the debate is largely moot. The reality was that outside the Special Operations community, few, if any, soldiers or Marines are trained or educated in the skill sets peculiar to an advisor. As mentioned, SF soldiers were in high demand for other duties and thus not available. Logically, the next best-qualified soldiers to perform this job were probably O/Cs from the Army's various Combat Training Centers (CTCs), but they too were needed at their places of duty to support the war effort. Even so, some were sent over to be advisors under Eaton.

Some people have suggested there may have been better options than DIVITs. DiRisio thought so. "I think a training support division, which runs lanes training, would have been a much better fit. . . ." Those soldiers are, in essence, O/Cs. They help train and evaluate units on collective training tasks and therefore might have made better advisors than DIVIT soldiers. The argument against TSDs is that the large majority of their battalions perform their missions with combat support and combat service support units. There are some TSD training battalions that work with National Guard Combat Arms units and those might have been the next best option after the CTC O/Cs. However, just like COL Stafford's 3d Brigade at Camp Atterbury, many of those units were already engaged in training National Guard units for duty in Iraq or Afghanistan. Their availability was limited as well. As DiRisio added after his comment above, ". . . it's not always about fit. Sometimes it's about availability and we were available."[2]

Even though advising a foreign army was not in a DIVIT's METL, the Iroquois Warriors certainly possessed some of the skills needed for the advisor duties to which they were assigned. Several IA units actually went through basic training with their 98th Division advisors. Many others had just completed basic training and were still in the crawl mode when their advisors arrived. Very few IA battalions had actually experienced combat before their new advisors showed up. As MAJ Swartwood discovered, even for the few units that had been in combat, there were still things the Iroquois Warriors could teach them. Those advisors who had been CAS3 and CGSC instructors had a great deal to offer the staffs of the units to which they were assigned.

Perhaps a more pertinent question here is not whether the 98th Division possessed the right skill sets for the initial rotation to Iraqi, but whether the 80th and 108th Divisions possessed the skill sets needed when they arrived. When the 80th Division arrived, the Iraqi units would have been a year older in age and experience. The skill sets and tactical and technical knowledge needed to advise them would have been more advanced. Instead of basic tactical knowledge at the platoon and company level, the advisors might need to advise and teach about integrating air support in battalion offensive operations. As each rotation takes place, the follow-on advisors would have to be ever more capable and knowledgeable about ground force operations at the appropriate levels (company, battalion, brigade, and division).

Of course, training skills were not the key requirement for success in an advisor mission. Schwitters explained the essence of what *was* required: "We needed people who were temperamentally and experientially trained to go in, put their arms around a bunch of folks, and develop relationships from which they could then influence action and behavior and develop capabilities." By that standard, few units, other than SF, would meet the need. One will search in vain for such a task on any conventional unit METL. Yet the need was there, so the Army did what it often does by taking units that are not trained to perform a certain mission or task and gives it to them anyway. That is the situation the Army has found itself in many times in the past, is finding itself in now, and will find itself in again in the future. The important thing, as Michael Howard said, is for units that get non-METL missions to get it right as quickly as possible.

MG James A. Kelly, now the Deputy Assistant Secretary of Defense for Reserve Affairs, recently described the old training model for RC units as "mobilize, train, deploy."[3] In other words, the idea was that the critical collective training required to make the unit actually deployable into a given theater would take place after the unit was mobilized and before it deployed. The model that USARC wants to move to is "train, mobilize, deploy," which means the unit would master its wartime METL tasks before it was mobilized. That approach is laudable and perhaps in many cases achievable. Unless the Army creates the FA-TRAC or similar command, it is a model that will not work for cases like the 98th Division in Iraq. As long as units are assigned to non-METL missions, there will always be a need for an extensive training period (approximately 45 to 90 days) to enable that unit to perform the mission to at least an adequate level. This is true of any unit, Active Component or Reserve Component.

Advisor Specific Issues

Training for the Advisor Mission

Despite the unfavorable evaluation that many 98th Division soldiers, and others, have expressed about the training at Camp Atterbury, the reality is that the training they received there was, at the very least, a solid foundation for many of the tactical and technical skills they needed in Iraq. That is not to say that the time allotted was always adequately used or that the classes were perfect, but the evidence indicates the training conducted was a good refresher for many reservists who had not touched a rifle, put on a protective mask, or conducted preventive maintenance checks and services on a military vehicle for years. The collective training was also a good springboard for the realistic training conducted in Kuwait. The training at Camp Virginia constituted what was in essence a mini-CTC event before the troops moved into the actual area of operations. The Camp Atterbury experience helped the Iroquois Warriors get through the "walk" level of those tasks, so they could maximize their training experience in Kuwait. They were far enough along in experience at Camp Virginia that they were not trying to play "catch up" on unfamiliar tasks taught in a very compressed and comprehensive way.

Unfortunately, the 98th Division ASTs did not get the benefit of the Phoenix Academy experience since it was established well after their arrival in Iraq. It seems odd that someone did not realize much earlier that education like that provided by the Phoenix Academy was needed. Nevertheless, once that shortfall was recognized, Schwitters and Sherlock moved quickly to make the academy a reality. It is impossible to surmise exactly what difference it would have made had the Iroquois Warriors gone through such a course, but it would have at least made them more familiar with the realities and responsibilities of the advisor mission before they arrived at their IA unit.

In planning for future advisor operations, perhaps even as part of a future FA-TRAC, the Army should plan for a Phoenix Academy-type course from the beginning of an operation to provide at least a minimal understanding of the complex nature of the advisor mission. The required education should include experiential events. The "building relationship" skills that Schwitters said were critical for advisors cannot be trained. They do not lend themselves well to the "task, condition, and standards" model. They are part of the art of war, not the science of war. Thus, they must be part of an education process, not a training event. This means that the subjects primarily require intellectual exercise, such as reading assignments and courses that provide an understanding of the country's culture, customs, and mores. Ideally, frequent and detailed interaction with seasoned advisors and a cross section of members of the target country would be best for helping the future advisor to understand how to build relationships with citizens and soldiers of that country.

Further, given information-age realities, an on-line advisor course that provides exposure to advisory experiences and responsibilities universal in nature would help soldiers in the future acquire knowledge earlier in the preparation process. Such a course would be especially valuable to RC soldiers.

Finally, the Army should consider developing doctrine that can be used by conventional forces on those occasions when they are assigned to an advisory-type mission. The doctrine can then form the foundation for developing training and education such as that provided at Camp Atterbury, Camp Virginia, and the Phoenix Academy.

Advisor Selection

In discussing the kinds of people needed to fill the job of an advisor, one hears most frequently two requirements: "They have to want to be an advisor," and "they have to be from among the best soldiers." If the mission is relatively small, those two requirements might be met through requesting volunteers and then screening the records of and interviewing those who volunteer. If the mission generally requires many soldiers, establishing a procedure to find out who wants to be there and defining whether a soldier is among the best is probably too cumbersome and slow. Also militating against such an approach is that such duties are not considered "plum" jobs and therefore not career enhancing. Few will actually volunteer and most of those will probably not be among the best—depending on the definition of "best."

When the 98th Division received the mission, the division staff did try to work those two requirements into their selection process. Most soldiers eventually assigned to the advisor teams were volunteers for the job. Some volunteers were actually screened out due to physical fitness scores, medical records, and other issues. The records for all advisors, including those few who did not volunteer, were screened to ensure the best possible mix of soldiers was being assigned to the teams. Of course, this process still did not ensure that everyone assigned to the ASTs wanted to be there, or were the "best," but it likely minimized or eliminated problems that would have arisen from a purely objective selection process that considered only soldiers' personnel files.

Advisor Logistics Support

Many of the 98th Division's advisors say that the logistics support to their team was inadequate at best and terrible at worst. Among their chief complaints was the lack of luxuries and distractions that normally grace any US installation. There was no Burger King or pizzeria. There was no movie theater or television. There was no post exchange at which to buy the niceties to which US soldiers have become accustomed. On the other hand, the necessities—food, water, and ammunition—were rarely, if ever, a problem. In fact, as a number of advisors related, they often ate with their Iraqi soldiers and their meals, ready to eat (MREs) piled up so there was always plenty of food. Actually, the lack of such facilities was arguably a good thing for an advisory effort. As Schwitters explained, setting up business in a "Little America" when advising foreign troops was not good practice because it runs contrary to the idea that the advisor should share the same deprivations as those he advises.

Soldiers selected for advisor duties need to understand that they will likely be operating in an environment that is Spartan in terms of creature comforts. The expectations of advisors should be that they will be sustained in more or less the same fashion and to the same level of comfort as those they are advising. Living beyond that level to any great degree begins to erode credibility with their advisees by creating envy and perhaps the impression that the advisor is too good to live as the locals do.

Reserve Component Specific Issues

Preparedness of Reserve Component Soldiers

The Reserve Components have made tremendous strides toward higher standards of professionalism over the past 30 years. Unlike their counterparts from the Vietnam and immediate Post-Vietnam era, National Guard and Army Reserve soldiers of today are largely indistinguishable from their active duty counterparts. Like the senior leaders of the Regular Army in the 1980s and 1990s, senior RC leaders of the same period strove to improve standards of readiness, conduct, appearance, and fitness in their commands, and they have succeeded. Granted, the reservist is sometimes not as well rounded in purely military experience as active duty soldiers and, collectively, reservists tend to be slightly older than regulars holding similar positions. But such is the nature of the Reserve Components and therefore is not likely to change.

There is a mindset among some reservists that being in the Reserves shields a soldier from overseas deployments, especially to combat zones. Since DESERT STORM, this mindset has been gradually dying away, especially among National Guard and USAR TOE units. The reality is that the US Army, as currently structured, cannot conduct any sizable operation without RC units. The Army has become too small in the post-Cold War era to operate without the Reserves, and it will likely remain so for the foreseeable future. Indeed, since 2003 the Army has assigned Guard and Reserve units to the Iraq and Afghanistan long-term rotation schedules and will continue to do so. Thus for TOE units, an active duty stint has become a fact for which RC soldiers must plan.

There are many TDA-type organizations, like the USAR training divisions, that historically have not deployed. The mobilization of the 98th Division, and of those divisions that followed it, illustrates that all reservists are now a possible source of manpower to help the war effort. The Reserve Components are truly an operational reserve and, unlike previous eras, will likely be used as such from now on.

Regular Army—Reserve Component Biases Analysis

Historically, tension between Regulars and part-time soldiers has existed virtually since the beginning of the Republic. Unfortunately, it remains today, despite the obvious advancements in professionalism and readiness made by the Reserve Components in the last 30 years. Primarily, Regular Army soldiers who often see Army Reservists and National Guardsmen as less disciplined, less prepared, less dedicated, and less competent generate most of the tension.

RC soldiers contribute to the tension as well. They are convinced the regulars do not value the contributions and capabilities they bring to the table that might be (and sometimes are) superior to what a Regular unit can provide. Thus, when they are activated and assigned to a Regular Army headquarters, they often arrive convinced they will be treated as second-class soldiers regardless of how well they perform.

Contributing to this historical tension is the experience of National Guard and Army Reserve units in previous conflicts. In World War I, many

National Guard units were broken up and consolidated with other units to meet the table of organization requirements of the newly adopted divisional structure. This action led to the loss of commands by a number of Guard regimental and brigade commanders when their units were made a part of others, causing animosity among both leaders and men. Later in the war, many other National Guard leaders, especially brigade commanders, were relieved for incompetence and replaced by Regular Army officers, which often caused further frustration for the Guardsmen whether the relieves were justified or not.

During the mobilization for World War II, once again many old National Guard units were organized out of existence. By the end of 1942, almost all of the original commanding generals of the 18 National Guard divisions and numerous brigade and regimental commanders were relieved for age and incompetence. Regardless of the propriety, those actions contributed to the National Guard's distrust of the Regular Army. In the case of the Army Reserve, none of its hundreds of units were activated for service under the officers who had served in them before the war. Reservists were brought on active duty only as individuals and rarely given commands of any significance. There were some but very few, especially if one considers that the vast majority of officers serving in the Army during World War II were reservists, yet few commands at regiment and above were held by Reserve officers.[4]

If one fast forwards to the first Gulf War and examines the experiences of the 48th and 256th Infantry Brigades, one sees fodder for both sides of the issue. A few units of the 256th Brigade demonstrated some serious leadership deficits and disciplinary problems. The 48th Brigade failed to measure up to the standards of the National Training Center (NTC). The NTC's Regular Army O/Cs gave the brigade low marks on most of its missions and the Guardsmen were quick to claim the regulars were just out to get them—to make the Guard look bad.

In some respects, the situation faced by the troops of the 98th Division does not seem too far removed from earlier times; for example, the decision not to deploy Robinson and the division headquarters to Iraq. In this case, however, the decision was probably a good one. There was no need for duplication of leadership and structure that already existed in CMATT. Also, sending those soldiers headed for the headquarters staffs and several other positions as individual fillers rather than as part of a unit deployment was also the best method to support the mission.

The reception of the division soldiers who arrived to supplement the MNSTC-I and CMATT headquarters was, for some, abrasive and cold.

They believed, and with some justification, that there was little effort to integrate the Iroquois Warriors into the headquarters in such a way to make them feel part of the team. This reinforced the natural tendency to try and maintain their identity as 98th Division soldiers. The desire to retain their identity may in turn have exacerbated the problem and caused at least one senior officer on the CMATT staff to accuse the Reserve personnel in that headquarters of setting up a parallel 98th Division communications system to pass division-specific information, which in fact was true.

The biases between regulars and reservists in the advisor teams appear to have been less pronounced, perhaps because of the proximity and sharing of danger; however, it did exist to some extent. MAJ Swartwood remembered there was some dissension between the regulars at brigade and his team simply because "we were reservists and they were Regular Army guys."[5] Some of the friction may have been justified as several Iroquois Warriors admitted that some team members probably complained about their situation more than they should have. Others indicated that some troops just did not want to be there and were not suitable to be advisors. That too, could have caused some ill will between the soldiers of the two components.

In fairness to the regulars, not all interaction between the two components was bad. Division soldiers, for example, were complimentary of the way LTG Petraeus seemed to interact with them. They truly believed he was glad they were there (and he admitted as much). Petraeus was able to get BG Sherlock assigned to a position of importance when he was assigned as the first CG of IAG (incidentally, a position also held by the ADC of each follow-on Reserve division). Additionally, regardless of their first impressions, many regulars warmed up to the reservists once they saw that the Iroquois Warriors were rolling up their sleeves and going to work trying to contribute to the war effort just like everybody else. The shame is that those impressions were not there initially, thus avoiding much antagonism and perhaps misunderstanding.

To help reduce this friction, the Army should look for ways to increase AC/RC interaction on a more formal basis during peacetime. After Vietnam, the US Army began to shift its focus back to fighting a Soviet invasion of Europe and a North Korean invasion of South Korea. The Reserve Components made up a major portion of the troops identified to be mobilized and deployed to either location to fight the war. As a result, a program called "Capstone" identified various RC units that would fall under Regular Army corps and divisions for mobilization purposes. Headquarters and subordinate units affiliated with Capstone RC units became involved in supporting those units' training, advising the units at training events, and conducting the external evaluation of the units during annual training (AT). As a result, Regular Army leaders at the brigade level and down had relatively frequent contact with RC personnel and organizations.

After the Berlin Wall came down and the Soviet threat died, the Capstone program also died. Though there was, for a time, an affiliation program, primarily for National Guard enhanced brigades, contact between regulars and reservists became less frequent. The primary contact between Reserve units and Regular Army units since 2001 (and perhaps even before) has been when an RC unit has shown up in theater to conduct actual operations under a Regular Amy headquarters (and sometimes vice-versa). As a result, few Regular Army personnel, outside those serving in TSDs, have an appreciation for the true nature and actual capabilities of RC units.

Exacerbating this problem has been that, historically, relatively few Regular Army officers ever serve a tour of duty with an RC unit. For Regulars, duty with the RC is not seen as career enhancing and few seek such an opportunity. In the case of many current senior Army leaders, their experience with and opinions about the Reserves were formed when most were lieutenants and captains in the immediate post-Vietnam era when the Capstone program was in effect. For many, and perhaps most, of them, that is the last time they have had any meaningful contact with an RC unit. Thus, their opinions were formed 25 to 35 years ago when many National Guard and Reserve units possessed the image of rolling to the field with ice chests full of soda and barbeque grills in the bustle racks—an image that is no longer valid. Many of those leaders have little or no first-hand understanding of the various problems that face an RC unit in terms of training, recruiting, retention, and readiness. Thus, a common prejudice against the Reserves is based on an inability to fully understand the true nature of RC units and their personnel, and the issues that militate against full readiness.[6]

Because of their lack of direct experience with Reserve units, Regular Army leaders also fail to understand that reservists will often come to them with valuable individual skills that are not readily apparent. For example, a group of reservists that are predominantly engineers may arrive for assignment to the command, but what is badly needed is a comptroller. It just may be that one of those engineers is a Wall-Street banking executive in his professional life and far more qualified for the position than any Regular Army finance officer. However, because the personnel manager only tries to fit round pegs in round holes, he fails to learn that one of those engineers is just the soldier he is looking for to fill the comptroller slot. Thus, the slot goes unfilled and the engineer officer, who may not have worked in his branch for years, now goes to the engineer staff.

Integration of RC units and personnel into a Regular Army command (and vice-versa incidentally) is a leadership issue. Any leader who recalls having his platoon or company cross-attached to another command vividly recalls how his unit, and he, was treated. If the gaining commander pulled in that platoon, fed it, armed it, and maintained it, that commander typically received a significantly increased capability to his command and a set of leaders and soldiers who were ready, willing, and able to be part of the team. If those troops were the last to be fed, could not get fuel, and were always given the worst missions, trust in the gaining unit would rapidly decline along with the willingness to do any more than what was specifically ordered.

Regular Army commanders and leaders should also be knowledgeable of what they are getting when an RC unit arrives and what they can truly expect in terms of capabilities. In the past, they could not expect a unit that has worked together for more than 38 or 39 days a year and that had gone through more than what was likely a minimally adequate mobilization training cycle somewhere before deployment. With the new Army Force Generation (ARFORGEN) model of training, this may not be the challenge it has been in the past.

Under ARFORGEN, each RC unit will enter a 6-year cycle that consists of three distinct phases or pools. The first phase consists of units in the Reset/Train pool. These units are in the process of recruiting and training at the individual level for about 3½ years. The units then enter the Ready Force pool where they are given additional resources that may include:

- Increases in specialty training, schools, and active duty positions for Active Guard-Reserve personnel.
- Increases in Active Component advisors.
- Increases in training days per year.
- Increases in training days per AT period.
- Increases in assigned equipment for training on collective tasks.
- Priority for school slots.
- Priority for mobile training teams.

These units will experience a higher operational tempo and more training at the higher levels of collective training tasks. At the end of this 1½-year period, the units enter the 1-year Available Force pool and are eligible for mobilization and deployment.[7]

Even with these additional resources, an RC unit will still not be at the same readiness level as their Active Component counterparts. Commanders must plan to give these units missions they can handle and give them greater responsibility as they grow in experience and capability. Most importantly, commanders and leaders must work to integrate these units and individuals into their commands as smoothly and efficiently as possible knowing that they might show up with the expectation of being treated differently than those units of soldiers habitually assigned to the commander's own organization. That expectation can be quickly quashed by accepting those RC units on an equal basis and making their leaders feel that way too. That sense of belonging will quickly communicate to the unit's subordinates and the integration will be as smooth as can be expected.

The attitude and conduct of RC unit leaders is equally important. Arriving with a defensive or protective attitude can cause the Regulars to feed any prejudices that might exist and can infect the unit's subordinate soldiers. Additionally, RC leaders should realize that they will likely have to integrate outsiders into their own ranks. Several reservists who were fillers to the 98th, for example, perceived some indifference toward them when it came to their integration into the various division teams. Some felt largely ignored or kept in the dark as to what their assignments would be until they arrived at Taji. Given the nature of Reserve mobilization requirements, it is likely there will always be some number of fillers needed to bring the unit up to strength. For the purposes of efficiency and the unit mission, IRR soldiers should be integrated just as if they had always been part of the organization.

Finally, it is interesting to note how much emphasis in the past 20 years has been put on the need for jointness in the US military. The idea is for senior leaders of each branch to come to know the capabilities, attitudes, obstacles, needs, and even the culture of the other services. This, in turn, should increase the capabilities of joint force operations and planning. Very little emphasis has been paid to the need of the Army's three components to really understand each other's capabilities, issues, attitudes, obstacles, and culture. That shortfall is particularly true for the Regular Army for several reasons. First, many reservists and Guardsmen have served in the Regular Army. They generally begin learning about the Active Component by living the experience. The same, of course, is not true for Regulars. Second, more positions are offered to reservists in an active duty environment than to Regulars to serve with Troop Program Unit (TPU) soldiers who are the bulk of RC personnel. Thus, Reserve leaders are far more exposed to the Regular Army than is the opposite case. Finally, the careers of Regular Army leaders who show promise are carefully managed and few end up serving with the Reserves. (General of the Army George C. Marshall, who served with the Illinois National Guard before World War II, was a notable exception.) Thus, most of them never have any meaningful experience with (and therefore an inadequate understanding of) the RC program and its units. Since these officers are required by law to serve in joint assignments before they can advance to the general officer ranks, the Army ends up with senior leaders who potentially understand more about the Air Force or Navy than they do about two-thirds of their own service.

Perhaps the Army should consider making a tour at the National Guard Bureau, in the Office of the Chief of the Army Reserve, at the US Army Reserve Command, and a few other select headquarters a requirement for promotion to brigadier general. Such assignments would be considered career-enhancing and thus expose some of those officers who will eventually rise to high commands (almost all of which will include RC units) to the realities of Reserve Component programs. One would surmise that it might also help decrease the historical tension between the components, thus making for a more efficient and capable Total Army.

Derivative Unit Identification Codes versus Unit Identification Codes Analysis

The 98th Division deployed about 750 troops (about 600 of which were originally assigned to the division) to Iraq on 125 DUICs. Some DUICs had only one person assigned to them. At least one DUIC was created for every subordinate unit in the division and some units had several DUICs. Additionally, the First Army created split DUICs when some division personnel who were sent to Fort Bliss were later required to go through the training at Camp Atterbury. New orders were cut creating sub-DUICs for those troops. What resulted was a personnel management nightmare for the division and the J-staff at MNSTC-I, because each soldier had to be tracked by the DUIC.

The 98th's G1 wanted to send the division's personnel over on five UICs. The plan was to transfer into those units all deploying personnel and transfer out nondeploying personnel to stay-behind units. This option allowed the division to send over personnel in recognized unit packages, making personnel management easier, and it would give those units combat credit for the deployment. Barring that, they wanted to create five DUICs, which would still make the personnel management of the deployment more efficient. USARC denied that too.

The net result of this, besides the management problems, was that neither the 98th Division nor any of its subordinate *units* deployed to Iraq.

In actuality 750 individual filler personnel, who just happened to be from the same command, were sent over for the mission. Only those units, if any, which contributed at least 65 percent of their assigned personnel to a DUIC that deployed to Iraq will receive campaign credit for what the troops accomplished, despite the fact that over 300 division soldiers served in combat, 5 of them were killed, and another 15 were wounded in action or suffered injuries.[8]

Collectively, division personnel are very proud of their service in Iraq and what they accomplished while there. Unit pride—esprit-de-corps—can be a combat multiplier. Ask any soldier who has served with the Big Red One or the Screaming Eagles. Soldiers are very proud of their units and especially their part in creating the legacy of that unit. That is as true for Army Reserve and National Guard units as it is for any Regular Army outfit. It certainly was (and is) true of the Iroquois Warriors. If anyone doubts that, one just needs to point to the efforts by division soldiers to be recognized as such by surreptitiously wearing the division patch even after orders were issued to remove them. While one cannot condone such actions, one can still respect the spirit behind it.

There were other problems associated with the use of DUICs as well. Sherlock described them in a 2006 interview:

> I think the worst thing we ever did was to get good at DUICs, but there's a larger problem than that. The way the Army deployed in 2002 and 2003 is that we ended up taking a lot of pieces and parts of units—Active, Guard and Reserve—as opposed to taking complete units. We also took a lot of capacity early, which burns some parts of the mobilization clock on soldiers. So as you had to go back and then get another military police or engineer unit, you ended up not having whole units to take. As such, you ended up taking individuals and filling out another derivative. And once you start into that process, you end up spending the rest of the time chasing your tail. Instead of taking the entire requirement for 750 soldiers, transfer-ring all of them into an AAUIC like the 2d Brigade of the 98th and deploying a brigade so you have a structure—a unit you can then still individually task organize to sup-port whatever MNSTC-I needed to do, because obviously you're going to meet the requirements on the ground—instead of that, we went in 125 derivatives of two, three, and four soldiers each, and then we also went with about 300 individual-based sets of orders. So instead of taking

what was envisioned as a unit-based solution, we became a unit pool for the solution.[9]

Sherlock went on to add,

> . . . it was hard on the soldiers because, in many cases, it brought on what I thought was the worst of both worlds. We were treated as a unit when it was convenient for us to be treated as a unit and we were treated as individuals when it was convenient for us to be treated as individuals. For example, when I went in and said, 'I need to look at equipping this' or 'I need this kind of support,' in some cases I would hear, 'Well, that's a 98th Division problem, deal with it.' And then when I would go in and say, 'Wait a minute, why are we taking this group of soldiers and re-missioning them and sending them somewhere else?' I was sometimes told, 'Well, you guys didn't come as a unit, you guys came as individuals, so we're going to use you as individuals.'[10]

Of course, there was no way to avoid entirely using DUICs in the situation faced by the 98th Division. Many of those requirements were clearly and simply individual-based and a DUIC was the best way to handle them. However, it would have been logical and relatively easy to identify several subordinate UICs and task organize the ASTs so that units were deployed vice individuals, thus allowing a unit command structure for management purposes and ensure that some of the division's subordinate units receive earned combat credit. As it stands now, most, if not all, campaign credit earned by the 98th's soldiers will disappear with MNSTC-I when it is disbanded on the conclusion of the Army's participation in the conflict.

The reason for the inability to credit properly the 98th Division units and soldiers for what they accomplished can be largely laid on the use of DUICs for deploying troops. The Army should seek ways to deploy units rather that individuals where possible, especially if a unit is contributing a large number of soldiers to the deployment. If that requires taking an existing organization like the 98th Division and task organizing it for the mission by reassigning personnel to a few subordinate units, where it can be done it should be done. For the sake of unit integrity and esprit-de-corps, the Army should strive to make a unit's contributions mean something more than a passing mention in the history books. To its credit, the Army has recognized the division's efforts with the Army Superior Unit Award, but no campaign streamer for Iraq will grace the division colors and may not for any of its subordinate units.

Assessing the Performance of the 98th Division

In various interviews and other discussions with soldiers associated with the 98th Division's mission to Iraq, it was apparent that the division's leaders, MG Robinson and BG Sherlock, were pushing hard to participate in LTG Helmly's concept of a FA-TRAC. Some people felt that the generals' intent in trying to get the division involved was driven by a desire to "save" the 98th Division. At the time, the DA and the USARC were considering (and are currently implementing) a series of changes that would considerably alter the configuration of the institutional and training support divisions in the USAR. Some divisions were to be downsized; others could be eliminated from the force structure. The belief among some people then, was that the two generals were trying to ensure the 98th Division was not eliminated as part of the restructuring plan—another illustration of the unit esprit in the division. Others intimated that the generals were simply trying to make the 98th a relevant part of the GWOT or perhaps they were just trying to support Helmly's efforts to get the Army Reserve out of its Cold War paradigm by taking on a nontraditional mission that seemed to generally fit the organization's METL. Still others just saw it as personal ambition.

Whatever the reason for their effort, the two generals were successful both in saving the division (although it appears now that it will be reduced to a one-star command and placed under a larger Army Reserve training command) and in getting the Iroquois Warriors more directly involved in the war effort. In retrospect, their efforts were timely from the standpoint that MNSTC-I needed to rapidly increase its capabilities in numerous areas at a critical time and the 98th Division was able to adequately fill many of those requirements. Whether the effort to get involved in the first place was a good idea or a bad one is arguable.

From the beginning, at least as far as Helmly and the division leaders were concerned, the USARC and FORSCOM headquarters were against the idea of using a USAR training division for reinforcing MNSTC-I. The arguments, as related before, were focused on the skill sets needed for the mission versus what the division could provide, the combat related aspects of the mission, and the need for the division to perform its TASS missions, among others. Not everybody in the MNSTC-I and subordinate headquarters was convinced it was a good idea either. Schwitters assessed the use of a DIVIT for the mission this way:

> . . . they were largely comprised of Total Army School System guys who taught Army schools within the Reserve Component, and we had drill sergeants—NCOs

and units—that were prepared to mobilize and take over the institutional training operations for the Army. Those aren't the skill sets that are uniquely suited to go into another culture, influence organizations and develop them in the manner that this mission required. They were, by experience and training, designed to give instruction or be drill sergeants, which weren't the skills we needed.

However, the general soberly added, " . . . while it wasn't a perfect solution, there wasn't a better one we could execute given the very clear and compelling timelines we had to operate against."[11]

Of course, there were those in the 98th Division itself who would agree with all or some of the foregoing arguments. Some of them chose to retire early and at least one refused to obey his mobilization orders. The vast majority of Iroquois Warrior soldiers, even those that might have disagreed with the idea of sending a training division to Iraq, patriotically answered their call and did their duty.

In spite of all the resistance to the idea from USARC, FORSCOM, and others, the gaining commander for whom the division's troops would work in Iraq clearly stood on the "good idea" side of the debate. Like Schwitters, Petraeus realized the DIVIT option was not the ideal solution to his needs. Still, he said of the Iroquois Warriors under his command, "We were happy to have them. We were just glad to get somebody over there to help us out—and the sooner the better." The general went on to say that, in retrospect, the division did a good job in Iraq:

I think they should be justly proud of what they did. In some cases they did missions for which they were completely suited; in other cases, just like everybody else in Iraq, they did missions that were not familiar to them and they responded admirably in each case. . . . To say we couldn't have done it without . . . the 98th would be a huge understatement, so they ought to look on this episode in their history with pride.[12]

Interviews conducted for this project with the members of the 98th Division reveal that those Iroquois Warriors who participated in the mission are indeed proud of their accomplishments and stand on the positive side too. Sherlock was particularly pleased with how quickly the division was able to deploy over there and pitch in:

On 18 June [LTG Cody] said, 'Okay, the mission is approved. Go do it.' Then less than a week later, we launched the first three of our 13-member survey teams to CRC, to Iraq less than 3 weeks later, and followed with the rest of the survey team about 2 weeks after that. So from being given mission approval to having people in Iraq was less than 3 weeks. From getting mission approval to having the survey completed in Iraq was about 7 weeks. And from getting mission approval to having the first soldiers on the ground in Iraq to start performing that mission was essentially 4 months. By mid-September we had soldiers arriving, which was a very fast flash-to-bang time had that been an Active Army unit. But it was also a very fast flash-to-bang time for what had been a generating force institutional training division that had not been heretofore thought of as an overseas deployment asset.[13]

The division was able to accomplish its assigned missions despite the lack of adequate information about the true nature of the mission and the relative inexperience of the soldiers selected to perform it. The overall experience was often likened by Robinson, Sherlock, and others, to building an aircraft as it was rolling down the runway on take-off. Still, when all was said and done, the soldiers of the 98th Division believed they had successfully accomplished everything that was asked of them. MAJ Loncle expressed his satisfaction this way:

> I think it was really successful given the limitations I saw. Could it have been better? Yes. There was a big disconnect between what we were told we were going to be doing and what actually happened. But when people hit the ground and figured out which direction was up, if you will, they all marched forward and did what they could do to various levels of success, no doubt. With the units I worked with, I know I saw improvement over the course of time we spent with them. I left them better than I found them, so I'll count that as success.[14]

MAJ McConnell was more emphatic. He said, "I really think the 98th Division made a huge impact and [provided] a great [example] as far as what can be done with American soldiers and institutional training divisions. I was very proud of that."[15]

When examining the results of the 98th Division's deployment to Iraq from 2004 to 2005, one notes that, while not everything went perfectly in each of the division's areas of endeavor, each mission was performed well enough to be deemed a success. This may seem to be damning with faint praise, but such is not the case. When one considers the obstacles facing the division in securing the mission; training for the mission; and deploying for, integrating into, and conducting the mission, it seems a wonder that its soldiers performed their myriad assignments as well as they did. The 98th Division's performance is a testament to the ever-increasing professionalism of the Army's Reserve Component soldiers and their leaders. The Iroquois Warriors should indeed be justly proud of what they accomplished.

Notes

1. Michael Howard, "Military Science in an Age of Peace," *Journal of the Royal United Services Institute for Defence Studies* 119 (March 1974) : 4.

2. LTC James DiRisio, interview by author, Headquarters, 98th Division (IT), Rochester, NY, 3 November 2006, 12.

3. MG James A. Kelly, interview by Laurence Lessard, Operational Leadership Experience Project, Combat Studies Institute, Fort Leavenworth, KS, 8 February 2007.

4. For an analysis of the relief of National Guard senior leaders in World Wars I and II from the National Guard perspective, see *The Minute Man in Peace and War: A History of the National Guard* by Jim Dan Hill, Stackpole Books, 1964. For another perspective on World War II, see Mark S. Watson, *United States Army in World War II, The War Department, Chief of Staff: Prewar Plans and Preparations*, Historical Division, US Army, 1950.

5. MAJ Roger Swartwood, interview by author, Headquarters, 98th Division (IT), Rochester, NY, 3 November 2006, 10.

6. To gain an appreciation of the lack of direct and prolonged experience senior Army leaders have with RC units, one only has to review the assignments listed on their official biographies. While these documents are not comprehensive in terms of an officer's actual contact with RC units and personnel, they are accurate in terms of which assignments the officer has had with an RC unit or headquarters whereby direct and prolonged contact is ensured.

7. Mr. Nathan Godwin, Headquarters, US Army Forces Command, telephone interview with the author, 3 April 2007.

8. Ms. Denise Harris, Policy Section, Military Awards Branch, US Army Human Resources Command, e-mail to author, Subject: Campaign Credit for the 98th Division, 19 March 2007; Headquarters, 98th Division, Excel Spreadsheet, "Active Casualty/Injury Report," 18 August 2006.

9. BG Richard Sherlock, interview by author, Office, Chief of the Army Reserve, Pentagon, Washington, DC, 16 November 2006, 12.

10. Ibid.

11. BG James Schwitters, telephone interview by author, Combat Studies Institute, Fort Leavenworth, KS, 13 December 2006, 2.

12. LTG David H. Petraeus, interview by author, Headquarters, Combined Arms Center, Fort Leavenworth, KS, 11 December 2006, 13–14.

13. Sherlock interview, 16 November 2006, 4.

14. MAJ Paul Loncle, interview by author, Headquarters, 98th Division (IT), Rochester, NY, 4 November 2006, 8.

15. MAJ Scott McConnell, telephone interview by author, Combat Studies Institute, Fort Leavenworth, KS, 12 December 2006, 13.

About the Author

Steven E. Clay, LTC (USA Retired), spent his 27-year Army career in mechanized infantry units (including two tours with the Big Red One) and in educating and training soldiers and leaders. From 1997 to 2006, he worked at the Combat Studies Institute (CSI), Fort Leavenworth, KS, in the following positions: executive officer; Chief, Staff Ride Team; and Chief, Research and Publications Team. He currently works for CSI as a contracted research historian. Mr. Clay's published works include *Blood and Sacrifice: A History of the 16th Infantry from the Civil War to the Gulf War* and is co-author of CSI's *Staff Ride Handbook for the Overland Campaign: A Study in Operational-Level Command.*

Glossary

1SG	first sergeant
2LT	second lieutenant
AAFES	Army and Air Force Exchange Service
AAR	after action report
ACR	Armored Cavalry Regiment
ADC	assistant division commander
ADVON	advanced party
AIT	advanced individual training
AKMTB	Al Kasik Military Training Base
ANA	Afghanistan National Army
AO	area of operations
AOR	area of responsibility
APFT	Army Physical Fitness Test
AR	Army regulation
ARFORGEN	Army Force Generation
ARTEP	Army Training and Evaluation Program
AST	Advisor Support Team
AT	annual training
BCT	basic combat training
BDU	battle dress uniform
BFT	Blue Force Tracker
BFV	Bradley Fighting Vehicle
BG	brigadier general
BIAP	Baghdad International Airport
Bn	battalion
C2	command and control
C3	command, control, communications
CAR	Chief, Army Reserve
CAS	Close Air Support
CAS3	Combined Arms and Services Staff School
CAV	Cavalry
CCC	Civilian Conservation Corps
CD	compact disc
CENTCOM	US Army Central Command
CFLCC	Coalition Forces Land Component Command
CG	commanding general
CGSC	Command and General Staff College
CGSOC	Command and General Staff Officer Course
CIF	Central Issue Facility
CJTF-7	Combined Joint Task Force-7
CLS	Combat Life Saver
CMATT	Coalition Military Assistance Transition Team
CMO	Civil Military Operations

CMTC	Combat Maneuver Training Center (Hohenfels, Germany)
COA	course of action
COIN	counterinsurgency
COL	colonel
Col.	colonel (Air Force and Marines)
CONUS	continental United States
COSCOM	Corps Support Command
COTTAD	Contingency Operation Temporary Tour of Active Duty
CP	command post
CPA	Coalition Provisional Authority
CPATT	Coalition Police Assistance Training Team
CPT	captain
CPX	command post exercise
CRC	Continental United States Replacement Center
CSM	command sergeant major
CSS	combat service support
CST	common specialist training
C-Staff	Combined Staff
	C1 = Personnel and Administration Section
	C2 = Intelligence Section
	C3 = Operations and Training Section
	C4 = Logistics Section
CTC	Combat Training Center
CTT	common task test
CXO	command executive officer
DA	Department of the Army
DEF	Defense
Div	Division
DIVIT	Division (Institutional Training)
DOD	Department of Defense
DUIC	Derivative Unit Identification Code
DVD	digital video disc
EOD	Explosive Ordnance Disposal
e.g.	for example
etc.	and so forth
FA-TRAC	Foreign Army-Training Assistance Command
FCP	Family Care Plan
FOB	Forward Operating Base
FORSCOM	Forces Command
FRG	family readiness group
FY	fiscal year
GEN	general
G-Staff	General Staff
	G1 = Personnel and Administration Section
	G2 = Intelligence Section

	G3 = Operations and Training Section
	G4 = Logistics Section
	G5 = Civil Affairs Section
	G6 = Communications Section
	G7 = Strategic Plans Section
GWOT	Global War on Terrorism
HHC	Headquarters and Headquarters Company
HMMWV	high-mobility multipurpose wheeled vehicle
HN	host nation
HQ	headquarters
HQDA	Headquarters, Department of the Army
HS	home station
IA	Iraqi Army
IAG	Iraq Advisor Group
ICDC	Iraqi Civilian Defense Corps
ID	infantry division
IDT	inactive duty training
i.e.	that is
IED	Improvised Explosive Device
IET	Initial Entry Training
IIF	Iraqi Intervention Force
ILE	Intermediate Level Education
IN	Indiana
INA	Iraqi National Army
ING	Iraqi National Guard
IP	Iraqi Police
IRR	Individual Ready Reserve
ISF	Iraqi Security Forces
ISO	in support of
IT	Institutional Training
IZ	International Zone
J-Staff	Joint Staff at MNSTC-I HQ:
	J1 = Personnel Directorate
	J2 = Intelligence Directorate
	J3 = Operations Directorate
	J4 = Logistics Directorate
	J5 = Plans Directorate
	J6 = Communications Directorate
	J7 = Force Development, Doctrine, and Training Directorate
JMD	Joint Manning Document
KBR	Kellogg, Brown and Root
KIA	killed in action
KMTB	Krikush Military Training Base
LAD	latest arrival date
LFX	live fire exercise

Lt. Col.	lieutenant colonel (Air Force and Marines)
LTC	lieutenant colonel (Army)
LTG	lieutenant general
MAJ	major
M/CM/S	mobility/countermobility/survivability
M-Day	mobilization day
MDMP	military decision making process
MEDEVAC	medical evacuation
METL	mission essential task list
MG	major general
MiTT	military transition team
MNC-I	Multi-National Corps-Iraq
MND-CS	Multi-National Division Central-South
MNF-I	Multi-National Forces-Iraq
MNSTC-I	Multi-National Security Transition Command-Iraq
Mob	mobilization
MOD	Ministry of Defense
MOI	Ministry of the Interior
MOS	military occupational specialty
MP	military police
MPRI	Military Professional Resources Incorporated
MRE	meal, ready to eat
MSC	Major Subordinate Command
MSG	master sergeant
MSN	mission
MTT	mobile training team
MWR	morale, welfare, and recreation
NATO	North Atlantic Treaty Organization
NAV	navigation
NBC	nuclear, biological, chemical
NCO	noncommissioned officer
NCOIC	noncommissioned officer in charge
NCOER	noncommissioned officer evaluation report
NCOES	Noncommissioned Officer Education System
NMTB	Numaniyah Military Training Base
NTC	National Training Center
NVG	night vision goggles
NY	New York
O/C	observer/controller
OCIE	organizational clothing and equipment
ODA	Operational Detachment-Alpha
OER	officer evaluation report
OES	Officer Education System
OIC	officer in charge
OIF	Operation IRAQI FREEDOM

OP	observation post
OPCON	operational control
OPSEC	operational security
OSUT	one station unit training
PCI	pre-combat inspection
PCS	permanent change of station
PD	professional development
PDSS	predeployment site survey
PE	practical exercise
PLDC	Primary Leadership Development Course
PMCS	preventive maintenance checks and services
POI	Program of Instruction
POW	prisoner of war
PTSR	post-mobilization training and support requirements
PX	Post Exchange
QRF	quick reaction force
RC	Reserve Component
rear CP	rear command post
RFF	request for forces
RFI	request for information
RIPTOA	Relief in Place/Transfer of Authority
ROE	rules of engagement
RPG	rocket-propelled grenade
RSOI	reception, staging, onward movement, and integration
S1	personnel staff officer
S2	intelligence staff officer
S3	operations staff officer
S4	logistics staff officer
SAPI	Small Arms Protective Insert
SAS	Special Air Service
SAW	squad automatic weapon
SCIF	Secure Compartmented Intelligence Facility
SF	Special Forces
SFC	sergeant first class
SGT	sergeant
SINCGARS	Single Channel Ground and Airborne Radio System
SIPRNET	secure internet protocol router network
SME	subject matter expert
SPTT	Special Police Transition Team
SRP	Soldier Readiness Program
SSG	staff sergeant
SSI-FWTS	shoulder-sleeve insignia-former wartime service
STX	situational training exercise
TACON	tactical control
TASS	Total Army School System

TCP	tactical control point
TDA	table of distribution and allowances
TF	task force
TMTB	Taji Military Training Base
TNG	training
TOC	tactical operations center
TOE	table of organization and equipment
TPU	Troop Program Unit
TRADOC	Training and Doctrine Command
TS	Training Support
TSD	Training Support Division
TSIRT	Theater Specific Individual Readiness Training
TSLT	Theater Specific Leadership Training
TTP	tactics, techniques, and procedures
TV	television
TY	training year
UAE	United Arab Emirates
UIC	Unit Identification Code
US	United States
USAF	United States Air Force
USAR	United States Army Reserve
USARC	United States Army Reserve Command
UXO	unexploded ordnance
USAREUR	United States Army Europe
VA	Virginia
VTC	video teleconference
WIA	wounded in action
XO	executive officer

Bibliography

Copies of all sources used in the research for this project (with the exception of those denoted by an asterisk [*]) are located in the *Iroquois Warriors in Iraq* file located in the Combined Arms Research Library archives, Fort Leavenworth, KS.

Primary Sources

Interviews and E-Mails

Arnold, COL Todd. Interview by author, 4 November 2006. Transcript. Operational Leadership Experience Project, Combat Studies Institute, Fort Leavenworth, KS. Available at http://www-cgsc.army.mil/carl/contentdm/home.htm (as of 1 March 2007).

_____. E-mail to author, 8 January 2007, 12:20 p.m. Subject: RE: 98th Division in Iraq. Combat Studies Institute, Fort Leavenworth, KS.

Baginski, LTC Theresa. Telephone interview by author, 4 November 2006. Transcript. Operational Leadership Experience Project, Combat Studies Institute, Fort Leavenworth, KS. Available at http://www-cgsc.army.mil/carl/contentdm/home.htm (as of 1 March 2007).

Bradley, MAJ Lawrence. Telephone interview by author, 7 February 2007. Synopsis transcript of interview. Combat Studies Institute, Fort Leavenworth, KS.

Castle, COL Edward. Interview by author, 5 November 2006. Transcript. Operational Leadership Experience Project, Combat Studies Institute, Fort Leavenworth, KS. Available at http://www-cgsc.army.mil/carl/contentdm/home.htm (as of 1 March 2007).

_____. E-mail to author, 10 February 2007, 11:20 a.m. Subject: RE: Question About Iraq. Combat Studies Institute, Fort Leavenworth, KS. Attachment: Consolidated Report, IED Ambush Attack of 3d Brigade, 5th Division (Iraqi Army), 8 July 2005.

Catalanotti, COL Robert. Interview by author, 3 November 2006. Transcript. Operational Leadership Experience Project, Combat Studies Institute, Fort Leavenworth, KS. Available at http://www-cgsc.army.mil/carl/contentdm/home.htm (as of 1 March 2007).

Chambers, John. Trip Report, Center for Army Lessons Learned. Subject: CALL AOB Trip Report 98th DIV (IT) 4–6 NOV 2005, Rochester, NY, 8 November 2005.

Charnock, SSG Brian. Interview by author, 4 November 2006. Transcript. Operational Leadership Experience Project, Combat Studies Institute, Fort Leavenworth, KS. Available at http://www-cgsc.army.mil/carl/contentdm/home.htm (as of 1 March 2007).

Christian, LTC Daniel. Interview by author, 3 November 2006. Transcript. Operational Leadership Experience Project, Combat Studies Institute, Fort Leavenworth, KS. Available at http://www-cgsc.army.mil/carl/contentdm/home.htm (as of 1 March 2007).

_____. E-mail to author, 7 February 2007, 11:00 a.m. Subject: RE: Questions About Your Brigade. Combat Studies Institute, Fort Leavenworth, KS.

Ciesinski, LTC Paul. Interview by Dr. Christopher Ives, 13 October 2006. Transcript. Operational Leadership Experience Project, Combat Studies Institute, Fort Leavenworth, KS. Available at http://www-cgsc.army.mil/carl/contentdm/home.htm (as of 1 March 2007).

Cipolla, BG Frank. Telephone interview by author, 20 November 2006. Transcript. Operational Leadership Experience Project, Combat Studies Institute, Fort Leavenworth, KS. Available at http://www-cgsc.army.mil/carl/contentdm/home.htm (as of 1 March 2007).

Curwen, LTC John C. Telephone interview by author, 8 February 2007. Transcript. Operational Leadership Experience Project, Combat Studies Institute, Fort Leavenworth, KS. Available at http://www-cgsc.army.mil/carl/contentdm/home.htm (as of 1 March 2007).

Daniels, COL Jody. Interview by author, 20 December 2006. Transcript. Operational Leadership Experience Project, Combat Studies Institute, Fort Leavenworth, KS. Available at http://www-cgsc.army.mil/carl/contentdm/home.htm (as of 1 March 2007).

_____. E-mail to author, 16 March 2007, 4:33 p.m. Subject: Your Interview Transcript. Combat Studies Institute, Fort Leavenworth, KS.

DeOliviera, COL Marcus. E-mail to author, 4 March 2007, 5:31 p.m. Subject: RE: Iraqi 1st Brigade. Combat Studies Institute, Fort Leavenworth, KS.

DiRisio, LTC James. Interview by author, 3 November 2006. Transcript. Operational Leadership Experience Project, Combat Studies Institute, Fort Leavenworth, KS. Available at http://www-cgsc.army.mil/carl/contentdm/home.htm (as of 1 March 2007).

_____. Telephone interview by author, 9 January 2007. Combat Studies Institute, Fort Leavenworth, KS.

_____. E-mail to author, 8 January 2007, 9:19 p.m. Subject: RE: 98th Division in Iraq. Combat Studies Institute, Fort Leavenworth, KS. Attachment: Summer 2004 Chronology, 98th Division, no date.

_____. E-mail to author, 9 January 2007, 1:22 p.m. Subject: RE: 98th Division in Iraq. Combat Studies Institute, Fort Leavenworth, KS.

_____. E-mail to author, 9 January 2007, 1:30 p.m. Subject: RE: 98th Division (IT) TOC. Combat Studies Institute, Fort Leavenworth, KS. Attachment: E-mail from COL Frank A. Cipolla to MAJ James M. DiRisio, 13 July 2004, 5:56 a.m. Subject: RE: 98th Division (IT) TOC.

_____. E-mail to author, 9 January 2007, 1:39 p.m. Subject: RE: Draft PowerPoint Presentation. Combat Studies Institute, Fort Leavenworth, KS. Attachment: E-mail from MAJ James M. DiRisio to LTC Jody Daniels, 29 July 2004, 12:28 p.m. Subject: RE: Draft PowerPoint Presentation.

_____. E-mail to author, 9 January 2007, 1:47 p.m. Subject: FW: Command Emphasis-Volunteer Statements SUSPENSE: 311200 AUG 04. Combat Studies Institute, Fort Leavenworth, KS. Attachment: E-mail from MAJ

James M. DiRisio to COL Robert Catalanotti, 30 August 2004, 7:59 p.m. Subject: FW: Command Emphasis-Volunteer Statements SUSPENSE: 311200 AUG 04.

_____. E-mail to author, 9 January 2007, 2:09 p.m. Subject: FW: DIV (IT) Contact. Combat Studies Institute, Fort Leavenworth, KS. Attachment: E-mail from LTC Brently White to MAJ James M. DiRisio, 06 July 2004, 12:04 a.m. Subject: FW: DIV (IT) Contact.

_____. E-mail to author, 24 January 2007, 2:57 p.m. Subject: RE: Convoy Training. Combat Studies Institute, Fort Leavenworth, KS.

_____. E-mail to author, 26 January 2007, 10:26 a.m. Subject: RE: CPATT. Combat Studies Institute, Fort Leavenworth, KS.

_____. E-mail to author, 29 January 2007, 10:38 a.m. Subject: RE: Dave Smith. Combat Studies Institute, Fort Leavenworth, KS.

_____. E-mail to author, 01 February 2007, 2:47 p.m. Subject: RE: Number of ASTs. Combat Studies Institute, Fort Leavenworth, KS.

_____. E-mail to author, 13 February 2007, 1:56 p.m. Subject: RE: Changes to the AST/MiTT Mission. Combat Studies Institute, Fort Leavenworth, KS. Attachments: Personnel Readiness Working Group (PRWG); Terms of Reference; PRWG Minutes 5 February 2005; English Version, MOD Unit Numbering Plan; 10 Division Proposed MOD Forces Organization Chart, version 3; MOD Office Call, 2 January 2005; MOD Office Call, 9 January 2005.

_____. E-mail to author, 13 February 2007, 2:34 p.m. Subject: RE: Changes to the AST/MiTT Mission. Combat Studies Institute, Fort Leavenworth, KS.

_____. E-mail to author, 29 March 2007, 1:50 p.m. Subject: RE: Taji BSU Commander Before Catalanotti. Combat Studies Institute, Fort Leavenworth, KS.

Eaton, MG (Retired) Paul. Interview by Contemporary Operations Study Team, 3 August 2006. Combat Studies Institute, Fort Leavenworth, KS.

Ewing, SFC Dennis. Interview by author, 4 November 2006. Transcript. Operational Leadership Experience Project, Combat Studies Institute, Fort Leavenworth, KS. Available at http://www-cgsc.army.mil/carl/contentdm/home.htm (as of 1 March 2007).

Friedman, LTC Joseph. Interview by author, 5 November 2006. Transcript. Operational Leadership Experience Project, Combat Studies Institute, Fort Leavenworth, KS. Available at http://www-cgsc.army.mil/carl/contentdm/home.htm (as of 1 March 2007).

_____. E-mail to author, 26 January 2007, 6:26 p.m. Subject: RE: Questions on the C2 Cell in Iraq. Combat Studies Institute, Fort Leavenworth, KS.

Godwin, Nathan. Headquarters, US Army Forces Command. Telephone interview by author, 3 April 2007. Combat Studies Institute, Fort Leavenworth, KS.

Harris, Denise E. E-mail to author, 19 March 2007, 8:42 a.m. Subject: RE: Campaign Credit for the 98th Division. Combat Studies Institute, Fort Leavenworth, KS.

Hauser, MAJ Shauna. Interview by John McCool, 29 November 2006. Transcript. Operational Leadership Experience Project, Combat Studies Institute, Fort Leavenworth, KS. Available at http://www-cgsc.army.mil/carl/contentdm/home.htm (as of 1 March 2007).

Helmly, MG James R. Telephone interview by author, 2 December 2006. Transcript. Operational Leadership Experience Project, Combat Studies Institute, Fort Leavenworth, KS. Available at http://www-cgsc.army.mil/carl/contentdm/home.htm (as of 1 March 2007).

Jones, MAJ Matthew. Interview by author, 4 November 2006. Transcript. Operational Leadership Experience Project, Combat Studies Institute, Fort Leavenworth, KS. Available at http://www-cgsc.army.mil/carl/contentdm/home.htm (as of 1 March 2007).

_____. Telephone interview by author, 16 January 2007. Synopsis transcript of interview. Combat Studies Institute, Fort Leavenworth, KS.

_____. E-mail to author, 25 January 2007, 8:27 a.m. Subject: RE: Division Organization. Combat Studies Institute, Fort Leavenworth, KS. Attachment: 98th Division (IT) Organization Charts, 16 October 2003.

_____. E-mail to author, 30 January 2007, 10:24 a.m. Subject: RE: Flights into Kuwait. Combat Studies Institute, Fort Leavenworth, KS.

_____. E-mail to author, 06 February 2007, 3:10 p.m. Subject: RE: 7th Brigade. Combat Studies Institute, Fort Leavenworth, KS.

_____. E-mail to author, 21 March 2007. Subject: Question About Advisors. Combat Studies Institute, Fort Leavenworth, KS.

Kelly, MG James A. Interview by Laurence Lessard, 8 February 2007. Transcript. Operational Leadership Experience Project, Combat Studies Institute, Fort Leavenworth, KS. Available at http://www-cgsc.army.mil/carl/contentdm/home.htm (as of 1 March 2007).

Kelly, COL Lawrence. Telephone interview by author, 4 November 2006. Transcript. Operational Leadership Experience Project, Combat Studies Institute, Fort Leavenworth, KS. Available at http://www-cgsc.army.mil/carl/contentdm/home.htm (as of 1 March 2007).

Loncle, MAJ Paul. Interview by author, 4 November 2006. Transcript. Operational Leadership Experience Project, Combat Studies Institute, Fort Leavenworth, KS. Available at http://www-cgsc.army.mil/carl/contentdm/home.htm (as of 1 March 2007).

McConnell, MAJ Scott. Telephone interview by author, 12 December 2006. Transcript. Operational Leadership Experience Project, Combat Studies Institute, Fort Leavenworth, KS. Available at http://www-cgsc.army.mil/carl/contentdm/home.htm (as of 1 March 2007).

_____. E-mail to author, 8 February 2007, 8:12 a.m. Subject: Questions About the 5th Division. Combat Studies Institute, Fort Leavenworth, KS. Attachment: Command Brief, 5th Division IAF Update, 3 March 2005.

_____. E-mail to author, 8 February 2007, 8:18 a.m. Subject: One More File That May Help. Combat Studies Institute, Fort Leavenworth, KS. Attachment: 5th Division Grand Scheme, Modified.

_____. E-mail to author, 12 February 2007, 7:23 a.m. Subject: 5th Division Counterparts. Combat Studies Institute, Fort Leavenworth, KS.

McLaren, MG John P., Jr. Telephone interview by author, 14 November 2006. Transcript. Operational Leadership Experience Project, Combat Studies Institute, Fort Leavenworth, KS. Available at http://www-cgsc.army.mil/ carl/contentdm/home.htm (as of 1 March 2007).

Monczynski, LTC Richard F. Telephone interview by author, 18 January 2007. Transcript. Operational Leadership Experience Project, Combat Studies Institute, Fort Leavenworth, KS. Available at http://www-cgsc.army.mil/ carl/contentdm/home.htm (as of 1 March 2007).

Morales, LTC Antonio. Telephone interview by author, 16 January 2007. Synopsis transcript of interview. Combat Studies Institute, Fort Leavenworth, KS.

_____. Interview by author, 30 January 2007. Transcript. Operational Leadership Experience Project, Combat Studies Institute, Fort Leavenworth, KS. Available at http://www-cgsc.army.mil/carl/contentdm/home.htm (as of 1 March 2007).

Newsome, CSM Milton. Interview by author, 3 November 2006. Transcript. Operational Leadership Experience Project, Combat Studies Institute, Fort Leavenworth, KS. Available at http://www-cgsc.army.mil/carl/ contentdm/home.htm (as of 1 March 2007).

Parsons, COL (Retired) Bradford. Telephone interview by author, 3 November 2006. Transcript. Operational Leadership Experience Project, Combat Studies Institute, Fort Leavenworth, KS. Available at http://www-cgsc. army.mil/carl/contentdm/home.htm (as of 1 March 2007).

_____. Telephone interview by author, 17 January 2007. Transcript. Operational Leadership Experience Project, Combat Studies Institute, Fort Leavenworth, KS. Available at http://www-cgsc.army.mil/carl/ contentdm/home.htm (as of 1 March 2007).

Petraeus, LTG David H. Interview by author, 11 December 2006. Transcript. Operational Leadership Experience Project, Combat Studies Institute, Fort Leavenworth, KS. Available at http://www-cgsc.army.mil/carl/ contentdm/home.htm (as of 1 March 2007).

Ryan, COL Sean. Interview by author, 21 December 2006. Transcript. Operational Leadership Experience Project, Combat Studies Institute, Fort Leavenworth, KS. Available at http://www-cgsc.army.mil/carl/ contentdm/home.htm (as of 1 March 2007).

Schwitters, BG James. Telephone interview by author, 13 December 2006. Transcript. Operational Leadership Experience Project, Combat Studies Institute, Fort Leavenworth, KS. Available at http://www-cgsc.army.mil/ carl/contentdm/home.htm (as of 1 March 2007).

Semler, LTC Christopher. E-mail to author, 12 February 2007, 2:13 p.m. Subject: RE: Questions. Combat Studies Institute, Fort Leavenworth, KS.

Sherlock, BG Richard. Interview by author, 16 November 2006. Transcript. Operational Leadership Experience Project, Combat Studies Institute,

Fort Leavenworth, KS. Available at http://www-cgsc.army.mil/carl/contentdm/home.htm (as of 1 March 2007).

Shipman, COL Douglas. Interview by author, 3 November 2006. Transcript. Operational Leadership Experience Project, Combat Studies Institute, Fort Leavenworth, KS. Available at http://www-cgsc.army.mil/carl/contentdm/home.htm (as of 1 March 2007).

_____. Telephone interview by author, 14 February 2007. Synopsis transcript of interview. Combat Studies Institute, Fort Leavenworth, KS.

_____. E-mail to author, 24 January 2007, 8:43 a.m. Subject: RE: Your Interview Transcript. Combat Studies Institute, Fort Leavenworth, KS.

_____. E-mail to author, 24 January 2007, 9:04 a.m. Subject: RE: Comparison of 2d and 3d Divisions. Combat Studies Institute, Fort Leavenworth, KS.

Stafford, COL Charles A. Telephone interview by author, 8 December 2006. Transcript. Operational Leadership Experience Project, Combat Studies Institute, Fort Leavenworth, KS. Available at http://www-cgsc.army.mil/carl/contentdm/home.htm (as of 1 March 2007).

_____. E-mail to author, 17 January 2007, 2:18 p.m. Subject: 98th Division (IT) Documents 1. Combat Studies Institute, Fort Leavenworth, KS. Attachment: 98th Division, Briefing, "The Foreign Army Training Command, Proposed Timeline and Operational Concepts," 8 July 2004.

_____. E-mail to author, 17 January 2007, 2:35 p.m. Subject: 98th Division (IT) Documents 2. Combat Studies Institute, Fort Leavenworth, KS. Attachment: 98th Division AST 35-Day Training Plan Matrix, Version 1.

_____. E-mail to author, 17 January 2007, 2:43 p.m. Subject: 98th Division (IT) Documents 3. Combat Studies Institute, Fort Leavenworth, KS. Attachment: First Army, Briefing, "FA-TRAC Mobilization/Deployment Model," undated.

_____. E-mail to author, 17 January 2007, 2:45 p.m. Subject: 98th Division (IT) Documents 4. Combat Studies Institute, Fort Leavenworth, KS. Attachment: Memorandum, Headquarters, 98th Division (Institutional Training), AFRC-TNY-CMD, Subject: Identification and Selection of Advisor Support Teams (AST) in Support of Operation Iraqi Freedom for Soldiers Outside the 98th Division, 19 August 2004.

_____. E-mail to author, 17 January 2007, 3:30 p.m. Subject: 98th Division (IT) Documents 5. Combat Studies Institute, Fort Leavenworth, KS. Attachment: 98th Division, Briefing, "Foreign Army Training Command in Support of MNSTC-I/CMATT," 25 August 2004.

_____. E-mail to author, 17 January 2007, 3:36 p.m. Subject: 98th Division (IT) Documents 6. Combat Studies Institute, Fort Leavenworth, KS. Attachment: Memorandum, Headquarters, 98th Division (Institutional Training), AFRC-TNY-CMD, Subject: 98th DIV (IT) Support to MNSTC-I (Multi-National Security Transition Command-Iraq), 21 August 2004.

_____. E-mail to author, 19 January 2007, 10:14 p.m. Subject: 98th Division

(IT) Documents 5. Combat Studies Institute, Fort Leavenworth, KS. Attachment: E-mail, COL Charles Stafford to LTC Keith Sharples, Subject: New Guy Stuff, 25 August 2004.

_____. E-mail to author, 19 January 2007, 10:22 p.m. Subject: 35 Day Training Plan. Combat Studies Institute, Fort Leavenworth, KS. Attachment: E-mail, LTC Steven G. Sorrell to 85th Div (TS), Subject: 35 Day Training Plan, 24 August 2004.

_____. E-mail to author, 23 January 2007, 10:25 a.m. Subject: 98th Division (IT)-3d Brigade Organization. Combat Studies Institute, Fort Leavenworth, KS. Attachment: 3d Brigade, 85th Divsion (TS), Briefing, "98th Division (IT) Mobilization," undated.

_____. E-mail to author, 23 January 2007, 12:27 p.m. Subject: 98th Division (IT)-3d Brigade Organization. Combat Studies Institute, Fort Leavenworth, KS.

_____. Telephone interview by author, 28 March 2007. Combat Studies Institute, Fort Leavenworth, KS.

_____. E-mail to author, 30 March 2007, 6:38 p.m. Subject: Training Requirements. Combat Studies Institute, Fort Leavenworth, KS.

Swartwood, MAJ Roger. Interview by author, 3 November 2006. Transcript. Operational Leadership Experience Project, Combat Studies Institute, Fort Leavenworth, KS. Available at http://www-cgsc.army.mil/carl/contentdm/home.htm (as of 1 March 2007).

_____. E-mail to author, 29 March 2007, 10:39 a.m. Subject: Question About AST Training. Combat Studies Institute, Fort Leavenworth, KS.

Tennyson, MAJ Jeffrey. Interview by author, 3 November 2006. Transcript. Operational Leadership Experience Project, Combat Studies Institute, Fort Leavenworth, KS. Available at http://www-cgsc.army.mil/carl/contentdm/home.htm (as of 1 March 2007).

Vernick, MAJ John. Interview by author, 5 November 2006. Transcript. Operational Leadership Experience Project, Combat Studies Institute, Fort Leavenworth, KS. Available at http://www-cgsc.army.mil/carl/contentdm/home.htm (as of 1 March 2007).

_____. Telephone interview by author, 10 January 2007. Synopsis transcript of interview. Combat Studies Institute, Fort Leavenworth, KS.

_____. E-mail to author, 19 January 2007, 2:03 p.m. Subject: Questions. Combat Studies Institute, Fort Leavenworth, KS.

Womack, Chaplain (COL) J. Paul. Written response to the author's queries, 31 January 2007.

Documents

Brown, SFC Andrew T. After Action Report, Subject: 98th Division AST Mobilization at Atterbury, IN, undated.

Headquarters, Department of the Army. DA Alert Order #549-04, Subject: Alert Order #549-04, DAMO-ODM, Washington, DC. Date/Time Group: 161816Z July 2004.

DiRisio, LTC James. "Summer 2004 Chronology, 98th Division," no date. See e-mail from LTC James DiRisio to author, 8 January 2007, 9:19 p.m. Subject: RE: 98th Division in Iraq. Combat Studies Institute, Fort Leavenworth, KS.

Eller, MAJ Michael L. "Consolidated Report, IED Ambush Attack of 3rd Brigade, 5th Division (Iraqi Army)," 8 July 2005. See e-mail from LTC Daniel Christian to author, 7 February 2007, 11:00 a.m. Subject: RE: Questions About Your Brigade. Combat Studies Institute, Fort Leavenworth, KS.

Headquarters, Coalition Military Assistance Transition Team. PowerPoint Brief, "10 Division Proposed MOD Forces Organization Chart, Version 3," 8 March 2005. See e-mail from LTC James DiRisio to author, 13 February 2007, 1:56 p.m. Subject: RE: Changes to the AST/MiTT Mission. Combat Studies Institute, Fort Leavenworth, KS.

_____. PowerPoint Brief, "Coalition Military Assistance Transition Team Command and Control Cell," undated.

_____. Information Paper, "Subject: Authorization and Wear of Shoulder Sleeve Insignia (SSI) for U.S. Army Personnel Belonging to the Coalition Military Assistance Training Team (CMATT)," 20 October 2004.

_____. PowerPoint Brief, "CMATT JMD Staff Brief," undated.

_____. PowerPoint Brief, "C2 Cell Mission Brief," undated.

Headquarters, First Army. PowerPoint Brief, "FA-TRAC Mobilization/Deployment Model," undated. See e-mail from COL Charles A. Stafford to author, 17 January 2007, 2:43 p.m. Subject: 98th Division (IT) Documents 3. Combat Studies Institute, Fort Leavenworth, KS.

Headquarters, US Army Forces Command. Message, Subject: Change 4 to Training Guidance for Follow-on Forces Deploying ISO Operation IRAQI FREEDOM. XX Sep 04. See e-mail from COL Charles A. Stafford to author, 30 March 2007, 6:38 p.m. Subject: Training Requirements. Combat Studies Institute, Fort Leavenworth, KS.

Headquarters, Multi-National Security Transition Command-Iraq. MOD Office Call Summary 2 January 2005. See e-mail from LTC James DiRisio to author, 13 February 2007, 1:56 p.m. Subject: RE: Changes to the AST/ MiTT Mission. Combat Studies Institute, Fort Leavenworth, KS.

_____. Fragmentary Order #15, Subject: Training Support Division Training Assessment, Baghdad, Iraq, Date/Time Group: 032100D June 2004.

_____. MOD Office Call 9 January 2005. See e-mail from LTC James DiRisio to author, 13 February 2007, 1:56 p.m. Subject: RE: Changes to the AST/ MiTT Mission. Combat Studies Institute, Fort Leavenworth, KS.

_____. Terms of Reference, Personnel Readiness Working Group, undated. See e-mail from LTC James DiRisio to author, 13 February 2007, 1:56 p.m. Subject: RE: Changes to the AST/MiTT Mission. Combat Studies Institute, Fort Leavenworth, KS.

_____. PowerPoint Brief. "Grand Scheme, 4.3."

Headquarters, Multi-National Security Transition Command-Iraq, Support Unit. PowerPoint Brief, "Assessment," 3 August 2004.

_____. MS Word Document, "Requirements Assessment," 3 August 2004.

_____. Excel Spread Sheet, "Army Support to MNSTC-I Requirements," undated.

Headquarters, 3d Brigade, 85th Division (Training Support). Briefing, "98th Division (IT) Mobilization," undated. See e-mail from COL Charles A. Stafford to author, 23 January 2007, 10:25 a.m. Subject: 98th Division (IT)-3d Brigade Organization. Combat Studies Institute, Fort Leavenworth, KS. Attachment: 3d Brigade, 85th Division (TS), Master Training Schedule, September—December 2004.

Headquarters, 5th Iraqi Division. PowerPoint Brief, "Command Brief, 5th Division IAF Update," 3 March 2005. See e-mail from MAJ Scott McConnell to author, 8 February 2007, 8:12 a.m. Subject: Questions About the 5th Division. Combat Studies Institute, Fort Leavenworth, KS.

_____. Briefing, "5th Division Grand Scheme, Modified." See e-mail from MAJ Scott McConnell to author, 8 February 2007, 8:18 a.m. Subject: One More File That May Help. Combat Studies Institute, Fort Leavenworth, KS.

Headquarters, 77th Regional Readiness Command. PowerPoint Brief, "Task Force Liberty, Soldier Readiness Program After Action Report, 2d Battalion, 390th Regiment, 2d Brigade, 98th Division," 10–12 July 2004.

Headquarters, 98th Division (Institutional Training). Annex A (Battle Roster) to Operations Plan 02-2004.

_____. MS Word Document. FA-TRAC, Foreign Army Training Assistance Command Lessons Learned, November 2004.

_____. Excel Spreadsheet, "98th Division AST 35-Day Training Plan Matrix, Version 1." See e-mail from COL Charles A. Stafford to author, 17 January 2007, 2:35 p.m. Subject: 98th Division (IT) Documents 2. Combat Studies Institute, Fort Leavenworth, KS.

_____. Excel Spreadsheet, "Active Casualty/Injury Report," 18 August 2006.

_____. Memorandum, AFRC-TNY-CMD, Subject: Identification and Selection of Advisor Support Teams (AST) in Support of Operation Iraqi Freedom for Soldiers Outside the 98th Division, 19 August 2004. See e-mail from COL Charles A. Stafford to author, 17 January 2004, 2:45 p.m. Subject: 98th Division (IT) Documents 4. Combat Studies Institute, Fort Leavenworth, KS.

_____. Memorandum, AFRC-TNY-CMD, Subject: 98th DIV (IT) Support to MNSTC-I (Multi-National Security Transition Command-Iraq), 21 August 2004. See e-mail from COL Charles A. Stafford to author, 17 January 2004, 3:36 p.m. Subject: 98th Division (IT) Documents 6. Combat Studies Institute, Fort Leavenworth, KS.

_____. Operations Order 05-24 (98th Division (IT) Redeployment Plan), Rochester, NY, 231700 July 2005.

_____. PowerPoint Brief, "Information Brief, 98th Division (IT) FA-TRAC and TY04/TY05 Missions," 14 September 2004.

_____. PowerPoint Brief, "Information Brief, 98th Division (IT) FA-TRAC and TY04/TY05 Missions," 2 October 2004.

_____. PowerPoint Brief, "98th Division (IT) Organization Charts," 16 October 2003. See e-mail from MAJ Matthew Jones to author, 25 January 2007, 8:27 a.m. Subject: RE: Division Organization. Combat Studies Institute, Fort Leavenworth, KS.

_____. PowerPoint Brief, "The Foreign Army Training Assistance Command, Proposed Timeline and Operational Concepts," 18 June 2004.

_____. PowerPoint Brief, "The Foreign Army Training Assistance Command, Proposed Timeline and Operational Concepts," 8 July 2004. See e-mail from COL Charles A. Stafford to author, 17 January 2007, 2:18 p.m. Subject: 98th Division (IT) Documents 1. Combat Studies Institute, Fort Leavenworth, KS.

_____. PowerPoint Brief, "Foreign Army Training Assistance Command in Support of MNSTC-I/CMATT," 25 August 2004. See e-mail from COL Charles A. Stafford to author, 17 January 2004, 3:30 p.m. Subject: 98th Division (IT) Documents 5. Combat Studies Institute, Fort Leavenworth, KS.

_____. PowerPoint Brief, "Foreign Army-Training Assistance Command (FA-TRAC) Review," undated.

_____. PowerPoint Brief, "OPLAN 04-XX (FA-TRAC) Mission Analysis Brief (Draft)," 07 July 2004.

_____. PowerPoint Brief, "OPLAN 04-XX (FA-TRAC) Course of Action Development Brief," 09 July 2004.

Iraq Reconstruction Management Office, Personnel Readiness Working Group (PRWG). Memorandum, Subject: Minutes from 6 February 2005 Meeting, 6 February 2005. See e-mail from LTC James DiRisio to author, 13 February 2007, 1:56 p.m. Subject: RE: Changes to the AST/MiTT Mission. Combat Studies Institute, Fort Leavenworth, KS.

Iraq Ministry of Defense. Excel Spreadsheet, MOD Unit Numbering Plan, English Version. See e-mail from LTC James DiRisio to author, 13 February 2007, 1:56 p.m. Subject: RE: Changes to the AST/MiTT Mission. Combat Studies Institute, Fort Leavenworth, KS.

Pinkela, MAJ Ken. PowerPoint Brief, "Foreign Army Training Assistance Command (FA-TRAC) Decision Brief to FDD Review Board," Office of the Chief, Army Reserve, 12 May 2004.

PowerPoint Chart, "AST Tool," 9 March 2005.

3d Brigade, 5th Division, "Significant Events Log, 1 Dec 04–25 Aug 05."

Secondary Sources

Books and Articles

*Army Knowledge On-line, General Officer Management Office website, BG James Schwitters.

*Center of Military History. *Order of Battle of the United States Land Forces in the World War.* Vol. 3, Pt. 2. Center of Military History Publication Number 23-4. Washington, DC: Government Printing Office, 1988.

Fallen Heroes Memorial. "Fallen Heroes of Operation Iraqi Freedom: Army Lt. Col. Terrence K. Crowe." http://www.fallenheroesmemorial.com/oif/ profiles/croweterrencek.html.

*Feasel, MAJ Laurence W. *Professionals on Review: An Historic Profile of the 98th "Iroquois" Division*. Rochester, NY: Headquarters, 98th Division, 1980.

Global Security, "Al Taji Army Airfield/Al Taji Camp." http://www.globalsecurity. org/military/world/iraq/al-taji.htm.

*Hansen, Timothy J. and Jocene D. Preston, ed. *An Encounter with History: The 98th Division and the Global War on Terrorism, 2001–2005*. Washington, DC: Government Printing Office, 2006.

Helmly, LTG James R. "Profound Change While Fighting the War." *Army*. October 2004, 103–14.

*Howard, Michael. "Military Science in an Age of Peace," *Journal of the Royal United Services Institute for Defence Studies*. As reprinted in *C600 Book of Readings,* US Army Command and General Staff College, Fort Leavenworth, Kansas.

The Middle Ground. Web log. http://themiddleground.blogspot.com/2004/10/ patriots-and-soldiers-iraq-fallen-49.html.

Molineaux, CPT Peter. "Iraqi Soldiers Wrap Up 'Operation COBWEB.'" *The Advisor*, Multi-National Security Transition Command-Iraq, 14 May 2005.

New York Times, 9 July 2004, "Rochester: 3,600 Face Prospect of Iraq Duty," 6.

Stars and Stripes. "Coming to Grips with a Close Call at Mosul." 11 October 2006. http://www.estripes.com/article.asp?section=104&article=33002 &archive=true.

MilitaryCity.com. "Honor the Fallen: Army Sergeant First Class Paul D. Karpowich." http://www.militarycity.com/valor/573046.html.

USA Today, "Army Reserve chief says force was not well-prepared for terror war," 16 September 2004. http://www.usatoday. com/news/washington/2004-09-16-army-reserve_x.htm.

With, SGT Julian. "Returning Home." *Times Union.com Blogs*, 25 July 2005. http://blogs.timesunion.com/wartime/?p=42.

Wong, Edward. "Ambush Kills 50 Iraq Soldiers Execution Style." *New York Times*, 25 October 2004.

Appendix A

Chronology

2003

Fall — LTG Helmly, CAR, developed FA-TRAC concept and discussed it with LTG Cody, ARSTAFF G3

2004

April — Draft FA-TRAC concept briefed at USAR conference, Fort Eustis, VA

28 April — OCAR FA-TRAC concept briefed to LTG Cody; Cody approves FA-TRAC concept; directs further development

12 May — FA-TRAC decision brief to OCAR Force Development Directorate

15 May — MNSTC-I headquarters activated in Baghdad

1 June — FA-TRAC concept briefing by BG Profit to LTG Petraeus (Cody, Helmly, Robinson, Sherlock present); Petraeus asks DA to send survey team to Iraq

3 June — HQ, MNSTC-I Fragmentary Order #15 issued

6 June — LTG Petraeus assumes command of MNSTC-I

15 June — 98th Division survey team concept brief to LTG Helmly

18 June — 98th Division survey team concept brief to LTG Cody; 98th directed to conduct survey of mission requirements in Iraq

21 June — Division TOC activated at Division HQ, Rochester, NY

23 June — Division ADVON Team mobilizes at Division HQ

26 June — Division ADVON Team moves to CRC Bliss

4 July — Division ADVON Team arrives in Iraq

6 July — Survey Team mobilizes at Division HQ

10 July — Survey Team moves to CRC Bliss

12 July — Stop-loss initiated

16 July — DA Alert Order #549-04 alerts 98th Division of possible activation

21 July — Survey Team arrives in Kuwait

24 July	Survey Team arrives in Iraq
29 July	First 98th Division coordination meeting with USARC and FORSCOM
3 August	Survey Team completes survey and Requirements Assessment
4 August	VTC between BG Sherlock (Iraq) and MG Robinson (Rochester)
5 August	Second 98th Division coordination meeting with USARC and FORSCOM
6 August	LTG Petraeus approves revised Requirements Assessment
7 August	Division Rear CP activated at Rochester
8–10 August	BG Sherlock and LTC Ryan present Requirements Assessment to USARC, FORSCOM, OCAR, and Army G3; 98th Division given go-ahead to conduct mission
9 August	Division notified by MG Wilson it would retain FY 05 TASS missions
@ 18 August	Postmobilization training plan approved by LTG Honoré; Camp Atterbury, IN, confirmed as mobilization training site
20 August	3d Brigade, 85th Division (TS) assigned mobilization training mission for the 98th Division
3 September	2300—98th Division receives DA mobilization order
8 September	CRC 1 initial mobilization at home stations (HS); begins HS training
	Mob 1 initial mobilization at HS; begins HS training
11 September	CRC 1 travels to Bliss
	Mob 1 travels to Camp Atterbury
18 September	Division Rear CP assumes mission from TOC
3 October	CRC 2 mobilizes at HS; begins HS training
	Mob 2 mobilizes at HS; begins HS training
6 October	CRC 2 travels to Bliss
	Mob 2 travels to Camp Atterbury
15 October	CRC 3 mobilizes at HS; begins HS training

18 October	Mob 3 mobilizes at HS; begins HS training
	CRC 3 travels to Bliss
	CRC 2 arrives in Kuwait
19 October	Mob 1 and Mob 2 arrive in Kuwait
20 October	Mob 3 travels to Camp Atterbury
23 October	CRC 1 arrives in Kuwait
30 October	CRC 3 arrives in Kuwait
@ 31 October	First 98th Division AST deploys to link up with Iraqi counterpart unit
5 November	Mob 4 and 4.5 mobilize at HS; begins HS training
7 November	Second Battle of Fallujah begins
8 November	Mob 4 and 4.5 travel to Camp Atterbury
28 November	Mob 3 arrives in Kuwait
16 December	Mob 4 and 4.5 arrive in Kuwait
December	GEN Casey directs formalization and standardization of AST concept across the Iraqi Army

2005

January	HQ, IAG begins to form
30 January	Iraqi Elections
@ 21 February	MiTT Leadership Conference
1 March	ASTs officially redesignated as MiTTs
4 March	Mob 4.6 mobilizes at HS; begins HS training
5 March	Mob 4.6 travels to Fort Hood
27 March	Mob 4.6 arrives in Kuwait
@ 30 March	Phoenix Academy starts classes
@ 1 April	MiTTS transferred from CMATT to MNC-I
	HQ, IAG established under MNSTC-I
@ 30 May	HQ, IAG transferred to MNC-I
23 July	98th Division issues OPORD 5-24, Redeployment Plan
August	Redeployment begins
October	Redeployment officially complete

Appendix B

98th Division Key Personnel, 2004–2005

Name	Division Position	Deployment Position(s)
MG Bruce E. Robinson	CG, 98th Div (IT)	Same
BG Richard Sherlock	ADC, 98th Div (IT)	Deputy CG, CMATT CG, IAG
COL Bradford Parsons	Div G3	OIC, 5th Div AST
COL Robert Catalanotti	CO, 1st Bde, 98th Div (IT)	Mobilization CO, Camp Atterbury Base Commander, TMTB
COL Frank Cipolla	CO, 2d Bde, 98th Div (IT)	OIC, ADVON Team OIC, C2 Cell
COL Edward P. Castle	Div G6	OIC, MOS/OES Training Teams
COL Sanford E. Holman	Div G4	OIC, 3d Div AST
LTC Todd Arnold	Civilian Executive Officer	Same
LTC Jody Daniels	Div Deputy Chief of Staff	Survey Team Ops Liaison Officer
LTC Antonio Morales	Div Assistant G3	OIC, C2 Cell—Kuwait CFLCC Liaison
LTC Douglas Shipman	S3, 1st Bde, 98th Div (IT)	XO, 3d Div AST OIC, 2d Div AST
LTC Richard Monczynski	Div Deputy G3	OIC, D-Rear CP
MAJ James DiRisio	G3 Plans Officer	XO to CG, CMATT
MAJ Matthew Jones	Assistant S3, 2d Bde, 98th Div (IT)	OIC, 18th Bn AST
CSM Milton Newsome	CSM, 6th Bde, 98th Div (IT)	CSM, TMTB

Appendix C

Redesignation of Iraqi Army Units, April 2005

The Iraqi Army underwent a major reorganization in April 2005 for the purposes of integrating the units of the Iraqi National Guard into the regular army. A uniform numbering system was implemented for the 10 existing divisions, and except for the divisions the unique designations were eliminated. The following information details the changes to the Iraqi Army units advised by soldiers of the 98th Division.

Original Designation	New Designation
1st Division	**Same**
1st Brigade	1st Brigade, 1st Division
1st Battalion	1st Battalion, 1st Brigade, 1st Division
2d Battalion	2d Battalion, 1st Brigade, 1st Division
4th Battalion	3d Battalion, 1st Brigade, 1st Division
2d Brigade	2d Brigade, 1st Division
3d Battalion	1st Battalion, 2d Brigade, 1st Division
8th Battalion	2d Battalion, 2d Brigade, 1st Division
9th Battalion	3d Battalion, 2d Brigade, 1st Division
6th Brigade	3d Brigade, 1st Division
22d Battalion	1st Battalion, 3d Brigade, 1st Division
23d Battalion	2d Battalion, 3d Brigade, 1st Division
24th Battalion	3d Battalion, 3d Brigade, 1st Division
7th Brigade*	4th Brigade, 1st Division
16th Battalion	1st Battalion, 4th Brigade, 1st Division
17th Battalion	2d Battalion, 4th Brigade, 1st Division
18th Battalion	3d Battalion, 4th Brigade, 1st Division
3d Division	**Same**
4th Brigade	1st Brigade, 3d Division
10th Battalion	1st Battalion, 1st Brigade, 3d Division
109th Battalion**	2d Battalion, 1st Brigade, 3d Division
12th Battalion	3d Battalion, 1st Brigade, 3d Division

*Formerly assigned to the 5th Division. Transferred to the 1st Division about 1 April 2005.

**Formerly an Iraqi National Guard battalion. Replaced the 11th Battalion about April 2004.

5th Brigade	2d Brigade, 3d Division
13th Battalion	1st Battalion, 2d Brigade, 3d Division
14th Battalion	2d Battalion, 2d Brigade, 3d Division
15th Battalion	3d Battalion, 2d Brigade, 3d Division
8th Brigade	3d Brigade, 3d Division
19th Battalion	1st Battalion, 3d Brigade, 3d Division
20th Battalion	2d Battalion, 3d Brigade, 3d Division
21st Battalion	3d Battalion, 3d Brigade, 3d Division
5th Division	**Same**
3d Brigade	1st Brigade, 5th Division
5th Battalion	1st Battalion, 1st Brigade, 5th Division
6th Battalion	2d Battalion, 1st Brigade, 5th Division
7th Battalion	3d Battalion, 1st Brigade, 5th Division
32d Brigade***	2d Brigade, 5th Division
204th Battalion	1st Battalion, 2d Brigade, 5th Division
205th Battalion	2d Battalion, 2d Brigade, 5th Division
206th Battalion	3d Battalion, 2d Brigade, 5th Division
9th Brigade	3d Brigade, 5th Division
25th Battalion	1st Battalion, 3d Brigade, 5th Division
26th Battalion	2d Battalion, 3d Brigade, 5th Division
27th Battalion	3d Battalion, 3d Brigade, 5th Division

***Formerly an Iraqi National Guard brigade. Replaced the 7th Brigade when it was transferred to the 1st Division in April 2004.

Index

Helmly, James R. (*see also* US Army Reserve Command, Office of Chief, Army Reserve), 7, 9, 11, 13, 28–29, 33, 39, 76, 209, 240, 247, 249
 his original concept of FA-TRAC, 1, 7, 224, 249
 on the Iraq War and the GWOT, 7, 17
 on readiness of USAR, 7
 and FA-TRAC briefs to Cody, 8
 on FORSCOM and USARC resistance to FA-TRAC, 8, 13, 25–26, 224
 directs 98th Division to develop survey team concept brief, 9
 at 9 August 2004 Requirements Assessment brief at the Pentagon, 37
 on the 98th Division, 9, 17, 38, 224
 on Camp Atterbury, 53
 efforts to reorganize the USAR, 224
HMMWV (M1114), 35, 62, 68, 88, 103, 117–118, 120, 124–125, 134, 142, 148–149, 154–155, 157, 160–161, 164, 175, 233
Henry, Peter A., 35–36, 91
Highway 1, 74, 92, 160
Hohenfels, Germany, 120, 131, 232
Holman, Sanford, 73, 160–161, 170–171, 253
Honoré, Russell, 50, 250
Howard, Michael, 208, 211, 228, 247
Hussein, Saddam, 83–84, 147, 154, 166, 204, 208

Improvised Explosive Device (IED), ix, 58, 62–63, 68, 74, 88, 99, 104, 131, 137, 147, 149–150, 164, 169, 181–182, 186, 191, 196, 233, 237, 244
Indianapolis, IN, 66, 202
Individual Ready Reserve (IRR), 18, 42, 141, 220, 233
Installations (US and Iraqi),
 Barracks
  Plattsburg Barracks, NY, 5
 Bases
  Al Kasik Military Training Base (AKMTB), Iraq, ix, 119, 159–162, 231
  Forward Operating Base (FOB), general, 141–142, 158, 160–161, 164, 232
  FOB Caldwell, Iraq, 108, 150
  FOB Marez, Iraq, 161, 164, 171
  FOB Shield, Iraq, 94
  FOB War Horse, Iraq, 105–108
  Kirkush Military Training Base (KMTB), Iraq, 108, 119, 123, 127–128, 131–132, 134–135, 140, 143, 149–151, 233
  Numaniyah Military Training Base (NMTB), Iraq, 97, 122, 136–137, 146, 148–149, 234
  Taji Military Training Base (TMTB), Iraq, 41, 69, 91, 95, 236, 253
 Camps
  Camp Atterbury, IN, v, vii–viii, 45–46, 51–58, 60–68, 71, 74–75, 77–78, 91, 100, 127–128, 141, 162, 178, 188, 203, 210, 212–213, 221, 243, 250–251, 253
  Camp Arifjan, Kuwait, 201

United States Army Reserve Command (USARC), 1, 7–8, 13–14, 25–28, 36–37, 41–42, 44–45, 48, 51, 212, 221, 224–225, 236, 250

United States Army Training and Doctrine Command (TRADOC), 7, 23, 236

Marshall, George C., 221

Marza, Brigadier General, 98–99

Mattydale, NY, 91

McConnell, Scott P., v, 77–79, 128, 130, 194–197, 199, 226, 228, 240, 245
    on training at Camp Atterbury, 56, 60–61, 63–64, 68
    on the "Green Hotel," 70
    on the true nature of the advisor mission, 73
    on the RIPTOA with early advisors, 121, 128
    on the staff of the 5th Division, 128–129
    on the "Ahmed-Parsons" plan, 130–131
    on working with the Marines, 140
    on working with the 5th Division, 143–144, 158, 191
    on the 42d Infantry Division, 152

McKiernan, David D., 26

McGrath, Philip S., 15, 100, 102

McLaren, John P., Jr., 78, 189–190, 199, 241

McMaster, H.R. (*see also* 3d Armored Cavalry Regiment), 169, 171

MEDEVAC operations, 149, 156, 182, 234

Metz, Thomas F., 151

Milano, Mike, 50

Military Occupational Specialty (MOS), 3, 36, 42, 51, 63, 73, 84, 88–89, 95–96, 98–100, 104, 108, 117–118, 203, 234, 253

Military Professional Resources Incorporated (MPRI) (*see also* Contractors), 67–68, 234

Military Transition Team (MiTT), 35, 108, 143, 148–149, 151–153, 155–156, 158, 168–171, 173–176, 183–184, 186–189, 192–193, 199, 201, 203, 234, 239, 244, 246, 251
    Equipment for, 148–149
    Life support to/logistics for, 151–153, 169
    Number of, 151, 153, 204
    Organization of, 35, 107, 187
    Redesignation from AST, 35, 107, 143, 167, 187

Miller, Brian, 96–99

Ministry of Defense (MOD), 87–89, 98–100, 103, 109, 119, 127, 171, 195, 234, 239, 244, 246

Ministry of the Interior (MOI), 83, 88–89, 94, 99, 147, 234

Mission Essential Task List (METL), 1, 32, 207, 210–212, 224, 234

Mission statement/requirements, 10, 25, 48, 50, 54, 69, 75–76, 93, 116, 151, 207–208, 210, 249
    98th Division, 19, 25, 37, 118
    Advisor Support Teams, 21, 32–33, 35, 46, 66, 71, 87, 91, 117, 137

C2 Cell, 115

MNSTC-I, 1, 3, 10, 19, 27, 31, 36–37, 42, 46, 51–52, 87, 94, 204

Mobilization, vii–viii, 1, 6, 13, 16–17, 20–24, 41–42, 44–46, 51–57, 63, 66, 76–77, 107, 178, 202, 215–217, 219–220, 222, 225, 234, 242–245, 250, 253

Mobilization (Mob) groups, 19, 51–52, 54, 63, 66, 74, 89, 91, 111–112, 116, 128, 141, 201–202, 209, 234

Mollineaux, Peter, 149

Monczynski, Richard F., 45, 51, 75, 201–202, 241, 253

Morales, Antonio L. "Tony," 15, 39, 76, 241, 253
    as member of the Survey Team, 34, 48, 50, 88
    on the postmobilization training plan, 34
    on training in Kuwait, 50, 48
    as CFLCC LNO, 50, 66, 88
    as C2 Cell representative in Kuwait, 66

Mosul, Iraq, 109, 119, 161–162, 164–165, 168–169, 174, 180, 197, 247

Mucciarone, Peter, 141–142, 174

Myers, Kevin, 96

Nassau, House of, 4

National Guard (*see also* US Army units), iii, v, 1, 4–5, 7–8, 46, 53–56, 58, 66, 119, 123, 125, 134, 150, 207–208, 210, 214–216, 218, 221–222, 228

National Guard Bureau, 221

Newsome, Milton, 91–93, 112, 241, 253

New York Times, 16, 28, 195, 247

North Atlantic Treaty Organization (NATO), 105, 234

Observer/controllers (O/C), 58, 119–120, 131, 209, 234

Office of the Assistant to the Chairman of the Joint Chiefs of Staff for Guard and Reserve Affairs, 16

Office of the Chief, Army Reserve (OCAR), 246, 249–250

Office of Security Transition (OST), 19, 29

O'Keefe, Stacy, 101, 104

Organized Reserves, 4–5, 111

Operations,
    AL FAJR, 132, 177
    DESERT FOX, 69
    COBWEB, ix, 146–148, 196, 247
    DESERT STORM, 215
    FISH NET II, 148
    IRAQI FREEDOM (OIF), 69, 75–76, 197–198, 234, 242, 244–245, 247
    OLYMPIC, 6
    PENINSULA, 147

Patch (shoulder sleeve insignia), 4, 14, 204, 222
    controversy over wear of, 85–86, 111

Parsons, Bradford, 28, 39, 50, 73, 75, 77, 97, 128, 134, 137, 194–197, 241, 253
    work with TOC, 13–17, 45–46

Professional Development (PD), 14, 19, 23, 26, 32, 37, 235
"40 plus 9," 23, 48, 60
Troy, William J., 34
Truhan, Mark, 105, 113
Turkey Village, 154

Unit Identification Code (UIC), 44, 221, 236
US Army Reserve (see also US Army units), iii, v, 1, 9, 221
US Army,
Numbered units:
Battalions:
    1st Battalion, 26th Infantry, 142
    1st Battalion, 30th Infantry, 134
    1st Battalion, 335th Regiment, 65
    1st Battalion, 390th Regiment, 58, 60, 135
    2d Battalion, 390th Regiment, 23, 29, 154, 245
    1st Battalion, 417th Regiment, 164
    6th Battalion, 98th Regiment, 15
    13th Battalion, 98th Regiment, 15
Brigades:
    1st Brigade, 1st Infantry Division, 204
    1st Brigade, 25th Infantry Division, 174
    1st Brigade, 80th Division (IT), 160
    1st Brigade, 98th Division (IT), 15, 58, 253
    2d Brigade, 98th Division (IT), 9, 29, 222, 245, 253
    3d Brigade, 1st Infantry Division, 106
    3d Brigade, 3d Infantry Division, 151
    3d Brigade, 85th Division (TS), 53–54, 57–59, 61–62, 64–66, 76–77, 210, 245, 250
    30th Infantry Brigade, 134, 150
    56th Brigade, 36th Division, 125
    48th Infantry Brigade, 216
    76th Infantry Brigade, 54, 58
    195th Infantry Brigade, 4
    256th Infantry Brigade, 216
    Aviation Brigade, 1st Cavalry Division, 69, 120
Divisions:
    1st Cavalry Division, 34–35, 69, 97, 120, 128, 137–138
    1st Infantry Division, 106, 142, 204
    3d Infantry Division, 107–108, 151, 181
    10th Mountain Division, 181, 187
    24th Infantry Division, 154,
    25th Infantry Division, 161, 168, 174, 180
    38th Infantry Division, 54
    42d Infantry Division, 46, 123, 151–152
    75th Division (Training Support), 91, 119

G☼ US GOVERNMENT PRINTING OFFICE: 2009—553-261